INTERACTIVE ORAL HISTORY INTERVIEWING

LEA'S COMMUNICATION SERIES
Jennings Bryant/Dolf Zillmann, General Editors

Select titles of related interest include:

Casmir • Building Communication Theories: A Socio/Cultural Approach

Cutlip • The Unseen Power: Public Relations. A History

Frey • Group Communication in Context: Studies of Natural Groups

Leeds-Hurwitz • Semiotics and Communication: Signs, Codes, Cultures

Vocate • Intrapersonal Communication: Different Voices, Different Minds

For a complete list of other titles in LEA's Communication Series, please contact Lawrence Erlbaum Associates, Publishers.

INTERACTIVE ORAL HISTORY INTERVIEWING

Edited by
Eva M. McMahan
University of Alabama
Kim Lacy Rogers
Dickinson College

IEA   LAWRENCE ERLBAUM ASSOCIATES, PUBLISHERS
1994   Hillsdale, New Jersey   Hove, UK

Lawrence Erlbaum Associates, Inc., Publishers
365 Broadway
Hillsdale, New Jersey 07642

Cover design by Kate Dusza

Library of Congress Cataloging-in-Publication Data

Interactive oral history interviewing / edited by Eva M. McMahan, Kim Lacy Rogers.
       p.   cm. -- (LEA's communication series)
    Includes bibliographical references and index.
    ISBN 0-8058-0576-1
    1. Oral history. 2. Interviewing. I. McMahan, Eva M.
  II. Rogers, Kim Lacy. III. Series.
  D16. 14. I55 1994
  907'.2--dc20   94-10437
                                             CIP

Books published by Lawrence Erlbaum Associates are printed on acid-free paper, and their bindings are chosen for strength and durability.

Printed in the United States of America
10 9 8 7 6 5 4 3 2 1

Contents

Preface

The chapters in this volume represent, in the broadest sense, an interpretive perspective of inquiry (Rabinow & Sullivan, 1979, 1987) that has flourished in oral history since the 1970s (Frisch, 1990; Grele, 1985; McMahan, 1989; Portelli, 1991; Thompson, 1988). This perspective considers oral history interviews as subjective, socially constructed, and emergent events; that is, understanding, interpretation, and meaning of lived experience are interactively constructed. Oral history, Portelli (1991) noted, "tells us less about *events* than about their *meaning*," and, hence, has a "*different* credibility" than written sources. "The importance of oral testimony may lie not in its adherence to fact but rather in its departure from it as imagination, symbolism, and desire emerge" (pp. 50–51).

The oral history interview is a unique documentary form in which the "evidence originates in the act of oral face-to-face communication" (McMahan, 1989, p. 5). The impetus for this collection was our fascination with the multifacted complexity of that method; and our belief that, despite many books that address methodological issues, no single work takes as its focus those complex, interactive processes that constitute the oral history interview. Our purpose in developing this volume, therefore, was to provide a variety of chapters that, taken together, address the possibilites and constraints inherent in oral history interviewing.

In chapter 1, "History and the Language of History in the Oral History Interview: Who Answers Whose Questions and Why?" Grele addresses power relations in interviewing. He reminds us that political ideology undergirds both the view of the historian and the narrator, and he demonstrates "how the political praxis of history is manipulated."

Culpepper Clark's chapter (2), "Reconstructing History: The Epitomizing Image," deals with the process of self-construction in the oral interview. Using a case study of efforts to desegregate the University of Alabama during the 1950s and early 1960s, he shows how narrators manipulate their recollections to construct their desired personal histories. The chapter serves as a cautionary discussion of narrators' willingness to change their stories to fit an altered historical context.

How narrators incorporate life-threatening events into their personal histories is the subject of chapter 3, "Trauma Redeemed: The Narrative Construction of Social Violence," by Rogers. By analyzing the narrative structure of interviews with African-American civil rights activists of the 1960s, she illuminates the narrative process by which narrators reconcile their experiences of victimization and trauma within a larger context of personal development and achievement in the civil rights movement.

In chapter 4, "Social Psychological Aspects of the Oral History Interview," Sypher, Hummert, and Williams turn our attention to how cognitive processes influence the interview. Based on a literature review of pertinent sociopsychological research, the authors discuss how individual memory, which is selective and constructive, affects accuracy and expression. In so doing, they provide suggestions for interviewers.

Chase and Bell (chapter 5) explore the relationship between narrators and interviewers in "Interpreting the Complexity of Women's Subjectivity." Using feminist social research as a starting point, they examine the potential problems associated with asking women narrators to talk about their experiences of subjection. Based on a self-reflexive critique of their own interviews, Chase and Bell show how interviewers' assumptions, despite being well-intentioned, can compromise narrators' responses.

Futtrell and Willard's chapter (6), "Intersubjectivity and Interviewing," takes a slightly different look at the relationship between interviewer and narrator. Defining *communication* as "the creation and negotiation of social selves and situations," the authors describe how interviewers and narrators construct "interactional texts" (Denzin, 1989). Analyzing selected ethnographic interviews with prisoners in nine maximum security prisons in the United States, Futtrell and Willard demonstrate that O'Keefe's message design logic "can be used to help establish intersubjectivity within the interview."

In chapter 7, "A Riot of Voices: Racial and Ethnic Variables in Interactive Oral History Interviewing," Hansen presents a personalized account of his experiences as a Caucasian male who interviewed Japanese Americans who had been interned at the Manzanar Relocation Center in California during World War II. Hansen's research indicates that even within a racially and ethnically homogeneous cohort of Japanese Americans, diverse communication styles and agendas can emerge during interviews. Hansen urges interviewers to be sensitive to the many nuances in cross-cultural interactions.

In "Envisioning Homestead" (chapter 8), Modell and Brodsky view interactive interviewing as a technique for generating personal and public memories. Their chapter describes the use of photographs as a "third voice" in the encounter between interviewers and narrators. They demonstrate that the use of photographs produced alternative memories among steelworkers and their families from Homestead, Pennsylvania. Hence, they argue that photographs can function not only as a methodological tool, but also as a conceptual device.

As stated earlier, *Interactive Oral History Interviewing* represents an attempt to unpack the dense interactive processes that influence oral history interviewing. Even so, we realize that this work leaves many topics untouched. The importance of social class and social power in interviews, the effects of aging and life-course stages on the interactive process, and cross-cultural and multicultural dynamics within interviews remain to be addressed by other scholars, as do questions related to narrative form and strategy, and the interactive effects of media in oral history interviewing. What we have achieved, however, is to call attention to certain significant variables that affect the interview process, and that must be given careful consideration by persons using the oral history interview method.

ACKNOWLEDGMENTS

We thank our series editors at Lawrence Erlbaum Associates, Inc., Dolf Zillmann and Jennings Bryant. We also thank Anita Abernathy and Gloria Keller of the University of Alabama and Vickie Kuhn and Gladys Cashman of Dickinson College, for their tireless and invaluable assistance in the preparation of the manuscript. We also thank Dickinson College for its support of this project with research and development grants.

Eva M. McMahan
Kim Lacy Rogers

REFERENCES

Denzin, N. K. (1989). *Interpretive interactionism.* Newbury Park, CA: Sage.

Frisch, M. (1990). *A shared authority: Essays in the craft and meaning of oral history and public history.* Albany: State University of New York Press.

Grele, R. J. (1985). *Envelopes of sound: The art of oral history* (2nd ed.). Chicago: Precedent Publishers.

McMahan, E. M. (1989). *Elite oral history discourse: A study of cooperation and coherence.* Tuscaloosa: The University of Alabama Press.

Portelli, A. (1991). *The death of Luigi Trastulli and other stories: Form and meaning in oral history.* Albany: State University of New York Press.

Rabinow, P., & Sullivan, W. M. (Eds.). (1979). *Interpretive social science: A reader.* Berkeley: University of California Press.

Rabinow, P., & Sullivan, W. M. (Eds.). (1987). *Interpretive social science: A second look.* Berkeley: University of California Press.

Thompson, P. (1988). *The voice of the past: Oral history* (2nd ed.). New York: Oxford University Press.

1

History and the Languages of History in the Oral History Interview: Who Answers Whose Questions and Why?*

Ronald J. Grele
Columbia University

Questions of memory, consciousness, and meaning in the oral history interview, of necessity, focus on two interrelated methodological issues: the role of the historian/interviewer in the creation of the document he or she is then called upon to interpret, and the creation of that document within a particular historical and social space and within a particular historical tradition (Friedlander, 1975; Frisch, 1979; Grele, 1985; Passerini, 1980, 1987; Portelli, 1981; Schrager, 1983). Most analysis of this type has highlighted the potential of the oral history process to change our conceptions of the traditional task of the historian, but, for the most part, we have been silent about the ways in which our own disciplinary discourse, its assumptions, and its context, influences that process. Our concern may be, as we tell ourselves, to map that area described by Harris (1985) "where memory, myth, ideology, language and historical cognition interact in a dialectical transformation of the word into a historical artifact" (pp. 6–7), but we have not been particularly concerned about how our own professional discourse may set the template for that map.

Thus, for all their unquestioned brilliance, works based on oral histories have veered between the poles of an enthusiastic populism, where the historian disappears in the name of giving voice to "the people," and a traditional conception of "objective" historiography, where the historian/author assumes a privileged position as interpreter of the interpretations of those he or she interviews. *All God's Dangers* by Rosengarten (1974), exemplifies the first pole. *Like a Family: The Making of a Southern Cotton Mill World* by Hall et al. (1987), the second. Both books are obviously sympathetic to the democratic impulses contained in the oral history process, but they do not reveal to us the hidden interaction between the participants to the interview that makes that democratic impulse a reality. There-

---

*For further comments by the author, please see the Afterword on p. 163.

fore, they do not, in the end, challenge methodological assumptions and professional practices that are less than democratic.

The problem of how to represent the interaction between the fieldworker and his or her informants is, obviously, not a problem limited to the oral history interview (Caplan, 1988; Clifford & Marcus, 1986; Glassie, 1982; Tedlock, 1979). But, it takes on a particular cultural meaning within the traditional debate within the historical profession over historical "objectivity" (Novick, 1988) and the ways in which those traditional attitudes have been used to answer questions raised by the movements of the 1960s, especially the civil rights movement and the women's movement, about the ideological assumptions of a history that ignored people whose past falls outside of the discourse of those who hold and exercise power. To open that discourse, it is first necessary for us to realize how we, as historians, are bounded and limited by it.

Elsewhere (Grele, 1985), I proposed that we examine the oral history interview as a "conversational narrative" jointly created by the interviewer and the interviewee, which contains an interrelated set of structures that define it as an object of study. The first set is the literary, grammatical, or linguistic structure uniting each word (sign) to every other. The second is the set of relationships established between interviewer and interviewee within the interview setting—the social structure of the interview. The third is the ideological structure of the historical narrative as it emerges through the conversation between interviewer and interviewee and the conversation of each of them with the larger cultural or historical traditions to which and through which they are speaking. This last set of relationships will reveal to us the political field of the interview within which the interview is embedded, what Langellier (1989) termed the *political praxis* of the personal narrative.

Langellier claimed:

> All personal narratives have a political function in that they produce a certain way of seeing the world which privileges certain interests (stories and meanings) over others, regardless of whether or not they contain explicit political content. The unmasking of ideology in the personal narrative requires an analysis of deep structure and meanings, within a discursive field of multiple texts and participants.... Telling personal narratives may legitimate dominant meanings or may resist dominant meanings in a transformation of meanings. The analysis of the enabling or constraining power of personal experience stories must consider the politics of their concrete and embodied performance rather than the texts isolated from contexts, or stories apart from discourse. (p. 271)

This notion of ideology as a socially structured system of meaning (Geertz, 1964) and, "the taking of sides in a struggle between embattled groups in a fragmented social life" (Jameson, 1981, p. 290), allows us to contextualize the narration within a set of larger social forces. To Langellier, it is a way in which one can relate the political praxis of the narrative to what Jameson called the discovery of the absolute horizon of reading and interpretation, or to Foucault's concept of a discursive field. Discourse in this sense is not, " a mere formalization of knowledge, its aim is the control and manipulation of knowledge, the body politic and, ultimately (although Foucault is evasive about this) the state" (Said, 1983, p. 188). "It is at once the object of struggle and the tool by which the struggle is conducted" (p. 216).

Because personal narratives (and the oral history interview is a personal narrative no matter how loose its structure may appear) are an occasion for the struggle for meaning and the control of interpretation as well as identity formation, they are deeply embedded in ideologies. Because ideologies represent the world as particular classes, factions, and/or interests wish that world to be, they exist in conflict with one another depending on the group consciousness of their spokespeople. Thus, an examination of the interview setting as an arena for the contesting of interpretation and therefore ideology will reveal to us how the political praxis of the history is manipulated. The fact is, that in most cases, the oral history interview is completed. The struggle inherent in the situation is managed to the satisfaction, more or less, of each of the partners. That completion would indicate that, despite a struggle for the assigning of meaning to aspects of the narrative, or the struggle for interpretative power, the partners feel that their conversations with one another and their conversation for the record have allowed each of them to legitimate the dominant meanings or to resist those meanings.

The situation in which this tension is most easily managed, a situation in which one of the partners simply overwhelms the other and no conflict over interpretation occurs, is, for reasons discussed elsewhere (Grele, 1985) an incomplete conversation. It contains none of the reciprocity that allows for response and denies to each partner the right to challenge the subjectivity of the interpretation and thereby reifies the ideology of one partner. To understand the ways in which political praxis emerges in the interview, we need a vision of the interview that encompasses the conflict inherent in the situation and links that conflict with the ways in which meaning is structured through the conflict itself.

The most sophisticated analysis, and the most intensive examination of the ways in which conflict is managed in the oral history interview, is the work of McMahan (1989). Concerned with many of the same issues as Langellier, McMahan focused her analysis solely on the oral history interview as a form of personal storytelling, and solely on elite interviewing in order to eliminate as many ideological variables as possible. Her aim is to integrate the discussion of conversational analysis, social processes, and narrative formation with the concepts of philosophical hermeneutics as developed by Hans-George Gadamer. In particular, McMahan is interested in three aspects of hermeneutic theory and how they apply to the interview: the performance of the interview within the universe of linguistic possibilities that mark the historicity of the human experience, the fact that the interpretation of historical phenomena is always guided by the biases that an interpreter has at a specific moment of time [ideology], and the contention that the act of interpretation must always be concerned not with the intended meaning, but what the intended meaning is about [deep structure].

McMahan defined the oral history interview as a situation of potential conflict that, through a series of conversational transformations and social strategies, both parties cooperate to convert into a situation of contrariety, a situation in which, for purposes of conducting the interview, they agree to disagree. Using the work of

Shutz and Kocklemas on the nature of intersubjectivity, and the ways in which people structure their worlds, McMahan lays the basis for a consideration of what Gadamer called the "hermeneutic conversation," and how it can be realized in the oral history interview. The hermeneutic conversation is a conversation in which the horizons of both partners (in this case the interviewer and the interviewee) are altered by appropriation of each other's text through a process of equal and active reciprocity (Linge, 1976). Its realization in the oral history interview is made possible by the situation of contrariety.

With these considerations in mind, McMahan analyzed a set of oral history interviews to ascertain the transformations involved in the process, and how they contribute to or deter the development of hermeneutic conversation. In this manner, she argued, we can understand the oral history interview as a communicative event, and the rules for making it such an event (i.e., an event in which actual communication takes place, where one has restored the possibility of response). We can also judge the usefulness of various strategies in producing such an event.

McMahan's analysis is an important step in the recognition of the ways in which ideology determines political praxis in the interview. She showed the intersubjective nature of the historical meaning and interpretation that emerges in the interview, and the dialectical manner in which it is produced. She was also able to illustrate how that interpretation is in fact the creation of social reality through the interplay of the historical views of both partners to the interview, and how the basic conflict over interpretation is mediated. In addition, whether intentional or not, her analysis has decidedly democratic overtones. Focused as it is on those interview situations in which both partners participate, in fact, privileging them, her analysis recognizes the necessity for participation and response on the part of both partners to the conversation. The view of the interview as an open set of transformations allows us to use the interview to move our understanding forward while not closing off the possibility of future interpretation. Much of what she said about the nature of conversation, and the ways in which meaning is achieved through talk, resonates with the deepest dreams of the participatory democracy and free speech movements.

Her analysis, however, stops short of a consideration of the interview itself as political praxis, in the sense of the term as used by Langellier (1989). While offering the possibility of such considerations, McMahan's interest is not in narrative as a way of approaching the political unconscious or as a system of actual power relations. To move to that deeper structural level it is necessary that we layer McMahan's theories with considerations of the political agendas of the partners in an oral history interview.

In the oral history interview, as contrasted to, let us say, the consciousness raising group (Langellier's main example),[1] the political situation is defined by the professional ideology of the historian/interviewer and the public ideology of the interviewee and the interplay between them and finds its expression in language in the conflict between two distinct views of what narrative is or should be, for historical

---

[1] For an interesting variant of this thesis, see Anguera (1988).

understanding, each reflecting a differing view of the role of language in the culture. The arena in which these conflicting views of narrative discourse are best seen is in the hidden conversations between the interviewer, interviewee, and the social world in which the interview takes place; that is, their conversations with and their meanings within the wider discourse of future users or readers (interpreters) of the interview.

Throughout her analysis of the oral history interview, McMahan noted the existence of this outside audience of potential users, but did not devote particular attention to the ways in which its existence influences the development of the hermeneutic conversation in the interview. The existence of that audience is, however, critical because it raises the level of ideological discourse beyond the immediate situation of the interview, and is, in effect, the audience of which the ideology is articulated. The interview itself is the vehicle for the integration of self and group identity and the audience is the group with which the partners seek to forge an identity. Ideologies, because they are located in the social world, no matter how complex that location, speak to some sense of solidarity with other members of a particular class or group (Jameson, 1981, p. 290) and in the oral history interview it is that class or group for which the historian serves as mediator to whom the interviewee speaks. The question is, to what group—for whom the interviewee serves as mediator—is the historian speaking?

The particular public political positions of the interviewer/historian and the interviewee are often easily revealed. Differences of class, race, and gender, in a social world conscious of the ways in which they are expressed, are often exposed as varying imperatives in the interview. In some cases, the social differences are so deep that the ideological conflict can never be healed. In other cases, agreement is so great there is little conflict. In most, however, the political agendas of both partners are fairly muted and emerge only with analysis.

But even then the conflict is often more subtle, especially when covered or obscured by the seeming innocuous rules of historical questions. Said (1983) argued:

> Everyone working in a field, by a process of acculturation, accepts certain guild standards by which the new and the not-new are recognizable. These standards are far from absolute, just as they are far from being fully conscious. They can be very harshly applied, nevertheless, particularly when the guild's corporate sense feels itself under attack.

These standards, what Foucault (1970) called the discourse of the disciplines, form the unstated ideological vision of the historian. In most interviews they are hegemonic; even the most cantankerous or ideologically distant interviewee will often look to the interviewer/historian for confirmation and guidance as to whether the information being conveyed and the interpretations being offered are the type desired by the historian.[2] In most cases it is agreed that the oral history interview will follow the rules of historical construction as laid down by the historical profession and interpreted by the historian. Such agreement obscures the ideological potency of

---

[2] For an analysis of the research interview and the relations between informant and researcher, see Mishler (1986).

the "professional" stance, and is an important part of the way in which decisions are made about who has the right to talk about what. Such power relations are potentially magnified in interviews with nonhegemonic populations or when they are interwoven with questions of class, race, or gender (Anderson, Armitage, Jack, & Wittner, 1987; Jefferson, 1984).

Keeping in mind the ways in which professional standards mask ideological issues, it is instructive to layer McMahan's use of particular interview segments in her discussion of hermeneutic conversation to try to uncover more of the political praxis of the interview. This particular layering may, in some sense, be unfair to McMahan because the examples I turn to are excerpts taken from interviews I conducted. When McMahan used them, she did not have the advantage of my own recollections of the interviewing situation and my thoughts about the political ambience of them. By this layering I do not mean to imply that her analysis is flawed—indeed, I hope to show that she did find, through her formal analysis, certain problems that, because she did not have the data, could not be discussed in a political language. By this layering, I hope to indicate the ways in which the professional attitudes of the historian become a matter of concern for the historical meaning of what the conversation is about (Mishler, 1986).

In the first case, McMahan quoted from an interview I conducted as part of the research for my doctoral thesis. The particular interview was with a former New Jersey congressman who had also played a role in the politics of the Democratic party in New Jersey when those politics revolved around the unseating of long-time boss Frank Hague. The purpose of the interview was to gather information for a thesis describing the development of "urban liberalism" in that particular congressional district. The dissertation was being directed by J. Joseph Huthmacher from whose work the concept of urban liberalism was derived. McMahan used this excerpt to show a pattern of requests for confirmation and clarification and how those requests are used to forward the conversation.

R: Those years were years of intensive battles within the labor movement over the issue of Communism and anti-Communist? [Request for confirmation]
E: Yes. [Grant]
R: Did that have any effect in the district? [Request for clarification]
E: I was not able to perceive that it had any appreciable effect in that respect. There was, of course, the battle within the electrical worker's union at that time but it seems to me that perhaps both factions then supported the party. [Grant]
R: You were active in the formation of the ADA? [Request for confirmation]
E: Yes. [Grant]

McMahan's formal analysis, it strikes me, is on target and it does explain the ways in which we both managed the conversation and struggled to interpret the event under discussion. Despite this, McMahan sensed that this segment failed to allow each of us to appropriate the perspective of the other, and thus did not yield hermeneutic conversation. I would argue that although the formal analysis may reveal this failure, it is only the political analysis that can explain it. As the interviewer, I was aware that the interview was to be read by my thesis committee (or at least some of the members of the committee), and that it most certainly was going to be read by Huthmacher with whom I had had some disagreements about the adequacy of urban liberalism as an explanatory theory for the politics of the New Deal Democratic party. On one level it was necessary for me to indicate to the members of my committee that I had asked the pertinent questions of my interviewee, that I had asked them in a manner consistent with the profession's view of "historical objectivity," and that I exhibited a competent grasp of the day-to-day events of the politics of that district at the time under discussion. On the other, I had to use those techniques to raise questions about the general interpretative framework of the most powerful member of that committee, who, in all fairness retained a remarkably even sense of humor about the situation, yet, was not about to let my own historical interpretation go unquestioned.

In essence, in the excerpt under investigation, I had decided (and I assume the members of my committee agreed because none of them raised a question) that the full story of the development of a liberal ideology within the Democratic party in New Jersey at that time necessitated a line of questioning about the role of the Congress of Industrial Organizations (CIO) in the development of that ideology, and the role of the Communist party in the development of the ideology of the CIO. An examination of the transcript, and McMahan's evidence, indicates that the congressman agreed to the legitimacy of that line of questioning. There was nothing in the set of questions decided upon by both interviewer and interviewee that would disturb the hegemonic discourse about the development of liberalism in the Democratic party in the 1930s and 1940s.

However, as a critic from the left, I was also interested in establishing that the Communist party, or members of that party, played some role, through a more or less class-conscious politics, in the development of the ideology of liberalism, a role not admitted by the concept of urban liberalism. I was also interested in discovering the ways in which anti-Communism became a part of liberal ideology, and how tensions over this issue within the labor movement and the Democratic party helped define urban liberalism by excluding class-conscious politics.

The congressman obviously disagreed with this agenda and interpretation, by arguing that the split in the labor movement over this issue had no effect because both factions continued to support the Democratic party. Stymied by this denial, and having no other evidence to support my case, I attempted to get at the issue of anti-Communism through a discussion of his membership in the Americans for Democratic Action, which at the time was a spearhead of anti-Communism among liberals within the Democratic party.

On the positive side, this exchange did give me some indication of the congressman's vision of the relationship between the labor movement and the Democratic party. On the negative side, however, it did lead me to ask three questions of the whole effort: Was he evading the issue? Was he ever in a position to participate in any of the debates over this issue? Could it be the case that the ideological debate among liberals over the issue of anti-Communism took place in another arena and that the local political level might not be the best place to search for evidence of its existence or effect? In any case, for our discussion, while on the formal level the excerpt shows a series of negotiations and responses, on the political level the conflicting views of the past and its meaning continued to discourage interpretative agreement. We could agree about the rules of the game, but not what the intended meaning was about. It is this impasse that McMahan sensed, but was unable to fully explain.

A second example is McMahan's use of an interview I did while working for the John F. Kennedy Library with Kennedy's first advisor on mental health and retardation. To McMahan, the excerpt, which is too long to quote here, is an example of topic management; which it certainly is. Again, however, some discussion of the interplay between professional concerns and historical interpretation, when interwoven with her formal analysis helps us to explain and appropriate the text more fully. Serendipity determined my participation in the interview. I happened to be going to California, where the interviewee lived, on a job interview and the timing was convenient. The interviewee had had a long and distinguished career in medicine and was, at that time, being interviewed on that career by the UCLA Oral History Program (the transcript when completed ran to more than 2,500 pages). His tenure at the Kennedy White House was brief and marked a small part of his career. Because I was somewhat unprepared to discuss the details of mental health policy and he had some difficulty recalling specifics of his brief tenure, we agreed, tacitly, that the interview would be conducted at a fairly abstract interpretative level mixed with any anecdotes or stories he happened to remember. In this sense, the most interesting part of the interview was the first 5 minutes when we both assessed the situation and came to this conclusion.

In the excerpt cited by McMahan, the concerns in my mind revolved around the close watch that members of the Kennedy administration exercised over the actions of the advisory council and its chairman. Others had told us that there was some concern on the part of the President and members of his family over the appointment because of the fact that one of the Kennedy sisters had been designated as mentally retarded, and because the family was unsure of the opinions of this particular advisor on a number of questions dealing with the care of mentally retarded young people. My aim in the interview was to discover whether or not this concern had been expressed directly and, if so, how he dealt with that concern. I also wanted his recollections of the effect that the rather limited range of activities allowed him and the council by the White House from the time of his appointment until the organization of a very successful White House conference on mental health and retardation, had upon his own career. I have no idea of how he interpreted my line of questioning, but his response was to frame the answer in terms of the usual limits a Republican might face within a Democratic administration. I am still unsure, after all these years, as to the meaning of that explanation. Can it be accepted at face value? Was it a way to mask his hurt at being treated with such suspicion? What the exchange does show is how easily questions can be handled within the ideological discourse of U.S. politics and party allegiances, despite the fact that most historians would tend to minimize the effect of those allegiances.

The point here is not to go through each interview excerpt used by McMahan to add information that only an interviewer would know and thereby divert attention from the strengths of that analysis. This layering has been undertaken to point out that questions of form are not prior to questions of ideology and that questions of ideology are not prior to questions of form. They emerge together in the dialectical relationship in the interview, and in the interaction between the partners in the interview as they explore the historical worlds in which each is embedded. For a successful hermeneutic analysis of an oral history interview these worlds and the ways in which they shape and determine the languages of the interview must be grasped.

The inherent unfairness of my use of these interviews, built as it is upon McMahan's use of the same material, points up a major issue for all fieldworkers, or anyone interested in discovering the generation of meaning in an interview encounter. The issue is what Rabinow (1986, p. 253) called, "corridor talk": the gossip about a fieldworker's field experience that is, "an important component of a person's reputation, and the material he or she uses [but] which is hardly ever written about 'seriously.'" The fact that we do not usually incorporate such "gossip" into our analyses of the question at hand obscures the internal and external dialogue of the interview. It also adds to the view, "widely held and generally reinforced by conventional fieldwork guides or manuals, that individuals can conduct fieldwork involving people studying people without being people" (Georges & Jones, 1980, p. 153). In oral history fieldwork, the situation is compounded by the initial archival assumption that the interviewer is simply a vessel through which information is conveyed to a larger audience of researchers, and by the fact that fieldworkers rarely, if ever, keep the kind of detailed fieldwork notes or journals kept by anthropologists and folklorists. Although many critics may wax poetic about the disappearing author, in this situation that disappearance leads to the dilemma posed earlier in our discussion of Rosengarten and the North Carolina collective. We are denied the necessary information that would allow us to uncover the political praxis of the interview and are thus unable to decipher the ideological contest over, and the context of, the interpretations being presented. In the first case, we are asked to believe that a folk ideology emerges spontaneously through experience but are never told why that happens or why it should be privileged over any other ideology. In the second we are denied the view of people grappling with the contradictions within their own historical visions and thus the view of them as fully active participants not only in their histories but in the search for meaning in that history. Our response to such works is therefore necessarily limited and the public discourse over its meaning is limited.

There are, of course, many examples of texts in which the fieldworker tells of his or her involvement in the creation of the documents upon which the text is based, and what that means for the interpretation being offered. Mintz's (1974) *Worker in the Cane* is an example of how a sympathetic fieldworker can handle the problem within a more or less traditional sense of text. Gluck's (1987) *Rosie the Riveter Revisited* is an example of how personal concerns and feminist theory can be mobilized to reveal the interplay between the historical views of interviewer and interviewee. *Black Mountain: An Exploration in Community* (Duberman, 1972) which is in many ways *sui generis*, is an attempt to fully develop what Tedlock (1979) called the dialogic nature of the text while consciously attempting to break the bounds of the professional historian's ideology.

Worker in the Cane is essentially a life history of Don Taso, a Puerto Rican sugar worker. As Mintz (1989), himself, has pointed out, the reception of the work has an ambiguous history. Criticized in 1960 when it was published because Mintz had become a friend of Taso and thus established close personal ties that compromised the basic aim of the fieldworker to maintain affectless ties to her informant, by the 1980s it was seen as an example of the anthropologist maintaining an unequal relationship between himself and his informant because Mintz rearranged the text for publication. Although it is true that Mintz arranged the material in a chronological order which it did not have when presented, he also reproduced the conversation in almost verbatim fashion to preserve the narrative. Throughout the work, and in his later comments on it, Mintz did not shirk from contemplation upon the ambiguity in the life history concerning the narrative roles of the informant and researcher, and is careful to note the continuing social division of labor, as Burgos (1988) termed it, within the emerging narrative.

In a break with standards of fieldwork of the time, he is careful to outline his growing friendship with Taso and how that friendship both expands the conversation and limits the development of the history itself, especially when Taso becomes somewhat unwilling to openly discuss his conversion to a form of pentecostal Protestantism that he knew Mintz viewed with a certain "sourness" (p. 5). Thus, the personal and the political boundaries of the cultural tension became objects of investigation themselves, and examples of the social relations of production that so fascinate Mintz in the full life history. In structuring the text, Mintz incorporated many of his questions into it so we, the readers, can judge the appropriateness of each response to the question asked. Most importantly, Mintz recognized the differing life views within the fieldwork situation without privileging either. By doing so he is able to place Taso's life story within the larger structure of the history of Puerto Rico and the history of sugar production in the Caribbean world. By highlighting his own participation in the creation of the text and his own disquiet about aspects of Taso's life, Mintz allowed Taso an independence of position and judgment denied in other texts that do not express this inherent conflict. This tension is also a bridge to larger questions about the ways in which the world created by Taso is changing, and an insight into that change, especially its limits. It thus unites the narrative with the events under discussion through the use of both biographies.

Mintz (1989) addressed directly the relations between researcher and informant.

To question one's project along the way is essential. But that question ought not, it seems to me, turn into a self-consciousness so sensitive that the purpose of the inquiry is forgotten while the methodology is being perfected. If that self-consciousness settles too heavily upon the ethnographer's worries about who he or she really is, then one runs the risk of being reduced to communicating mostly about oneself. Then it is the informant who may become background....

...Anthropology must be humanistic in its orientation. But anthropology must be scientific.... If one believes in causation in human events, if one believes that history is not simply what people feel it is, then one is prepared to interpret in a manner that allows others to judge the interpretations for themselves on a basis that provides at least some opportunity for proof or disproof. (p. 794)

Although Mintz raised a number of questions about power in his discussion of *Worker in the Cane*, the ideology of the profession as it operates in fieldwork is not one of his concerns. Gluck's work is much more personal, narrowing the distance and perspective Mintz has maintained and consciously attempting to bridge gaps between herself as professional historian and her informants as storytellers. Essentially a compilation of edited interview segments, *Rosie the Riveter Revisited* tells the stories of several women who worked in the aircraft industry in the Los Angeles area during World War II. The book is infused with the ideology of feminism, in particular the notion of the necessity to merge the personal and the political. Gluck prefaced each account with commentary on her own impressions of the woman being interviewed, the role of the interviewing process in the life of the woman who is telling her story, and the storytelling abilities of the particular informant. One of the exceptional aspects of the crafting of the book is that after Gluck had recorded and transcribed the interviews she then returned to the people interviewed to jointly edit the final text. This allowed them a certain shared power over the ways in which they were presented to the larger public. Unfortunately, Gluck did not tell us in what ways this helped shape the interpretation of the experiences under study. This procedure, however, did allow Gluck to escape from the tendency to reify the moment of production or presentation as the only moment in which meaning is expressed in continuing dialogue. Her attempt to bring herself into the text and share with her informants the shaping of the text derives from a deeply ethical sense of her responsibilities to those she interviewed that is at odds with a view of them as solely informants. "I tell my students," she wrote, "that we are giving something very important back to the people we interview. Yet, at times, I worry that we may, to some degree, be exploiting those we interview" (pp. 26–27).

The most radical example of the attempt to transcend the usual limits of the definitions of personal and professional relations established by the disciplinary ideology is Duberman's (1972) *Black Mountain*. Roundly criticized when it was published in 1972—Conkin (1973) called it "embarrassing," "pretentious," "the very epitome of bad taste"—most reviewers missed the brilliance of what Duberman had done. It is an extraordinary example of how a historian who is aware of the subjectivity of the historical enterprise, and the ways in which multiple agendas create multiple meanings in an interview, creates a text that attempts to contain and exhibit those various and contradictory meanings. If the meaning of words, ultimately, depends on the concrete situation in which they are spoken, how does the historian craft his or her presentation to show the fullness of those concrete situations and the full range of contradictions within them while still adhering to the conventions of his or her calling. If these conventions dictate that the historian should not appear in the text, Duberman's answer is that he cannot abide by those conventions.

To Duberman, the history of Black Mountain, an experimental college in North Carolina that attracted to its staff and student body a remarkable group of intellectuals and artists, is contested territory. And he is deeply involved for personal and political reasons in that contestation. Thus, throughout the work, Duberman stepped aside to meditate upon the progress of the work. He consciously broke his narrative in order to add his own impressions of its form and emergence to it. In the process, he created a new text and brought into the open his own personal history, his political attitudes, his sexual orientation, in short, all of his "prejudices." He then, at some length, discussed the ways in which they have become part of his work. Oddly enough, this very subjectivity, his own consciousness of his own prejudices and their effects on the prejudices of others, transforms them into objects of study, and the initial objects of study, the people who made the history of Black Mountain, become the subjects of the analysis.

Fully conscious of the ways in which *Black Mountain* is a confrontation with the normal standards of professional discourse, Duberman told us in his introduction that he had to put the work aside for a number of years because he found that his early work did not catch the range of commentary and interaction he desired. Returning to it, he returned with the aim of breaking through the disciplinary boundaries. The difficulty of the task is noted in the following excerpt from his journal, which he cited in the book.

My Journal, Monday, August 3, 1970: The data is taking over again. Or rather, my compulsiveness about being totally accurate and inclusive. I start letting myself go [but] get deflected into incorporating...material into earlier sections; mostly additional citations to footnotes rather than changing interpretations—just the kind of silly "iceberg" scholarship...that I rhetorically scorn. By the time I come back to the question that had started to excite me, I'm laden with repetitive information to other people's reactions to other issues. How can I explore theirs and mine simultaneously? I don't want to evade or distort their views, but I don't want fidelity to theirs to take over, to obliterate mine.... It's an example of how destructive so-called "professional training" can be; it initiates you into and confirms the rightness of techniques previously used by others. Yet, there aren't any techniques, only personalities. (pp. 89–90)

Duberman is not an oral historian. He is a historian who has conducted a series of interviews as part of a research project. But, his insights into the nature of the process and the difficulty of representing the excitement of fieldwork and the promise of the interview within the traditional forms of historical narrative are brilliant. His attempt to try to represent that process in his book in such a way that he remains true to the circumstances of the creation of the information he is using, offers us an important commentary upon our work. That he cannot fully resolve the contradictions should not surprise us. His achievement is that he has laid bare the contradictions involved in the usual assumptions about authority and power in historical presentation.

In the following excerpt of an interview from *Black Mountain*, chosen at random, and not a very good one, we can see the contradiction. And, because the excerpt is so typical of many that we find in our own work, we can see our own contradictions as well. This particular segment is from an interview Duberman conducted with David Weinrib, a sculptor, in which Duberman asked Weinrib to describe a musical event mounted by John Cage at Black Mountain, an event that became a part of the folklore of the college.

Weinrib: There were a lot of people looking at clocks, And there was a podium. I mean a lectern, and Cage was at it.... It was to the side...And he started to lecture.... He read it. And as he was reading it things started to happen. But he just kept reading, as I remember, all evening.

Duberman: What was the content? Do you remember?

Weinrib: I don't remember. Except there was — there was some quotations from Meister Eckhart... I don't remember much else about the content. It was cut into very often. But he just kept reading. And there was a number of things that happened. And there was Rauschenberg with an old Gramophone that he'd dug up. And every now and then...he'd wind it up and play this section of an old record...

Duberman: What was he playing?

Weinrib: Just old hokey records, as I remember.

Duberman: Old popular records?

Weinrib: Old records. I'm sure he bought them with the machine. 1920s. 1930s. Then Cunningham danced around the whole area.

Duberman: Around this core of chairs?

Weinrib: Yes, danced and —

Duberman: Were there aisles in between?

Weinrib: No. I remember we all sort of sat together.

Duberman: In the center?

Etc., etc.(p. 354)

What Duberman did here was simply an exaggerated version of what I was doing when I interviewed the congressman quoted earlier, what Mintz did in a much more subdued fashion, and what Gluck must have done in the interviewing sessions but edited out of the published presentation. In his concern for analysis, he has destroyed the story as story. Because we feel we have some commitment to the documentary impulse, we cannot allow the narrative to wander too far, to become too complicated, before we intervene to ascertain the context of the events under discussion, the actual time of their occurance, and the details of each. The oral history is a narrative and also an analysis. The analysis of the narrator is embedded in the story he or she tells, the analysis of the historian is embedded in the questions asked. Those questions break the narrative with analysis. If the oral history is a conversational narrative, the conversation is often at odds with the drive for narrative. The ideological conflict takes the form of the basic conflict of the interview.

Although we destroy story as story, our interviewees will move quickly to restore that narrativity. "Where was I?" they ask, and go on with their telling. Our role in building the narrative is crucial. Yet, the manner in which we attempt to build it, to add detail to it, to force memory to its limit, is by the destruction of the vary narrativity of the narrative. We do not treat it as an unfolding story in which we are being swept along, but as an object of analysis and deconstruction. The production of real narrative, in which narrative schemes govern the construction of the testimony, is rare in oral history, and the reason is that the interviewer refuses to allow it to develop.

Oral history interviewing is part of the historical enterprise. Thus, the historian/interviewer is trapped in the language, practices and ideology of the profession. That ideology, most baldly stated by Fischer (1970) is that history is not storytelling but problem solving. Historians work in the everyday public language of the culture and have never, despite many noble or ignoble attempts, devised a specialized language for themselves. Yet, within the profession a sharp distinction is often drawn between analytic history and narrative history, and between narrative and analysis within a particular historical work (Hexter, 1971).[3] This distinction, Susman (1964) argued, is deeply embedded in the profession and expresses our differing views of a usable past. Because it is in the realm of language that we find the location of the basic ideological conflict in the interview, these distinctions become crucial. The language of history used by the interviewer is the language of analysis. Its form is the question. The language of history used by the interviewee is the language of narrative. Its form is the story. Each has a teleology operating within it (Gadamer, 1976). Thus, if we can understand the ways in which these conflicting languages of history ebb and flow within the interview, we can understand the ways in which each partner, beneath the guise of politeness, is contesting for control of the interview, and thus control of the interpretation. We can see the political praxis of the interview.

This contest, of course, is often unstated. Based as it is in our acculturated mode of asking questions or of telling stories we fail to recognize its political nature. But, when placed in an arena of contradiction and contrariety, its ideological nature is revealed. In this manner, we see the ways in which interviewer and interviewee conspire to legitimate dominant meanings, or delegitimate them, or confront each other in ideological disputation. In either case, the interplay between these languages allows us to discover the fit between both interviewer and interviewee and the world as they experience it (Langellier, 1989).

Alessandro Portelli (1981) argued that, "[t]o tell a story is to take arms against the threat of time" (p. 162). But in an interview, we force the story into time, to

---

[3]Recent debates over the ways in which various theories of deconstruction have affected the historical profession have done nothing to break the narrative/analysis discourse. See for example Harlan (1989) and Appleby (1989).

contextualize it and thereby disarm the storyteller. The consequences of this situation are ambiguous. Do we, thereby, as Ricoeur (1984) would have it, aid in the emplotment of the incident into a unified and complete story? Do we thus aid in the creation of a more coherent structure to the life story being told? (Roos, 1989) Or are we undermining the possibility of self-presentation and forcing the story into well-worn paths? In situations where we are interviewing people who speak within the dominant or hegemonic discourse, the use of the language of analysis allows us to question that discourse, to contest the ideology, to explore the contradictions inherent in it, to discover its social roots—to demystify it. In situations where we are interviewing people who are attempting to break through the mounds of the hegemonic discourse, or people whose dissent is not clearly articulated because they are rarely given the opportunity to respond, our analytic stance can undermine their confidence in their ability to tell the tale, to configure their world. We can thereby reinforce the dominant discourse just by doing what we usually do. The power we exercise to contest interpretation is not only interpretative—it is social and political.

Obviously, this dilemma is not limited to oral history. Feminist scholars in many disciplines have raised similar issues about male and female language and how that language is a reflection of social power (Caplan, 1988). It is a variant of issues now being raised in the attack on critical legal studies for use of a language, which is the language of professionally trained White males, and the drive to include other discourses, mostly narrative, in those studies (Crenshaw, 1988). The question to be faced is whether or not the return of narrativity is to be as welcome among hegemonic classes, and equally privileged (Wilkie, 1973).

The question of power in the interview is more complex than social form or conversational dominance. The languages of history, analytic or narrative, are the languages through which we and our interviewees as citizens and historians, filter our experiences, thereby defining them, and through which we express our own world views and ideologies. The tension that emerges reflects deeper social tensions and thus the question of sharing power in the interview is simply one form of the question of sharing power in the social order. We are caught in a bind. If we intervene in the building of the narrative, we intrude ourselves and our ideology into the process. If we do not, we abnegate our responsibility as critics of mystification.

There may be no satisfactory answer to this contradiction, although differing solutions have been proposed. Some fieldworkers, in anthropology in particular, have argued that no solution is possible when the fieldworker studies other cultures and they should withdraw from that work. Others would withdraw the power of interpretation from the fieldworker altogether, as if that were possible. Rosaldo (1980) proposed that we seek the possibility of a final narrative as an "analytic narrative" (p. 89). Engaged scholars might argue, as does Jameson (1981) that, ideological struggle is not first and foremost, "a matter of moral choice but of taking sides in a struggle between embattled groups" (p. 290). Thus, the decision to encourage or discourage narrative, to intervene in the storytelling, would rest upon one's desire to buttress or undermine the class position that is being articulated. Rabinow (1986, pp. 256–258, 261) outlined four different postures, each with its own problematic. "But," he added, "the problem is precisely to decide if it is actually suitable to place oneself within a 'we' in order to assert the principles one recognizes and the values one accepts; or if it is not, rather, necessary to make the future formation of a 'we' possible."

The debates in anthropology have been summarized and the various positions critiqued by Dwyer (1982, pp. 255–286). Faced with the same dilemma of the relationship between "self" and "other" Dwyer urged us to recognize that,

> ...in the personal confrontation between Self and Other, the barrier between the two is broken down as the parties interact, daily, with one another; also the illusion of an objective self becomes untenable, because mere participation in the confrontation inevitably locates the self culturally as the 'outsider' intruding on the Other's terrain, and historically as a representative of a society that has a prior history of intrusion. (p. 274)

Dwyer turned to the dialogical characteristics of such confrontations to outline an argument for the "recursive nature of meaning" (p. 275). In this sense, each moment of contact is part of a larger project in which each partner to the confrontation orients and reorients the project in new directions.

Recent work in oral history points to the same direction, yet elaborates a sophisticated set of considerations on the nature of the dialogue in the oral history interview. In *The Death of Luigi Trastulli* (1991) Portelli developed the historiographical and political implications of such a dialogic perspective. Closely based on his own fieldwork experiences, Portelli accented the role of equality and difference in field research.

> The two concepts are related. Only equality prepares us to accept difference in terms other than hierarchy and subordination; on the other hand, without difference there is no equality—only sameness, which is a much less worthwhile ideal. Only equality makes the interview credible, but only difference makes it relevant. Fieldwork is meaningful as the encounter of two subjects who recognize each other as subjects, and therefore separate, and seek to build their equality upon their difference in order to work together. (p. 43)

In this situation, both the observer and the observed "may be stimulated to think new thoughts about themselves" (p. 43). The dialogue is, in effect, never ending as both parties search for ways to appropriate the narratives of the other. In an attempt to develop the concept of dialogue and to actualize it in their fieldwork, both Dwyer and Portelli gave numerous examples of the ways in which they opened themselves and their projects to the people with whom they worked so that speech and counterspeech were given full rein in formulating the analysis they developed on the societies whose narratives they sought to uncover and explain.

Unlike other fieldwork sciences, however, oral history has always had a public character. From its origins in archival practice, oral history has always presented itself and its product—the interview—to a larger public for its use, be that public the people interviewed or other historians. In this sense, the oral historian, because he or she has never exercised source monopoly, has attempted to continue the dialogue over the meaning of the testimony by bringing colleagues or the citizens themselves into the dialogue. The project is, thus, never finished. In his recent work, *A Shared Authority* (1989), Frisch presented us with a number of examples of how this was done and the effects on the historical consciousness of both the historians involved and the communities studied. Frisch's works serve to remind us of the public nature of our work. If the solution to the dilemmas of how we remain true to the best of the traditions of the profession while remaining true to the testimony we are given and the world from which it emerges is in some form of a dialogic approach, then it is incumbent upon us to always remind ourselves of the public nature of our work and its role in the larger social and political milieu in which we work.

REFERENCES

Anderson, K., Armitage, S., Jack, D., & Wittner, J. (1987). Beginning where we are: Feminist methodology in oral history. *Oral History Review*, 103–128.

Anguera, K. (1988). To make the personal political: The use of testimony as a consciousness-raising tool against sexual aggression in Puerto Rico. *Oral History Review*, 65–94.

Appleby, J. O. (1989). One good turn deserves another: Moving beyond the linguistic; a response to David Harlan. *American Historical Review*, 94(5), 1326–1332.

Burgos, M. (1988). Life stories, narrativity, and the search for self. *Publications of the Research Unit for Contemporary Culture*, 9.

Caplan, P. (1988). Engendering knowledge: The politics of ethnography. *Anthropology Today*, 4(6), 8–17.

Clifford, J., & Marcus, G. E., (Eds.). (1986). *Writing culture: The poetics and politics of ethnography*. Berkeley: University of California.

Conkin, P. (1973). Review of *Black Mountain*. *Journal of American History*, 60, 512.

Crenshaw, K. W. (1988). Race, reform and retrenchment: Transformation and legitimation in anti-discrimination law. *Harvard Law Review*, 101 (7), 1331–1387.

Duberman, M. (1972). *Black Mountain: An exploration in community*. New York: Dutton.

Dwyer, K. (1982). *Moroccan dialogues: Anthropoł ʾgy in question*. Prospect Heights, IL: Waveland Press.

Fischer, D. H. (1970). *Historian's fallacies: Toward a logic of historical thought*. New York: Harper & Row.

Foucault, M. (1970). *The order of Things: The archelolgy of the human sciences*. New York: Vintage.

Friedlander, P. (1975). *The emergence of a UAW local: A study in class and culture*. Pittsburgh: University of Pittsburg Press.

Frisch, M. (1979). Oral History and *Hard Times*: A review essay. *Oral History Review*, 53–69.

Frisch, M. (1989). *A shared authority: Essays in the craft and meaning of oral history and public history*. Albany: State University of New York Press.

Gadamer, H-G. (1976). *Philosophical hermeneutics* (D.E. Linge, Trans.). Berkeley: University of California.

Geertz, C. (1964). Ideology as a cultural system. In D. Apter (Ed.), *Ideology and discontent* (pp. 47–65). Glencoe, IL: The Free Press.

Georges, R. A., & Jones, M. O. (1980). *People studying people: The human element in fieldwork*. Berkeley: University of California.

Glassie, H. (1982). *Passing the time in Ballymenone: Culture and history of an Ulster community*. Philadelphia: University of Pennsylvania.

Grele, R. J. (1978). Can anyone over thirty be trusted? *Oral History Review*, 36–44.

Grele, R. J. (1985). *Envelopes of sound: The art of oral history*. New York: Praeger.

Gluck, S. B. (1987). *Rosie the riveter revisited: Women, the war and social change*. Boston, MA: Twayne.

Hall, J. D., Leloudis, J., Korstad, R., Murphy, M., Jones, L. & Daly, C.B. (1987). *Like a family: The making of a southern cotton mill world*. Chapel Hill: University of North Carolina.

Harlan, D. (1989). Intellectual history and the return of literature. *American Historical Review*, 94(3), 581–609.

Harris, A. (1985). Introduction. In R.J. Grele, *Envelopes of sound: The art of oral history*. New York: Praeger.

Hexter, J. H. (1971). *Doing history*. Bloomington: University of Indiana.

Huthmacher, J. J. (1968). *Senator Robert F. Wagner and the rise of urban liberalism*. New York: Atheneum.

Jameson, F. (1981). *The political unconscious: Narrative as a socially symbolic art*. Ithaca, NY: Cornell.

Jefferson, A. W. (1984). Echoes from the south: The history and methodology of the Duke University oral history program. *Oral History Review*, 43–62.

Labov, W. (1972). *Language in the inner city*. Philadelphia: University of Pennsylvania.

Langellier, K. M. (1989). Personal narratives: perspectives on theory and research. *Text and Performance Quarterly*. 9(4), 243–276.

Linge, D. E. (1976). Introduction. In H-G. Gadamer, *Philosophical hermeneutics* (pp. xi–lviii). Berkeley: University of California.

McMahan, E. M. (1989). *Oral history discourse: A study of cooperation and coherence*. Tuscaloosa: University of Alabama.

Mintz, S. W. (1974). *Worker in the cane: A Puerto Rican life history*. New York: Norton.

Mintz, S. W. (1989). The sensation of moving while standing still. *American Ethnologist, 16*(4), 786–796.

Mishler, E. G. (1986). *Research interviewing: Context and narrative*. Cambridge, MA: Harvard University Press.

Novick, P. (1988). *That noble dream: The "objectivity question" and the historical profession*. New York: Cambridge University Press.

Passerini, L. (1980). Italian working class culture between the wars: Consensus to fascism and work ideology. *International Journal of Oral History* 1(1), 1–27.

Passerini, L. (1987). *Fascism in popular memory: The cultural experience of the Turin working class*. Cambridge: Cambridge University Press.

Portelli, A. (1981). The time of my life: Functions of time in oral history. *International Journal of Oral History* 2(3), 162–180.

Portelli, A. (1991). *The death of Luigi Trastulli and other stories: Form and meaning in oral history*. Albany: State University of New York Press.

Rabinow, P. (1986). Representations are social facts: Modernity and post-modernity in anthropology. In J. Clifford and G.E. Marcus (Eds.), *Writing culture: The poetics and politics of ethnography* (pp. 234–261). Berkeley: University of California.

Ricoeur, P. (1984). *Time and narrative* (Vol 1., K. Mc Laughlin & D. Pellauer, Trans.). Chicago: University of Chicago Press.

Roos, J. P. (1989). *Life story vs. society: a methodological Bermuda triangle*. Paper presented at the Vienna Center Seminar on the Study of Change in Forms of Life, Vienna.

Rosaldo, R. (1980). Doing oral history. *Social Analysis 4*, 89–99.

Rosengarten, T. (1974). *All God's dangers*. New York: Random House.

Schrager, S. (1983). What is social in oral history? *International Journal of Oral History*, 4(2), 76–98.

Said, E. W. (1983). *The world, the text and the critic*. Cambridge, MA: Harvard University Press.

Susman, W. I. (1964). History and the american intellectual: Uses of usable past. *American Quarterly*. 16(2), 231–250.

Tedlock, D. (1979). The analogical tradition and the emergence of dialogical anthropology. *Journal of Anthropological Research, 35*, 387–410.

Wilkie, J. W. (1973). *Elitelore*. Los Angeles: Latin American Studies Center, University of California.

2

Reconstructing History: The Epitomizing Image

E. Culpepper Clark
University of Alabama

All acts of historical preservation (by which I mean any commitment of thought, no matter how trivial, to a fixed medium) are governed by the prospect of future remembrance, and unless an individual is pathological, the motive in being remembered is to be remembered well—a good father, a good mother, a good teacher, a good president. From diaries to memos, from letters to oral history transcripts, people appeal to a universal audience for validation of their self-worth.

It is this concern for remembrance that gives history its psychological dimension. As Erikson (1975) noted in a social context, historians "are practitioners of a restorative art which transforms the fragmentation of the past and the peculiarities of those who make history into such wholeness of meaning as mankind seeks" (p. 114).The same may be said of history's psychological dimension. The act of remembering is therapy for the psyche, a Proustian search for lost time. It takes our individuated acts in any given moment, especially any bad things we have done, and connects those acts with the wholeness of our being in time, a wholeness expressed in our nobler, loftier senses of self. It is protective and restorative, and although it admits of negative self-disclosure (conceding bad things about one's self), even negative disclosures bend to the higher imperative of self-knowledge through self-justification. "We must always remember," Erikson observed, "that the autobiographer has not agreed to a therapeutic contract by which he promises to put into words all that 'comes to mind'" (p. 123). Finding a past that one can live with, and coming to terms with the past—these necessary acts of the well-adjusted person require that the past not simply be rediscovered but redeemed.

Despite recognition of a kinship between the oral history interview and psychoanalysis (Lomax & Morrissey, 1989), there is some reluctance among oral historians to concede its therapeutic value. This reluctance, however, derives from the historians's particular interest in memory, not the interviewee's. For the informant, the therapeutic dimension is always present as he or she strives for a holistic view of self through a synchronic adjustment of past and present. As Portelli (1981) wrote, "The historian is mainly interested in reconstructing the past; the speaker seeks to project an image" (pp. 165–166). It is this imperative that distinguishes texts created about the past from texts created in the initial upsurge of events, and even in the latter instance, there is always the psychodynamic prospect of future remembrance to be considered. Portelli again said, "The telling of a story preserves the teller from oblivion; a story builds the identity of the teller and the legacy he will leave in time to come" (p. 162). It makes the narrator/interviewee a self-interested autobiographer as well as a participant and for that reason filters the past in ways that call for heightened skepticism of the interviewee's end product, the oral history transcript.

In writing about desegregation at the University of Alabama, I often wished my informants were unavailable and longed for the simplicity of archival research. I would not then be bothered with the contrast between their unfolding, not-yet-finished truths and the documentary trail of what they had done at some particular moment in time. This tension between memory and its subject matter, past thoughts and actions, is especially taut in a drama like civil rights where good and evil are sharply etched and where ending up on the "right" side can be so important in establishing self-worth. In fact, the pressure to be identified with history's right side can occasion a change in the memory of material conditions. The change itself may appear small, even trivial, but because it alters what Burke (1969) called, in the dramatistic sense, an "epitomizing image," "an episode that symbolically represents...the course of the plot" (p. 339), it can transform the whole story. In fact, it is necessary that an alteration be subtle so as to avoid bigger variances that are more readily detectable, both to the reader/listener and to the individual making the alteration. (I suspect most who alter texts would deny having made a change).

To demonstrate both the nature of the epitomizing image and its transforming potential, it is necessary to show a compelling motive for changing the way the past is remembered (that is, why some actions are better altered than excused) and to locate an anecdote that has the power to change the larger story by subsuming its ambiance in a single example. To accomplish this objective, I use my experience in writing the story of desegregation at the University of Alabama. (To avoid emcumbering the text, primary sources that follow and the narrative they support can be indexed in Clark, 1993.)

In 1953, two women, both recent graduates of all-Black Miles Memorial College in Birmingham, applied for admission to the University of Alabama. Three years later they became the first African-American students ordered admitted to a previously all-White institution under the implementation decree of *Brown v. Board of Education*. In what became known as the Autherine Lucy episode, this first attempt at desegregation ended in failure after 3 days of tumultuous disorder on the Tuscaloosa campus. Seven years later, on June 11, 1963, Vivian Malone and James Hood walked past George Wallace as he made good on his promise to stand in the schoolhouse door. These two dramatic events, each coming as it did on the heels of a dramatic campaign in the civil rights movement, the Montgomery Bus Boycott for the Lucy episode and the Birmingham confrontation between Martin Luther King, Jr., and Bull Connor for the schoolhouse door, etched in the public mind a lasting association between the University of Alabama and the forces of massive resistance. This associative guilt made it all the more imperative that a lore develop to explain the university's actions in the desegregation crisis of the 1950s and early 1960s. After all, a university's reputation hinges on its identification with the established values of a dominant culture, especially a culture that appears to be on the winning side of history.

Various organizations and individuals have evolved lores to explain what happened in Tuscaloosa—NAACP officials, African-American student applicants, massive resisters, a handful of liberal dissenters, and the university community. Of all these accounts, none reveals more of the psychological dynamics of remembering than that developed by the university's administration and echoed by its faculty. This study explores the recent memory of two chief actors in the university's desegregation ordeal and squares their memory against the documentary trail created at the time. Vice President James Jefferson Bennett and President Frank Anthony Rose set the official tone and directed the university's response. Like most in the university family, Rose and Bennett styled themselves as moderates, even progressives on the question of race relations, but they also saw themselves as pragmatists. They might best be termed *strategic moderates*. They steered a course between the Scylla of entrenched segregation and the Charybdis of social change. To stay in office (and thereby to maintain their moderating influence), they placated the overwhelming desire of Whites to maintain segregation, while convincing themselves that they were biding time, waiting for the right moment to do the right thing. In so doing, they took actions, some of them unconscionable by present lights, that are best forgotten in the interest of future remembrance.

THE TROUBLED MEMORY OF 1956

The key administrator was Vice President Bennett, a tough ex-marine, professor of law, and from 1954 through 1963, an administrator of considerable influence. He served as legislative liaison for the university during the gubernatorial administrations of James Folsom, John Patterson, and Wallace, and although he had come to the university as a freshman on the same train with George Wallace, he despised the governor, especially after the 1962 campaign in which Wallace fulfilled his pledge not to be "out-niggered." Bennett was an active Episcopalian and professed his church's more advanced positions on human rights. In the 1956 Autherine Lucy debacle, he personally risked danger to protect Lucy from the mob. No one could doubt his conviction or his courage, neither could any one doubt his pragmatism or his ambition.

In the 6 months following Autherine Lucy's expulsion (caused in part by an unwise and untrue allegation brought against the university by her attorneys, Thurgood Marshall, Constance Baker Motley, and Arthur Shores), the university received three applications from African-American students they considered both qualified and serious. In each instance they hired private detectives to do background investigations, and in each instance they got the kind of information necessary to undo the applicants. As chief assistant to the university president, Bennett became progressively more involved as the individual cases developed. Depths to which Bennett and the university sank in these three instances created a compelling motive in later years to change memory in such a way as to identify themselves with the forces of civic virtue.

In the first case, Ruby Steadman Peters, a 40-year-old woman, asked to take courses at the extension center in Birmingham. She wished to transfer credits back to Alabama State College for Negroes in Montgomery so that she could complete her degree in education more expeditiously. She even agreed to take the courses by correspondence or by television to avoid interracial contact in the classroom. The university's Board of Trustees agreed to consider her application but soon developed information from investigators that could be embarrassing for her. The president pro tem of the board asked two prominent White men, each with good connections in the African-American community, to visit her. One of the men served as judge of Birmingham's debtors court and later would be appointed to the federal bench by John F. Kennedy. The other was president of a savings and loan company that held Peter's mortgage and handled most of the credit arrangements for the realty company where she worked. She decided to withdraw her application. On learning of her decision, the president pro tem wrote the judge and the banker to say thanks "for the excellent manner in which you have handled these negotiations leading up to this happy conclusion. Please convey our thanks also to our other friends, who assisted you in this undertaking."

The second applicant, Billy Joe Nabors, had the backing of Allan Knight Chalmers. Chalmers was a long-time diplomat of the civil rights movement with excellent connections in Alabama. He had chaired the Scottsboro Defense Committee, a support group for the "Scottsboro boys," for over a decade and became friends with the Grover Hall newspaper family in Montgomery and other influential Alabamians. At the time of the Nabors case, he chaired the fund-raising arm of the NAACP Legal Defense and Educational Fund and was a member of Boston University's theology faculty. He also served as a trustee of Talladega College, a small Black college 40 miles east of Birmingham, where Nabors attended school. At first, the university's president at that time, Oliver Cromwell Carmichael, and Bennett responded favorably to Chalmers' offer to find "the right Negro applicant." But when trustees learned of Nabors' application, they launched another investigation. Among other things, they learned that Nabors, who came from a large, poor family in the city of Talladega, was $50 in arrears to the laundry where he worked and had acquired a reputation in the local school system for having a temper. As it turned out, the information proved sufficient to undo the application—perhaps a fortunate outcome in that Nabors went on to graduate from Howard University's law school.

The final application taken seriously that year came from Joseph Louis Epps, a pre-med student at Morehouse College in Atlanta. A native of Birmingham, Epps received the support of Emory Jackson, editor of the *Birmingham World* and a recognized leader in the African-American community. Jackson had graduated from Morehouse in the 1930s and belonged to the same fraternity young Epps had joined. Epps' mother got things started in late July by requesting an application form for her son. President Carmichael told the Board in early September that Epps was the most qualified applicant to date and observed that "Bennett has made a preliminary investigation of applicant Epps without being able to find any evidence that would warrant rejection of his application." What happened next is worth telling in detail because it reveals the lengths to which university officials went in placating White sentiment. Their actions also stand in marked contrast to the way these officials remember what happened.

On the day Carmichael told the board about Epps, Bennett began logging his activities on the case; not detailed notes, but revealing nonetheless. Under the heading 9/6/56, Bennett jotted down his first contact with Sam Christian, a private investigator, and with Dr. James Sussex, a psychiatrist at University Hospital in Birmingham. Dr. Sussex was treating Ruby Anna Epps, the young man's mother. The next day, September 7, Sussex called Bennett to say that he had talked with the mother who had just been visited by Emory Jackson. She told the doctor that she did not want her boy to go to the university, that she expected him back from Atlanta tomorrow, and that she would bring him to Dr. Sussex if that proved "necessary to keep him in Atlanta." Bennett also talked with the private investigator and the president pro tem of the board that day but did not reveal the substance of those conversations.

Nothing happened on the 8th. Bennett merely noted that Epps was "not yet back in town." Then on the 9th, the university received a letter from Epps "demanding action"; whereupon Bennett went to Birmingham to see Dr. Sussex. Sussex got in touch with the mother who in turn agreed to have her son call when he arrived. In the meantime, Sussex had written a letter to the mother requesting a delay or postponement of the application. The next day, September 10, the doctor and the mother talked and she assured him that her son had agreed to stay at Morehouse. She also said that she would bring him in to see the doctor the following day at 1:00 p.m. At 2:30 on September 11, Sussex called Bennett to say that the young man had come in alone. Bennett's notes create a graphic sketch of what happened in the doctor's office: "[Epps] had over one hour w/Dr. Boy uncertain what to do. Word is out among NAACP. [Emory] Jackson and others putting heavy pressure. Tried to keep him from seeing Dr. Mother shifts from one side to other—typical of paranoid. Dr. impressed on boy that his admission might put mother in asylum. Boy agrees to give decision to Sussex at 8 tonight."

At 10:00 p.m. Bennett called only to learn that the doctor had not yet heard from the boy. Sussex in turn called Epps' mother using the "pretext that he had been out" and thought she might have called while he was away from the phone. Sussex learned that Epps had been with Emory Jackson ever since leaving the doctor's office but that he would call the next day. When Epps did not call, Sussex phoned him at home. Epps told the doctor that he would go back to Morehouse but that he would not withdraw his application. In reporting these results to Bennett, Sussex speculated "that Jackson has gotten the boy to leave the door open, hoping to change his mind over [the] weekend." Bennett mused, "We can hope he doesn't, but should be ready with decision if he does."

Of course, one could construct an explanation in which the doctor learned of the highly charged situation into which young Epps was headed and tried to stop the application in the interest of the mother's health—she did need professional care. But the evidential fragments that reveal the doctor's thinking are, if anything, seamier than the actions he took. In an earlier conversation, Sussex told Bennett that the mother was "obese, 43–44 yrs of age & looks like the 'Aunt Jemima type.'" Not surprisingly, the doctor's callousness was exceeded by the private investigator and his informants. They reported Ruby Epps as proudest of her son who was well behaved and did not run around, but found that the father, a coal miner, although "a good man, runs around." A White man described the Epps family as an "average Negro family, the mother is crazy & police quiet her from time to time." Two Negroes were interviewed: "one of these was chased by mother w/knife—1 negro lives close by—mother's crazy—drinks liquor in front yard & curses—doesn't care about what children do."

Poignantly, the mother, who by testimony of informants did not care, had written Governor Folsom on August 5 to get the governor to intervene in her son's behalf. She told the governor of her letter to the president of the university and of his "most promising note" in return. She also reported a letter to the state superintendent of education who had suggested "a college in the East" with state aid—assistance she already had asked for and been refused. She told Folsom, who had a reputation as the South's most forward thinking governor on the race question, that she had lived a Christian life and raised her children to do the same. She assured the governor that she was against "mixed marriages," but for "democracy." "I believe in what is right," she explained, "but to deny my son the right to a good education is hard to bear." "Stick to your guns," she urged. "God can't use no cowards in his kingdom."

The university's experience in the Peters, Nabors, and Epps cases convinced officials that stopping African-American applicants would not be difficult, Autherine Lucy's class action victory in the courtroom notwithstanding. In June 1956, the NAACP ceased to operate in Alabama by injunctive order of a state circuit judge. Absent NAACP support or assistance from federal authority, applicants like Peters, Nabors, and Epps were left to the mercy of a university that was determined by policy of its trustees not to admit African-American applicants until compelled by another court order. Individual petitions could be defeated in the same manner as Peters, Nabors, and Epps. In fact, such extraordinary measures were not needed because until 1963 no applicant received any organized support. It remained easy enough simply to pigeonhole the applications that arrived every year, or after 1960, simply file them with the Security Division of the Department of Public Safety.

THE "EPITOMIZING IMAGE"

Despite the university's obvious resistance to desegregation, and because of it, a lore has developed that casts the university's administration as instruments of its own salvation from segregation. To make the story work, university officials had to place themselves at the center of the drama, a drama in which they became victims of extremists on both sides—influential, diehard segregationists on the one hand and pushy NAACP chiefs on the other. Despite their victimization, the story goes, good judgment and careful planning prevailed in the end. Like all lores, there is some truth in the legend. Administrative officials did have to contend with a group of five especially influential trustees who melded board leadership to prevailing White sentiment and determined to resist by all legal means any change in the racial status quo. Moreover, the NAACP showed little regard for local constraints and by its own admission exercised poor judgment at several crucial turns. Also, in the final drama, when the NAACP Legal Defense Fund reentered the case and when the Kennedy administration, among other steps, threatened grants for space-related research, university officials did hurry off to Washington to plan for Wallace's promised stand in the schoolhouse door. But these facts have been enlarged to create a story of active involvement in ending segregation.

Like all lores, it is sustained by a powerful image, a representation that establishes the truth of a story through exemplification. It has the power of illustration, of converting abstract discussions of good and evil into concrete visualizations. It induces the response "I see" for "I understand." And because these images, like all pictures, are a matter of perception, they cannot be controverted readily in an interview unless one is prepared to say, "you're a liar" or "you have faulty memory." They possess the persuasive force of the eyewitness. To deny the truth of the example requires an unpleasant *ad hominem*, a willingness to attack the narrator's competence or motivation. The image as anecdote comes into being out of someone's memory and is buttressed by the authority of its creator, usually someone in a position to know or observe. It is the refrain of the Vietnam veteran, "I was there, I ought to know." Absent concrete counterproof, only a skeptic qua cynic would question the authenticity of such accounts. Put another way, these accounts are sustained by the gullible side of human nature, the side that knows not to believe the newspapers, but does anyhow. This credulity is a necessary condition of communication, for without it common understandings cannot exist.

Of course, any and all stories are freighted with examples, but only a few prove pivotal. Standing alone, an epitomizing image may seem trivial, but by conscious or subconscious intent of the narrator(s) it becomes the fulcrum on which an entire lore is leveraged. In the Autherine Lucy episode, the university's failure to secure the campus made it necessary to counter the public appearance of having given affront to innocence. Lucy's calm demeanor and solitary courage provided a sharp contrast to the shrill and dangerous mob that formed and that resulted in Lucy's eventual expulsion by the board of trustees. To counter this negative impression, the university developed a storyline, which it came to believe, that Lucy's application was not seriously motivated and that the university, not Lucy, was the ultimate victim of circumstances.

To question Lucy's motive, it was necessary to show that she did not act alone, that her enrollment was by committee, financed and paid for by the NAACP. In so doing, university officials talked about the manner in which she appeared for registration: driven to campus in a Cadillac, overdressed for the occasion, accompanied by advisers, given preferential treatment during registration, and making tuition payment with crisp, $100 bills. In court the university argued that her behavior amounted to incitement. Although each count in the university's bill of particulars had its answer (the Cadillac was taken when a Chevrolet would not start, she dressed in her Sunday best to avoid seeming too casual, the university itself decided that she should not stand in line for registration, and the new bills were acquired for fear that the university would refuse a personal check), the account of her registration became the university's standard example to contrast Lucy's effrontery with the national media's portrayal of victimization.

As important as the story of Lucy's registration, the need to counter the image of innocence defiled moved to even more specific detail. A true epitomizing image in a historical narrative is one that contending parties agree to be important. If told by one side, it will be told with explanation or modification by the other, but both will agree in broad outline that it happened and that it is important. These anecdotes are so salient that a historian cannot, indeed will not neglect them. They dramatize the historian's sense of truth in such compelling fashion that they will be used regardless of the truth of their content. As the case in point, Autherine Lucy tells a harrowing tale of near death at the hands of a frenzied mob. She recounts how she had to dash from a car into one building while the mob hurled eggs, rocks, tomatoes, and any other missiles they could get in their hands:

So, anyway, I jumped out of the car and ran for the building, and I got to the door and felt that I had made it and just then I found something hitting me on my shoulder. At the time I didn't know what it was, I didn't take time to stop and see, but it really didn't hurt so I kept going. I ran up the steps and to the door and got inside the door and someone locked it. I don't remember who, it might have been the instructor, but as I went in someone locked the door behind me to keep the crowd from following me, but they were right behind me, because I could hear them say,"Let's kill her," "let's kill her," and [the sound of their voices] following me up those steps. So you might know that I was very much afraid at this time. I sat there and tried to [compose] myself and naturally the next thing that I thought of doing was saying a prayer. And I can remember, not the exact words, but I can remember in this prayer that I asked to be able to see the time when I would be able to complete my work on the campus, but that if it was not the will of God that I do this, that he give me courage to accept it, because this was a time when I really felt then that I might not get out of it...alive. Of course, I wanted to, but I wanted the courage to accept death at that point if it had to be that way. And when I finally gained my composure, I looked down on my coat. I had a green, pretty coat—not this color [pointing to some fabric] but sort of an aqua-looking color. I looked down on this coat and there was egg that had dripped all the way down on this coat. And I gathered from the look of the egg that it must have been a rotten one, because, you know, naturally when an egg is not rotten you have the yoke and then the white. They're separated. But this was just a yellowish-looking egg that ran down on the coat.

At the center of this story is a heroine under attack. It is not the threats that rivet nor even the prayer-provoking fear of death. In the end it is the pretty green coat down which runs the contents of a rotten egg; visually, vividly symbolizing feminine virtue befouled. The narrative is abhorrent to a male-centered culture that makes much of women as a protected gender—it jars even White supremacists. It is a story so compelling that a historian cannot pass it up. It is a tale so representative that it must be rejoined by any who are made to look bad by it. On first hearing it, I knew that, as a historian, I would use it even after I had heard the rejoinder; not because I believed Lucy to be more truthful, but because in the absence of compelling counterproof, it illustrated what I believed to be the larger truth of Lucy's victimage.

The denial, or at least the modification of Lucy's story, came from Jefferson Bennett. For his part, Bennett acknowledged the general outline of Lucy's account and conceded the element of danger. The most repeated testimony from the subsequent court hearing was his statement that on two occasions Lucy was "twenty seconds from death." However, Bennett's accounts then, and even more so later, emphasized the protection the university afforded Lucy, especially his own derring-do before the mob. To maintain the image of Lucy as a protected woman, although one whose conduct itself provoked the crowd, it became necessary to deny the only evidence that she had been physically struck by the mob (*viz*, the story of the dripping, rotten egg, a small detail that loomed large). In remarks prepared for a group of students in 1983, Bennett denied that Lucy had ever been hit by an egg:

> I parked the car so that it was facing away from the rear of the building and [Dean of Women] Sarah Healy and Autherine, with her books, dashed into the side door of Graves Hall annex and that door was then locked. Autherine later said that she was hit with an egg; Sarah and I don't remember that. I think that the egg came along with the total drastic turmoil that she was experiencing. I went back to the car and became the only target the mob had left. You see, she was gone but I was there.

Bennett goes on to recount the details of his confrontation with the mob, but already he had made his point. Lucy only thought, perhaps in the swirl of events even fabricated, that she had been hit by an egg. In fact, the kernel notion in Bennett's remarks was that Lucy had been protected from the consequences of her own provocative behavior. Through memory, Bennett transformed himself (and by extension the university) into the mob's target. "she was gone but I was there." Lucy, and all she represented, had been de-centered. Bennett and the university now occupied center stage in the desegregation drama.

Although Bennett's personal courage throughout the Lucy crisis cannot be doubted, his story can. Less than a week after the dramatic events occurred in February 1956, Bennett provided a written deposition for university lawyers. In his report, Bennett said that as he, Lucy, and Healy got out of the car and approached a side door, they were "discovered by the crowd which had begun to assemble in the front of the building" and turmoil ensued. As they hurried to the building, "Dean Healy and Autherine Lucy were struck by eggs just as they went into the door. They locked the door and I turned back toward the automobile." Why did Bennett change his story? A case can be made that he simply forgot such a small detail. But why did he feel it necessary to deny such a small matter? The answer may lie in the fact that he had heard Lucy (now Autherine Lucy Foster) address the same students a short time before and reacted to the dramatic centerpiece of her story. He correctly sensed it to be an epitomizing image, an example that had to be altered to restore not only the university's view of what happened but his own personal sense of wholeness. For Bennett the issue seemed to have become as much a matter of gender as race, perhaps even more so on this key point, and therefore his story now had to embrace the whole cultural matrix that undergirded White, male supremacy, a matrix that despite his progressive views for the time bound him in later years to reconstruct his fragmented past in such a way as to restore a semblance of wholeness to the life of power and influence he had lived. By his reckoning, the power to do what was right temporarily escheated to a society of such extremes as to render him and his university powerless to do the right thing. Thus he, even more than Lucy, became the victim. By agitating for her rights, she had everything to gain. By offering her protection, which she required both because she was a woman and African American, he stood to lose everything.

AN ESCALATING TALE

If Bennett changed details to make his story come out right, Frank Anthony Rose constructed a myth of heroic proportions from whole cloth. Rose was appointed president of the University to take office January 1, 1958. Carmichael had resigned at the end of 1956, a thoroughly defeated and broken man. Rose remembered informal discussions with board members, including the board's chief resister, that resulted in a charge that Rose bring about a peaceful resolution of the inevitable desegregation. He further remembers soliciting African-American applications from the Southern Christian Leadership Conference and from the Southern Regional Council. Unfortunately, so the story goes, none of the applicants supplied proved qualified. Still, Rose remembered well his determination to get the job done. In the fall of 1962, he recalled John Kennedy asking him not to proceed because of the Ole Miss crisis and because of the situation brewing in Cuba. Again in the spring of 1963, Kennedy importuned Rose to wait until the fall of 1963, rather than the summer term, but this time Rose absolutely refused to delay further.

Rose's story is rich in detail, anecdote, and names dropped with familiarity, and comports well with expectation. The problem is that none of it is true. Applications were not sought. In fact, Rose told the board of trustees in the fall of 1962 and again in the winter of 1963 with George Wallace present, that the university's vigilance had resulted in over 230 applications being turned aside. Rose shared J. Edgar Hoover's doubts about Martin Luther King and the SCLC's loyalty and believed the SRC to be infiltrated by Communists. Moreover, Vivian Malone, whom Rose later hailed as a godsent applicant, had applied to study at the Mobile branch as early as 1961. Clearly, many qualified applicants had presented their credentials, but instead of evaluating their qualifications, the Rose administration systematically turned their names over to the Security Division of the State Department of Public Safety for investigation. Moreover, Rose closed the processing of applications early in the summer, fall, and winter of 1962–1963, in order to avoid consideration of African-American applicants. Rose wrote to Major W. R. Jones, head of the Security Division, and explained, "The closing of the enrollment, as you know, has always been our practice and is one of our legal steps. You know us well enough to know that we don't need any encouragement or advice on closing our registration." The conversations with President Kennedy are doubtful. Rose did know Robert Kennedy. The United States Junior Chamber of Commerce had named both Outstanding Young Men of the Year in 1954. They met on that occasion and maintained an acquaintance that proved helpful in planning for the stand in the schoolhouse door. There is, however, no evidence that President Kennedy ever advised delay, and every evidence that the Kennedy administration pushed the university in the winter of 1963 to finish the business that summer. Robert Kennedy did believe the Rose administration to be helpful in the final drama, but even at that, he thought Rose himself to be curiously and unnecessarily helping Wallace in the closing act.

A few years ago, I participated in an interview with Rose. Although in poor health, he still possessed the charm and charisma that marked his administration. He was relaxed, his voice quiet but still resonating authority, his recall sharp and vivid. As I listened to him, I began to suspect, even regret, some of the conclusions I had formed over 3 years of archival research, especially those I had proclaimed in a symposium that commemorated the 25th anniversary of Wallace's stand in the schoolhouse door. But sometime in the second hour of conversation my regret turned to frustration as I realized that so little of what was being said squared with the archival trail, and I began to wonder how a naive interviewer, one not familiar with the documentary fragments, could disambiguate the truth from so compelling a story. I began to realize that this interview was therapy for Rose, a cover-up, a redemption of time.

LESSONS FOR THE HISTORIAN AND A NOTE ON BURKE

Of course, too much can be made of the eccentric memory of a single person, but each part of the story Rose told established the larger lore about the university's behavior in its desegregation ordeal. It became the accepted wisdom of what happened. Naive, nonconfrontational interviewing would further sediment this understanding and confound historical reconstruction. The motive to distort is understandable and therapeutic (i.e., it adjusts the facts with the preferred image of one's life). Because most university officials worked hard to assist the Kennedy administration in the final days, they believed themselves to have facilitated desegregation from the beginning. They do not choose to remember that they were not part of the solution, and thereby became an integral part of the problem. Or as their mothers could have told them: Wanting something to end right does not make it end right. The lore they created, because it is so intertwined with self-image, is not easily shaken. Rose's memory was beyond an interviewer's power to influence. Bennett conceded that some things, such as the Epps episode, were simply too painful to remember, certainly too painful to record, and though he would not confirm the account of what happened, neither would he deny it. Rose and Bennett, through the reconstruction of memory, have settled accounts with posterity.

Burke's "epitomizing image" is a useful concept for understanding pivotal narratives imbeded within larger texts. Burke did not develop fully the concept. In fact, like many of Burke's ideas, it was a nugget dropped along the trail. He stumbled on the idea in reading Richard Wright's *Native Son*. Burke was looking for the "logically prior" beginning to a story. "A beginning," he observed, "should 'implicitly contain' its ending..." (p. 338). The kernel notion is that writing a book is like retracing one's step (i.e., if one begins with a sentence or idea or anecdote, the beginning itself stands subject to the interrogation: Why did you begin with this?—and so on until one arrives at the "logically prior" beginning, which Burke then declares the "epitomizing image." What I have done is adapt this notion. Where I may differ from Burke is in my idea that an epitomizing image may occur at any point in the text—it could be used as an introductory image (that would be one of its tests), but it is not necessary so long as it could serve as "the imagistic source out of which the story flowed" (p. 339).

REFERENCES

Burke, K. (1969). *A grammar of motives*. Berkeley: University of California Press.

Clark, E. C. (1993). *The schoolhouse door: Segregation's last stand at the University of Alabama*. New York: Oxford University Press.

Erikson, E. H. (1975). *Life history and the historical moment*. New York: Norton.

Lomax, J. W., & Morrissey, C. T. (1989). The interview as inquiry for psychiatrists and oral historians: Convergence and divergence in skills and goals. *The Public Historian, 2*(1), 17–24.

Portelli, A. (1981). "The time of my life": Functions of time in oral history. *International Journal of Oral History, 2*(3), 162–180.

3

Trauma Redeemed: The Narrative Construction of Social Violence

Kim Lacy Rogers
Dickinson College

In recent years, we have increasingly become exposed to the life narratives of people who have survived nearly unbearable experiences of violence and emotional devastation. Talk show guests, autobiographers, novelists, and academics of various persuasions have related the stories of disaster victims, Holocaust survivors, combat veterans, victims of political terrorism, and rape and incest survivors to an avid and interested public. Psychologists have shown a particular interest in the way that these life stories reflect a successful and creative adaptation to both the initial episodes of stress, and to later experiences of grief and loss (Aberbach, 1989; Storr, 1988). Psychologists and historians have analyzed the personal narratives of trauma survivors in order to understand the methods individuals use to give meaning to experiences that have threatened them with annihilation and destruction (Herman, 1992; Leydesdorff, 1992; Lifton, 1979; Mollica, 1988; Ochberg, 1988).

In this chapter, I examine the oral narratives of five African-American women and men who were active in the civil rights movement in the deep south in the 1960s. At various times in their 5 years with the movement in New Orleans and rural Louisiana and Mississippi, these individuals experienced terrorism and violence from segregationist Whites, and some suffered from battle fatigue due to continual exposures to danger and loss (Carson, 1981; Rogers, 1993). Mid-life interviews with seven former members of New Orleans' chapter of the pacifist, interracial Congress of Racial Equality (CORE) and two of their lawyers—known collectively in New Orleans as the CORE family—illustrate the incorporation of collective and individual trauma into mature personal narratives.

I argue that activists have developed two narrative forms to encapsulate their complex experiences within the civil rights movement—trauma narratives and narratives of redemption. I further argue that mid-life narratives indicate that

31

activists have used these episodes of trauma and redemption to frame and contextualize their life trajectories as consistent with their youthful politics. Several have described their careers and political activities as efforts that enable them to support the indigenous culture of Black New Orleans. Such activities refocus their movement concerns into work that combines social generativity and creativity—two of the major tasks of successful mid-life functioning (Erikson, 1965; Storr, 1988). Among the variety of life stories that New Orleans' former CORE activists have lived out, individual redemption narratives connect the youthful activists to mature adult roles and careers. These redemption narratives—which uniquely and personally recount the gifts and benefits of the civil rights movement—have provided a direction, a content, and a continuing social and emotional model for adult development and personal relationships (Polkinghorne, 1988).

The trauma narrative is a genre that permeates our culture through its prominence in very literal war stories, in Holocaust narratives, in sagas of political prisoners, and in tales told by survivors of rape, incest, natural disasters, and other forms of social and personal violence. Such narratives are central to the emotional impact conveyed by dramatic autobiographies of civil rights leaders (Farmer, 1985; Sellers, 1973, 1990), and by the video footage in the documentary "Eyes on the Prize" series. Herman (1992) described traumatic events as "extraordinary...because they overwhelm the ordinary adaptations to life." She said that such experiences "generally involve threats to life or bodily integrity, or a close personal encounter with violence and death. They confront human beings with extremities of helplessness and terror, and evoke responses of catastrophe" (p. 33).

Traumatic events frequently leave their survivors with memories that seem frozen in time and "encoded in the form of vivid sensations and images." These characteristics predominate because, due to the stress of trauma, "the nervous system reverts to...sensory and iconic forms of memory" (Herman, 1992, pp. 38–39). Survivors of the terrorism that threatened many activists and killed a number of local and national leaders frequently relate their most frightening experiences in this fashion. Often, their stories of fear and danger are set apart from previous and subsequent stories by language use, tense, and form of address—as though these experiences are isolated in memory. Frequently, narrators switch from a first-person, past-tense form of address to a second-person, present tense. The vivid imagistic descriptions in these narratives gives an otherworldly quality to appalling scenes of violence and terror.

These trauma narratives are usually integrated into a larger personal history through the redemption narratives that frequently follow them. These narratives focus on either physical rescue or preservation from evil, or on the redemptive aspects of relationships that save the narrator from fear, isolation, or emotional collapse in the face of violence or death. Such stories focus on emotional states and bonds, and on processes of growth and development that compensate for and contradict the threats to the self that were generated by terrorism. Often, redemption narratives include descriptions of emotional and psychic epiphanies and connections, and of complex emotional and psychological victories that become embodied in individual lives (Rogers, 1989, 1993). Often, redemption narratives function in an educational or inspirational way: Activists discover the meaning of their sacrifices in their relationships within the movement, and in their ties to local people in the communities in which they worked. Thus, the psychic and emotional wounds inflicted upon activists are both explained and to some extent healed by the love and connection that they received through the movement.

For some individuals, redemption narratives provide the "turning point" that inspires or frames subsequent personal choices: Activists' intense experiences within the movement lead them to direct their adult energies into actions that are consistent with their movement ideals—as "cultural workers," educators, or lawyers and professionals who work to better the local African-American community (Rogers, 1989, 1993; see also McAdam, 1988).

MEMORIES OF VIOLENCE AND REDEMPTION: MOVEMENT STORIES

Terrorism and violence were real threats for civil rights activists in many parts of the south. In the 1950s and 1960s, at least 30 people were murdered by White Southerners for attempting to win civil and political rights for African Americans. The deep south states of Alabama, Mississippi, and Louisiana achieved a justly deserved notoriety for the numerous violent attacks that their White residents, vigilante groups, and law enforcement officials made on civil rights activists (Branch, 1988; Chestnutt & Cass, 1990). Dave Dennis, a CORE field secretary, described the Mississippi Freedom Summer project of 1964 as "a war... Every time people got up in the morning, you didn't know if you were going to see 'em again or not.... Everything was a risk" (Raines, 1977, p. 302). According to Cleveland Sellers (1973/1990), a leader of the Student Nonviolent Coordinating Committee (SNCC), Freedom Summer produced "one thousand arrests, thirty-five shooting incidents, thirty homes and other buildings bombed; thirty-five churches burned, eighty beatings, and at least six persons murdered" (p.94). In rural Louisiana, where CORE organizers worked in the rigidly segregated communities of Plaquemine, Monroe, Arcadia, and Bogalusa, CORE organizers and volunteers were routinely harassed, shot at, beaten, jailed under flimsy pretenses, and given severe sentences for imaginary transgressions (Peck, 1964). Many of the "war stories"—the trauma narratives of the movement—came from young organizers' efforts to win rights for African Americans in these small towns and rural counties of the deep south.

Jerome Smith was a member of New Orleans' CORE chapter from 1960 through 1962, and worked in CORE's Mississippi campaigns in 1963 and 1964. A former student and longshoreman, Smith participated in CORE's dangerous Freedom Ride from Montgomery to Jackson in 1961, and served a sentence in Mississippi's Parchman Penitentiary. In 1988, he recalled a brutal beating he received in McComb, Mississippi, after a Freedom Ride to the town's bus station in 1961:

> I can remember times when your testicles and your rectum would be, and everything on you would be tight as a vise, a choke, and all, and your whole person would have a kind of paralysis, and then seeing the spirit of something would seep in—and you

would just open up, move into it...I remember something like that, I was sitting on this bus in McComb, and we used to have breathing exercises and stuff. And I was on the bus; I was so tight, so tense, so rigid and everything I did was paralyzed by the moment. And when I got off the bus, I saw these men coming at me. I just remember fixing my tie. I got a newspaper, and I smiled at em, and I thought of George (Raymond). George was with me. I just thought about George, and I just got *loose*. I went into the bus station, and when we got into the bus station, it just took us over. I can just remember the women howling, "Kill him! Kill him! Kill him!" And they had me down, and I remember George jumping from table to table and counter to counter and probably if George hadn't been so elusive, they would've killed me.... By George moving, I was able to work my way to the door and to the streets. (Smith, 1988b)

In the midst of the terror and brutality of the mob attack, Smith recalled finding comfort—and, ultimately, survival—through his relationships with movement colleagues. In McComb, his life was ultimately saved by an older African-American man who had a local reputation as an "Uncle Tom":

The streets were swollen with whites, and Klans, whatever, and he came with this truck, and because he had played this role all his life—the so-called "Tom" role—he was the only one could get through. No one else would have been allowed through, 'cause he was like the invisible man, he was like Uncle Remus, so if Uncle Remus wouldnta came through, I would be dead. He didn't get outa his truck. He just simply asked me if I could hear him. I said, "Yes." I remembered mumbling something. He said, "when you feel the truck, just roll over." And they (the whites) was not paying any attention. They was going after the others. And I was just able to just flip over into the back of the truck, into this pig slop. And that's how my life was saved, because if he wouldnta come, if somebody else woulda come, they wouldnta entered.... (But) by him coming through, they allowed him to come through the crowd, and to get to the head of the crowd, which was near the door I was coming out. (Smith, 1988b)

In this narrative, Smith's experience of danger is contradicted and corrected twice, first by his gratitude to his CORE colleague, then by his very literal rescue by the older African-American man. Such a strategy works to distance the narrator from the very real threat to the self that the trauma narrative both invokes and recalls. Still other devices that narrators used to distance themselves from their memories of fear and terror included humor, an affectless irony, or statements of solidarity and recollections of solidarity and collective purpose. Sometimes these distancing devices are part of a redemption narrative; sometimes not. Occasionally, recollections of danger, solidarity, and a defusing humor are mixed, as when Smith recalled several fast getaways that he made with Matt Suarez in Mississippi between 1963 and 1964. Suarez, a member of New Orleans' CORE, and later a CORE field secretary, had a reputation for outrunning pursuing police or white vigilantes on the winding back roads of rural Mississippi. Said Smith,

I remember the time when the troopers had my picture. One night I had to sneak out. Flukie (Matt Suarez) was staying on the Jackson (State) University campus and they were moving me from house to house and ultimately brought me to a professor's house, and Flukie came, and they had to get me out in one of those station wagons that Lorraine Hansberry and Lena Horne helped us to get, to get out of town. So I got in the back, and they covered me with blankets, and I remember telling Flukie, "Man, stop, I prefer goin to jail. You gonna kill me." But he never would stop, even when we were goin up to Neshoba County, trying to get information on Chaney, Goodman, and Schwerner.[1] Dave Dennis had organized this fact-finding group—it was Dave, Flukie, and (Rudy) Lombard came with us. We was drivin', and I remember saying, "Man, friendship gonna *kill* me." I mean, what could we do? We all talking about how stupid we was, following Dave up there (to Neshoba County). But anyway, we went. We was just so close to each other. (Smith, 1988b)

Smith worried about his friends' safety, and his own. "We had been through so much, even before the Mississippi thing, we didn't think we were gonna live to be 30 years old. We used to have discussions around that" (Smith, 1988b). Nevertheless, he put his experiences in the perspective of the long history of African Americans in the southern states. Even though he faced death a number of times, Smith felt that "the greatest struggles had been done by those who came before us. Many times I used to count trees when we were walkin in the woods in Mississippi, and I would see them as places where all the unknown people had been hung" (Smith, 1988b).

For Smith, as for many of the other activists in CORE and in the Student Non-Violent Coordinating Committee (SNCC), the rural African-American folk of Mississippi, Alabama, and Louisiana proved to be a redemptive presence and inspiration. Through African-American farmers and sharecroppers, Smith and others connected with an African-American folk tradition that their own parents had recently left, as they had moved from rural into urban areas (Carson, 1981). Smith found an education in Mississippi: He could "see people who were drenched in the sophistication of books, learning from people who could not spell their name, about the books they read" (Smith, 1988a). The African-American Mississippians helped to explain the personal dangers and traumas that the CORE activists experienced through a long history of redemptive communal and religious suffering. Smith recalled "being trapped in Smith County," and

this man came, an old man where I went to church. And he said, "they're lookin' for you, and I'll bring you back." So this old minister walked me through the woods. I don't know how many miles we walked, we got to an opening. He said, "I'm gonna leave here, and say a prayer for you before I leave." I said, "You know, I feel real bad,

---

[1]James Chaney, Andrew Goodman, and Mickey Schwerner were three CORE members who disappeared in June 1964, and were murdered by the local Ku Klux Klan near Philadelphia, Mississippi. Chaney was an African-American Mississippian. Goodman and Schwerner were Northern White volunteers for the Council of Federated Organizations' Freedom Summer Project, which drew 800 White volunteers to Mississippi to register African-American voters and to teach in Freedom Schools. The bodies of Chaney, Goodman, and Schwerner were discovered later that summer. The murders and extreme violence against African-American and White activists in the state drew national attention to racial repression in Mississippi and in the South.

you have to go back by yourself." He said, "Well, you have to go *on* by yourself. But I'm not really by myself." So he took out his Bible, say, "I have strength in this. And if this doesn't react quick enough"—speaking about his Bible—he had this gun. And we stood there laughing. And he say, "But you moving forward, and all you have is *you*. So I'm more concerned about you than about myself." Say, "but even much more than that, son, I'm just so glad you're here. So glad that all of y'all are here. And death don't really mean nothin' to me. I'm just so glad that I was able to *see*."... And he was the one who used to tell me, "you know, you really a church. You know all of y'all are church." And he stayed and watched me walk. I discovered that he actually sat there until I cleared and that meant that he sat there for awhile, cause he could see me for quite awhile. (Smith, 1988b)

In the various campaigns between 1960 and 1964, Smith drew close to his colleagues from the New Orleans CORE chapter. He worked closely with Dave Dennis, Ike Reynolds, Rudy Lombard, and George Raymond, Jr., and with Alice, Jean, and Shirley Thompson. Of this group, he recalled that "we were like the direct actionists of reputation. We were looked upon as people whose feet were constantly in the dust; we were always standing in the fire. And the kind of allegiance we had to each other was known throughout the country, wherever we went.... We just had a great comfort in being with each other, regardless of what the situation was" (Smith, 1988b). Smith said that his relationships in the movement,

> gave you a strength, definitely, it was a fact of strength. A sense of not being alone. It gave you a confirmation; it certified your purpose. It minimized your fear, helped you to overcome your fear. There was a collective strength, even when you were by yourself, that minimized your fear. Just the thought that wherever the action was, somebody would be there with you, and if they were not there, they were on their way. Even if they were not, there was a comfort and commitment, and there was always the knowledge that you would be rescued or helped—and celebrated. Not celebrated in the public sense, but celebrated in the sense of knowing that we were like each other's saviors. (Smith, 1988b)

Smith's colleagues related similar stories of terror from their work in rural areas. In August of 1963, CORE organizers worked with African-American ministers in Plaquemine, Louisiana, to register the town's African-American voters and to desegregate public facilities. On September 1, local police brutally dispersed a group of African-American protestors as they attempted to march from the Plymouth Rock Baptist Church to the downtown. Mounted state police pursued the marchers back to the church (Farmer, 1985). Rudy Lombard (1979) recalled that the troopers then

> *stormed* the church. They rode some horses into the church, with cattle prods. They were trampling people. A number of us retreated to the parsonage, and they fired teargas into all the windows, and about kicked the doors in. Eventually, it was bad enough that some of us spent the night in a fig tree. The cops were running all around. And they got [CORE National Director James] Farmer out of there...it was really chaotic. (Lombard, 1979)

CORE lawyers Lolis Elie and Robert Collins had gone to Plaquemine to assist the organizers and the local African-American ministers. On the night of September 1, the police and state troopers scoured the African-American community for Farmer after their attack on the church and its parsonage. Farmer and a number of other people took refuge in an African- American-owned funeral home. Lolis Elie (1970) was among the people who packed the funeral parlour after running from the gas-filled parsonage:

> When I opened the door I went in there and it was a wake. I was really almost hysterical. I remember thinking that the child in the casket was better off than anyone else...I was looking out the window, and I could see troopers on horses—any black person they saw, they would jam against the wall [with a] cattle prod, and the other started beating them with a billy club.... Then a trooper stormed up to that door and they said, "We want that nigra Farmer." I saw one of the most courageous acts of my life. It was the lady who owned the funeral home who said, "You have no right to come into my funeral home making that noise, making that disturbance." He said, "there's a disturbance in here." She said, "There ain't no disturbance but the disturbance you are causing." I've never seen anyone more courageous than that. I think the troopers were going to kill Farmer. (Elie, 1970)

Elie's partner, Robert Collins (1988), recalled a scene of confusion and panic as the mounted police charged into the crowd of African-American protestors:

> When we got there, they'd already had a wave of people who had gone downtown and there were policemen on horseback who had teargassed these people, and ran into the crowds, and some people were injured. The thing I remember about it, there was an ambulance, with a red light, twirling around, and these hundreds and hundreds of people in the street and in the churchyard. All of a sudden they said, "The horses are coming! The horses are coming!" The state police surrounded the church square, and herded all these hundreds of people in there, and they started lobbing these teargas canisters, they were shooting them into the crowd, and just forming clouds of teargas. You can imagine the panic that caused. It was absolutely the scene of a nightmare.... The whole square was surrounded. The state police had on their gas masks. If you can visualize anything more terrifying that policemen on horseback with gas masks on, running people down.

The CORE leaders and the director of the funeral home smuggled James Farmer out of town in a hearse that trailed Elie and his partners Collins and Nils Douglas. Then, said Elie (1970), "we all met at my house and got drunk or tried to within ten minutes."

While Elie used humor to deflect the impact of his Plaquemine story, Collins played down the emotional consequences. When asked how the experience affected him, Collins (1988) replied, "it was strange, it was strange. It was exciting, but we were taking some big chances." When asked whether he felt marginalized as a result of this kind of danger, Collins replied, "I guess I did. People thought we were taking big chances, which we were, I guess. Cause we could have been lynched."

Lombard (1979) described his own response to the police attacks in Plaquemine.
A few nights afterward, he said,

> We marched on the jail. We had a federal injunction banning further demonstrations
> and marches, but we marched anyway. Everybody was so shocked. And when we got
> to the jail, they [the police] were so shocked [because] we just walked right into the
> middle of them. They didn't arrest us.
>   They had done everything they could. They had trampled people, teargassed em,
> and beat em. We were determined not to give up.... Nobody expected us to come back
> after all of that brutality. A federal injunction prohibited it. But we did.

In 1988, Lombard explained that he and his colleagues felt compelled to return
to the most difficult and dangerous areas. Like war veterans who survive life-threatening experiences, and then choose to return to combat, the young activists seem
to have been drawn back into danger by their loyalty to their colleagues, and by
their own belief in the moral imperative to test themselves through struggle:

> If there was a situation that spoke to danger, that was probably where we wanted to
> be. We thought it was important to grab this thing by the throat. So if it was dangerous,
> that only meant that it had to be dealt with. And if you were serious, you weren't
> gonna be intimidated by anything.

Like Smith, Collins, Lombard, and Elie related their experiences of terror with
language that distanced them from its effect. Their descriptions alternately displace,
elevate, or mute their immediate emotional responses, and thus heighten the unreal
quality of the events. Doris Jean Castle-Scott (1989) used similar strategies to
describe her feelings about the Freedom Rides from Montgomery to Jackson in
1961. She recalled her impressions as the train from New Orleans approached
Montgomery:

> We were scared to death...and you approach Montgomery, and you see all these blue
> shirts with sticks in their hands who are the state troopers, and you don't know what
> their orders are, you know? But nevertheless, you don't waver one way or the other,
> you just do it.... We had to be out of our minds.

Like Smith, the other CORE narrators used narratives of redemption to describe
the relationships they developed within CORE and the larger movement—their
colleagues and friends were sources of love, inspiration, and courage. Elie felt that
he and his friends had become "self-actualized" in the movement. Elie, his partners,
and the young people in CORE formed "a community" within New Orleans, and
this "collectivity" provided Elie with "spiritual growth" as well as emotional and
intellectual development in the heady movement years (Elie, 1988a). "My close
friends said, 'Let's play out our high side. Let's strive to become better human
beings' " (Elie, 1988b). For Lombard, the movement became "an education" that
was "better than school." Within CORE, he met "the most incredible human beings,
which is an education you can't buy, but can only discover as you struggle against

things which oppress you. I think people who are noble, and who are worth knowing and loving, find those situations, and gravitate toward them" (Lombard, 1988). In 1989, Castle-Scott recalled both the emotional bonding and the psychic defenses that cemented the close relationships among movement activists:

> The friendships were understood. They didn't have to be explained or anything. People got close to one another out of need. Somehow or other we never lost that. You know, you needed certain kinds of people around you, with you. You may no longer have a need for that now, but that person has never lost their meaning in your life because they fulfilled that need at that particular time. And I think that's something different from childhood friendships, high school, college.... One of the things I think is really really interesting about the group here, as a group, we really really really never talk about the fear and the damage that we experienced as a direct result of being involved in the civil rights movement. And when we do, we always do it in a joking way. I don't know if that says something about what we were afraid to face, or not.

In each of these instances, narrators relate stories of terror and fear, yet integrate the emotional impact of the narratives through the use of humor, and irony, or through the recollection of solidarity. The strategies preserve the agency of the self even while individuals describe experiences that endangered their lives (Bruner, 1990). Yet all relate that they achieved a greater emotional and personal life through the relationships they developed and maintained through the movement. In this sense, then, the narratives of redemption and of redemptive relationships both compensate for and give meaning to the terror that activists experienced. Further, the lessons of the redemptive narratives both explained and counterbalanced the often disappointing years of the late 1960s and 1970s, when many of the idealists of CORE experienced disillusionment and despair as their early hopes for racial justice were exploded by continued white repression, assassinations, and other losses.

THE MORNING AFTER: LESSONS OF THE 1960S AND 1970S

Smith had numerous disappointments in his years after the epiphanies and trials of the movement. In the 1970s, he felt a great despair when he realized that the energy and collective solidarity of the movement had ended. In the late 1980s, he was also angered by conservative national politics and racial policies that had left the "plantation...very much intact." But even though Smith saw his personal life as "more a kind of sorrow song than a joy song," he saw his life as fulfilling and consistent with his movement beliefs. The movement, he said, "is like the lifebreath of my existence. I believe that life is struggle, and that it will define its method and means of breaking the chains of slavery" (Smith, 1988a). In 1988, Smith ran Tamborine and Fan, a learning center and summer camp for the children of the downtown neighborhoods where he had grown up. There, he taught African-American and African history to African-American children, and celebrated the struggles of Nelson Mandela and the African National Congress (ANC) in South Africa. Smith's programs were modeled after those of the Freedom Schools that had been operated by SNCC and CORE in Mississippi. Smith (1988b) claimed that his movement experiences had

> made me one with the place I'm sitting now. It made me know, too, that the life of struggle is always living. And it made me always be loyal to the gifts of that experience, and to maintain that service. It made me always want to touch the streets of struggle, not to be a stranger to the streets of struggle, not to be a stranger to the streets where destruction, or even madness, may be. And if anything, to this day I try to function in a way that I honor those moments and even the blood that was lost. That is why I'm able to move in the way that I move now.

Elie, who had begun exploring the teachings of the Nation of Islam and Elijah Muhammad as early as 1963, had decided before 1968 that racial integration was both undesirable and impossible (Elie, 1988a). In the early 1970s, he had experienced severe emotional losses as his father died, his marriage ended, and the law firm of Collins, Douglas and Elie dissolved. He dealt with these crises by retreating completely from the city's blossoming African-American political organizations, and by reading deeply in psychology, African history, and African-American history. In the 1970s and 1980s, he had become increasingly interested in preserving and enhancing local African-American culture. He had joined the Congo Square Writers' Union, a local African-American writers' workshop, in the 1970s. By the late 1980s, he maintained an active law practice, but he was disappointed and disillusioned by the opportunism of African-American political organizations and their candidates in the local political theater. Elie maintained that his own growth and development had come as a result of the close friendships he had maintained in the movement. By 1988, his closest friend was Lombard; two other very close friends from CORE, Richard and Oretha Castle Haley, had recently died. Elie's relationships with the Haleys, Lombard, and a few other movement colleagues had taught him to keep a moral account of himself. "You have to be accountable to your friends who are dead," he said. "Because it's bound to happen. They're gonna die depending on you." Although he regretted not having "more material resources" as he neared age 60, Elie felt that "to have become a self-actualized person is worth almost any price." He had become an African-American nationalist in the 1960s. In the late 1980s, he remained a nationalist and Pan-Africanist in philosophy, an admirer of W.E.B. DuBois, Marcus Garvey, and Elijah Muhammad—apostles of African-American pride, celebrators of African-American culture, and proponents of community development and self-defense. Of his own life, Elie (1988b) said that "I'm proud and happy that in my very minor way, I sought to move human beings forward."

Lombard had begun to doubt the efficacy of nonviolence and racial integration in 1963 and 1964, and he later realized that "nobody *intended* for us to be equal.... *Nobody's* gonna share any decision-making, and *no* white person's ever gonna live by a decision *you* make" (Lombard, 1979). After Lombard completed his doctorate in urban studies at Syracuse University, he returned to New Orleans, and spent the 1970s and 1980s between New Orleans and Los Angeles. In the late 1970s, he worked with the city's Black Creole chefs to produce a cookbook, *Creole Feast*, that focused a spotlight on the city's traditional Franco-African cuisine. In 1986, he ran unsuccessfully for mayor against two African-American candidates as a protest against the direction of African-American politics in the city—which he saw as both corrupt and ineffectual, and thus a betrayal of the movement's aims. Dismissed as a "gadfly" by the press, he received 1% of the vote (Rogers, 1993). In 1988, Lombard worked as a financial planner and businessman, with interests in both Los Angeles and New Orleans. He retained a passionate interest in African-American culture and politics, and felt that CORE, and his relationships in the movement

> gave us a vehicle for confronting the things we were supposedly to fear the most. And it has been a hallmark in my own life. I don't have many fears, and haven't had any since the 1960s. It demonstrated an opportunity to grab hold of whatever it is you were fearful of, individually and collectively. And I think you find out who you are in adverse circumstances—if you have anything you can admire about yourself. And the other thing is, if you can understand what that was about, it will hold you in good stead. It was an incredible context in which to mature as a person, and I would say that an extraordinary group of people came to terms with themselves there, and discovered America there.... I think you came away with some courage, and with a profound understanding of the nature of the society in which you have found yourself, and which you are forced to deal with if you choose to stay in it, especially if you choose to change it. (Lombard, 1988)

Lombard felt that his current struggles were related to those of the past: "I thought it was important to be counted among the number of people who stood up against this terrible system that we describe as segregation. It was important to me then, and its important to me now that I was part of that." He maintained that his adult identity had been forged by his experiences in the movement, and he still described his life as "a struggle"—the code word for the numerous efforts that activists made to transform U.S. society (Lombard, 1988).

In 1989, Castle-Scott worked as a night admissions administrator at New Orleans' Charity Hospital. She had worked at social service jobs since her return to New Orleans in the late 1960s. Her early optimism about the possibilities for real change for African Americans had been eroded by the continual violence inflicted by Whites against African-American activists throughout the 1960s. She remembered rage when Martin Luther King was assassinated:

> The night that King died, I can remember a meeting at my sister's house at which we seriously, *seriously*, entertained trying to identify a white person that we could kill that would hurt white people as much as that death had hurt black people.... The closest person we came to was [Republican Senator] Everett Dirksen, and that sonofabitch *died* the next week. That's the honest to god truth. That was the frustration at that particular time...King was the only somebody that was saying,

"please, let's give it a chance, let's try again." Everybody else was saying, "burn, kill"—and you had no reason not to. You had no reason not to. (Castle-Scott, 1989)

Castle-Scott had become involved in the civil rights movement by "following my big sister, Oretha," a strong-willed and dynamic local and regional CORE leader. In the years after her return to New Orleans, Castle-Scott occasionally worked with the African-American political campaigns and issues that her sister and her husband Richard Haley supported. After the Haleys' deaths in 1987 and 1988, Castle-Scott withdrew from most political activity. She maintained that the lessons of her movement years had been life changing and enduring. Without the movement, she admitted, she might have had a comfortable, predictable middle-class life,

> but I don't know if I would have been as valuable to myself as I feel that I am, because I did experience what I experienced in the civil rights movement. I don't think that I would have had the opportunity to grow out of myself both inwardly and outwardly. And by grow, I guess I can only define that by saying that everything I have come to know I have come to understand that I was decisional about it. And the things that were problematic within myself, I had to look inwardly for solutions to them.... It wasn't so much getting in touch with myself as it was drawing on the resources I possessed and understanding how I could utilize those resources for things that were important to me.

Collins (1988) believed that he and his partners were trying to "push the system as far as it could go" through legal change in the 1960s. "Somebody had to do it," he said. "There were a lot of people who didn't have the courage, who weren't willing to make the sacrifice, and I guess we were just crazy enough to try it at the time." After 1964, northern lawyers affiliated with the Lawyers' Constitutional Defense Committee (LCDC) came south to assist Collins, Douglas, and Elie and other embattled southern lawyers in civil rights cases. For Collins, this was a period of great learning and growth, as well as danger and crisis (Collins, 1988).

In 1988, Collins was a federal judge for the Eastern District of Louisiana; in 1978, he had been confirmed as the first African-American federal judge in the deep south since Reconstruction. Collins' political trajectory followed a now-familiar progression "from protest to politics," as he moved from representing CORE and other civil rights groups to organizing the Community Organization for Urban Politics (COUP), an African-American political organization, in New Orleans in 1969 (Piliawsky & Stekler, 1991). After 30 years in the law, Collins admitted that he was a happy man, fulfilled in his work and in his personal life. He saw his position as a federal judge as a logical extension of the movement's goals:

> it's all about the same thing. Getting your just desserts. You know, justice could not just be obtained through demonstrations. It had to be obtained through political power. Obtaining political power and using it wisely.

CONCLUSION

The terror and trauma that activists experienced in the movement were given collective and historic meaning by their colleagues and by allies in the African-American communities in which they worked. The movement subculture validated and honored activists for their efforts, and placed them in a long African-American religious tradition of redemptive suffering and personal sacrifice for the community (Cone, 1991).

By 1978 and 1988, a number of the former CORE activists had publicly related their trauma and redemption narratives at least several times. Their "war stories" were familiar to the members of the local "CORE family," and had also been shared with the larger African-American and White communities in New Orleans.[2] The continuing closeness of the former CORE activists and their mutual validation of each other's experiences have helped to integrate their memories of terrorism into fulfilling life stories. Such support and affirmation are critical elements in the integration of trauma because they validate the perspective of the survivor (Herman, 1992; McCann & Pearlman, 1990). Clearly, the CORE narrators received this kind of collective support in the movement, and their sense of closeness to their colleagues gave their experiences a political, racial, historic, and religious context. Thus, the contemporary experience of trauma was given meaning and made endurable by close relationships with movement colleagues and with other African Americans (Rogers, 1989, 1993).

Mid-life narratives indicated that CORE activists had created lives that were consistent with their youthful values. Whether engaged as "culture workers," educators, or professionals, former activists expressed a consistency with and a fidelity to the values and lessons of the movement years. As middle-age adults, they described continuing experiences of personal development that complemented and extended the choices of their youth: Smith taught an Afro-centric curriculum that built upon the teachings of the Freedom Schools; Lombard ran for

---

[2]Lolis Elie, Oretha Castle Haley, Richard Haley, and Matteo Suarez had been interviewed by James Mosby and Robert Wright of the Civil Rights Documentation Project at the Moorland-Spingarn Research Center, Howard University, in 1969 and 1970. Jerome Smith had been interviewed in 1983, and Matt Suarez in 1977 by writer-activist Tom Dent. These interviews are part of the Thomas C. Dent Papers, Amistad Research Center, Tulane University, New Orleans, Louisiana. Matteo Suarez was interviewed in 1986 for Cagin and Dray's (1988) *We Are Not Afraid: The Story of Goodman, Schwerner, and Chaney and the Civil Rights Campaign for Mississippi.* I interviewed Lolis Elie, Oretha Castle Haley, Rudy Lombard, and Richard Haley in 1978 and 1979; Elie in 1980, and Elie, Matteo Suarez, Alice Thompson, Doratha Smith-Simmons, Jerome Smith in 1988, and Doris Jean Castle-Scott in 1989; I again interviewed Lolis Elie, Doratha Smith-Simmons, and Matteo Suarez in 1991. In 1986, the Drexel Center at Xavier University in New Orleans produced a film, *A House Divided*, on the civil rights struggle in New Orleans. Virgie Castle, Oretha Castle, Lolis Elie, Jerome Smith, and Rudy Lombard were interviewed for this film (Ware 1986). In 1989, station WWOZ in New Orleans interviewed Lolis Elie and Jerome Smith for a program, "The Civil Rights Movement Remembered." In June 1993, Elizabeth Mullener interviewed Lolis Elie for a series of stories on "The Myth of Race" in the New Orleans *Times-Picayune.*

political office, and maintained an active interest in the city's African-American cultural activities; Elie helped to support African-American arts and cultural developments in New Orleans, and his nationalism and Pan-Africanism were rooted in his movement experience. Collins saw a direct line between his work as a CORE attorney and his ascent to the federal judiciary. Castle-Scott traced her ability to use personal resources to accomplish social and individual goals to the lessons of the movement—which had expanded her own capacities for action and self-understanding (Rogers, 1993).

Slugoski and Ginsburg (1989) asserted that an individual's "sense of personal continuity is grounded in the self-narratives one generates, reinforced by the stability of one's social networks in one's society and institutions" (p.51). New Orleans' CORE activists constructed consistent movement stories, and maintained relationships within the local "CORE family" from the 1960s through the 1980s. Their mid-life stories shared similar narrative strategies and forms—and in all of these stories, the movement experience remained central to the shaping of their subsequent identities and career choices.

Tonkin (1992) observed that "It is not always easy or even possible to say how far tellers are authors of or authored by their telling" (p. 132). Clearly, the CORE narrators' stories of trauma and redemption have served as projective devices for their lives beyond the movement. These collectively shared narratives connect them to a communal history of resistance, sacrifice, and validation, and have served as models for personal and political choices in the years that followed their experiences of terror and solidarity. Such stories continue to be told as part of communal commemorations of the civil rights movement, and as personal narratives to interviewers who attempt to understand that experience and its meaning (Mullener, 1993; Rogers, 1982, 1993; WWOZ, 1989).

Oral historians engaged in research on social movements or on trauma should be aware of the power of collectively created understandings of historical experience, and hence the striking ability of specific narrative genres to provide a form for experience—a form that can evoke powerful individual and collective responses. Such forms as the trauma narrative and the redemption narrative have an emotional resonance for readers and listeners who are sensitive to the messages of southern African-American and White church cultures, to the oratory of leaders like Dr. Martin Luther King, Jr., and to the traditions of redemptive suffering and heroism that have become embodied in our national memory of the civil rights movement. Veterans of this experience have achieved social identities that "unify and give status" to their collective experience of crisis and its resolution (Tonkin, 1992, p. 134). Scholars who do not understand this critical feature of social movement narratives risk missing the vital connections between the collective experience of political activism and the interactive creation of memories and personal histories. From such relationships and memories, individuals shape their life stories—linking present and future to the transformative past.

REFERENCES

Aberbach, D. (1989). *Surviving trauma: Loss, literature, and psychoanalysis.* New Haven & London: Yale University Press.

Branch, T. (1988). *Parting the waters: America in the King years 1954–1963.* New York: Simon & Schuster.

Bruner, J. (1990). *The remembered self.* Paper presented at the Mellon Conference on "The Remembered Self," Atlanta, GA.

Cagin, S., & Dray, P. (1988). *We are not afraid: The story of Goodman, Schwerner, and Chavey and the civil rights campaign in Mississippi.* New York: MacMillan.

Carson, C. (1981). *In struggle: SNCC and the Black awakening of the 1960s.* New York: Oxford University Press.

Castle-Scott, D.J. (1989, January 19). Interview by K. L. Rogers, New Orleans. This interview, and others conducted by the author, is part of the Kim Lacy Rogers-Glenda B. Stevens Collection (RSC), Amistad Research Center, Tulane University, New Orleans.

Chestnutt, J. L. Jr., & Cass, J. (1990). *Black in Selma: The uncommon life of J. L. Chestnutt, Jr.* New York: Farrar, Straus & Giroux.

Collins, R. (1988, June 8). Interview by K. L. Rogers, 8 June, New Orleans. RSC.

Cone, J.H. (1991). *Martin & Malcolm & America: A dream or a nightmare.* Maryknoll, NY: Orbis Books.

Elie, L. E. (1970, May 26). Interview by J. Mosby, New Orleans. Civil Rights Documentation Project, Moorland-Spingarn Research Center, Howard University.

Elie, L. E. (1978, November 10). Interview by K. L. Rogers, New Orleans. RSC.

Elie, L. E. (1979a, April 24). Interview by K. L. Rogers, New Orleans. RSC.

Elie, L. E. (1979b, May 22). Interview by K. L. Rogers, New Orleans. RSC.

Elie, L. E. (1980, November 15). Interview by K. L. Rogers, New Orleans. RSC.

Elie, L. E. (1988a, June 29). Interview by K. L. Rogers, New Orleans. RSC.

Elie, L. E. (1988b, July 12). Interview by K. L. Rogers, New Orleans. RSC.

Elie, L. E. (1991, June 3). Interview by K. L. Rogers, Author's Collection.

Erikson, E. (1965). *Childhood and society.* Harmondsworth: Penguin.

Farmer, J. (1985). *Lay bare the heart: An autobiography of the civil rights movement.* New York: New American Library.

Haley, O.C. (1970, May 26). Interview by J. Mosby. Civil Rights Documentation Project.

Haley, O.C. (1978, November 27). Interview by K. L. Rogers, New Orleans.

Haley, R. (1969, August 12). Interview by R. Wright. Civil Rights Documentation Project.

Haley, R. (1979a, April 25). Interview by K. L. Rogers, New Orleans. RSC.

Haley, R. (1979b, May 9). Interview by K. L. Rogers, New Orleans. RSC.

Herman, J. (1992). *Trauma and recovery.* New York: Basic Books.

Leydesdorff, S. (1992). A shattered silence: The life stories of survivors of the Jewish proletariat in Amsterdam. In L. Passerini (Ed.), *International yearbook of oral history and life stories. Memory and totalitarianism* (pp 145–164). Oxford, UK: Oxford University Press.

Lifton, R. J. (1979). *The broken connection: On death and the continuity of life.* New York: Simon & Schuster.

Lombard, R. (1979, May 9). Interview by K. L. Rogers, New Orleans. RSC.

Lombard, R. (1988,June 7). Interview by K. L. Rogers, New Orleans. RSC.

McAdam, D., (1988). *Freedom summer.* New York: Oxford University Press.

McCann, L.I., & Pearlman, L.A. (1990). *Psychological trauma and the adult survivor: Theory, therapy and transformation.* New York: Brunner/Mazel.

Mollica, R. L. (1988). The trauma story: The psychiatric care of refugee survivors of violence and torture. In F. M. Ochberg (Ed.), *Post-traumatic therapy and victims of violence.* New York: Brunner/Mazel.

Mullener, E., (1993, June 16). Leaders on both sides smoothed way to integration. *The Times-Picayune,* pp. A 14–16.

Ochberg, F. M. (1988). Post-traumatic therapy and victims of violence. In F. M. Ochberg (Ed.), *Post-traumatic therapy and victims of violence* (pp. 3–19). New York: Brunner/Mazel.

Peck, J. (Ed.). (1964). *Louisiana—Summer, 1964: The students report to their home towns*. New York: Congress of Racial Equality (CORE).

Piliawsky, M., & Stekler, P. J. (1991). From Black politics to Blacks in the mainstream: The 1986 New Orleans mayoral election. *Western Journal of Black Studies, 15*(2), 114–21.

Polkinghorne, D. (1988). *Narrative knowing and the human sciences*. Albany, NY: State University of New York Press.

Raines, H. (1977). *My soul is rested: Movement days in the deep south remembered*. New York: Bantam Books.

Rogers, K. L. (1982). *Humanity and desire: Civil rights leaders and the desegregation of New Orleans, 1954-1966*. Unpublished doctoral dissertation, University of Minnesota, MN.

Rogers, K.L. (1989). 'You came away with some courage': Three lives in the civil rights movement. *Mid-America, 71*(3), 175–94.

Rogers, K. L. (1993). *Righteous lives: narratives of the New Orleans civil rights movement*. New York: New York University Press.

Salaam, K. Y. (1987, October 15-November 15). An Interview with "Big Duck" a.k.a. Jerome Smith. *The New Orleans Tribune*, pp. 35–38.

Sellers, C., with R. Terrell, (1973, 1990). *The river of no return: The autobiography of a Black militant and the life and death of SNCC*. Jackson & London: University of Mississippi Press. (Original work published 1973)

Shotter, J., & Gergen, K.J., (1989) *Texts of identity*. London & Beverly Hills: Sage.

Slugoski, B.R., & Ginsburg, G.P. (1989). Ego identity and explanatory speech. In J. Shotter & K. J. Gergen (Eds.), *Texts of identity* (pp. 37–55). London & Beverly Hills: Sage.

Smith, J. (1983, September 23). Interview by T. Dent. Thomas C. Dent Papers, Amistad Research Center, Tulane University.

Smith, J. (1988a, July 8). Interview by K. L. Rogers, New Orleans. RSC.

Smith, J. (1988b, July 26). Interview by K. L. Rogers, New Orleans. RSC.

Smith-Simmons, D. (1988, July 27). Interview by K. L. Rogers, New Orleans. RSC.

Smith-Simmons, D. (1991, June 5). Interview by K. L. Rogers, New Orleans. Author's Collection.

Storr, A. (1988). *Churchill's black dog, Kafka's mice, and other phenomena of the human mind*. New York: Grove Press.

Suarez, M. (1969, August 11). Interview by R. Wright, Civil Rights Documentation Project.

Suarez, M. (1977). Interview by T. Dent. Thomas C. Dent Papers.

Suarez, M. (1988, June 20). Interview by K. L. Rogers, New Orleans. R.S.C.

Suarez, M. (1991, June 7). Interview by K. L. Rogers, New Orleans. Author's Collection.

Thompson, A. (1988, July 25). Interview by K. L. Rogers, New Orleans. RSC.

Tonkin, E. (1992). *Narrating our pasts: The social construction of oral history*. Cambridge: Cambridge University Press.

Ware, B. (Producer & Director). (1986). *A house divided*. [Film]. New Orleans: Xavier University.

WWOZ, New Orleans (Radio Program). (1989, January 16). *The civil rights movement remembered*. (Cassette Recording).

4

Social Psychological Aspects of the Oral History Interview

Howard E. Sypher
Mary Lee Hummert
University of Kansas

Sheryl L. Williams
Illinois State University

Interpersonal interactions are extremely complex, often unpredictable, and although they can be very distressing, they are simultaneously central to our lives and to our satisfaction with our lives. These interactions come in many forms, discussions, rituals, and so on, that are guided more or less by cultural norms or rules of conduct.

Interviews have an inherent advantage over most other kinds of interpersonal encounters. That advantage lies in the situational constraints inherent in "doing an interview" or in "interviewing." Interviews are not impromptu. Interviews involve assigned roles, those of interviewer and interviewee. The principal responsibility of the oral history interviewer is to acquire information and the principal responsibility of the interviewee is to provide that information. In cognitive terms, there are "scripts" for interviews that are easily accessible, and the interview in general has less inherent uncertainty as a result of such scripts than do many other types of encounters. Of course, the interviewing process is actually more complex than this simplistic overview suggests. For example, we may find that expectations associated with interviews prove to be stumbling blocks even when good faith efforts to succeed are made on behalf of both parties.

Often interviews, like other less specialized interactions, flow well. In a good interview, there is almost a synchrony as interviewee and interviewer "hit it off" and seem to anticipate each other's next move or question. The participants appear to fit effortlessly into their roles and participate fully in the elicitation of pertinent information, beliefs, opinions, and so forth. Other times, the interview is painful, almost like an old-fashioned trip to the dentist and the painful extraction of molars. Obviously, we wish to avoid such encounters, but, often as not, we seem to have a bad interaction despite the interactants' intent or communication skills.

Yet, the process or form of the interview is not the only place where failure to achieve an optimal level of performance can occur. We may participate in a smooth interpersonally satisfactory interview that does not achieve the goal of acquiring acceptable information. That is, we may ask people questions and they may give us answers but realize after the interview that we did not probe successfully to tease out some important bit of information or insight that the respondent had available. We might get only part of the picture when more complete data, potentially accessible only just beneath the surface (or a question away!), would have given us a clearer understanding of an issue, problem, or individual.

This chapter outlines (albeit briefly) a cognitive social psychological view of the interview process. We attempt to identify the determinants of successful social interaction in the interview and focus on the part that cognition (on-line and memory-based) plays in helping and/or hindering the process of information acquisition.

THE PROCESS OF INTERVIEWING

Since the 1970s, communication researchers have devoted considerable attention to the process of social interaction in general and to the process of interviewing in particular. Research on social interaction has been undertaken from a variety of perspectives including symbolic interactionism, ethnomethodology, developmental psychology, and others. Interviewing research has also been the domain of inquiry for divergent groups including those whose sole purpose is to describe the dynamics of the employment interview to survey researchers who hope to identify sources of reporting error (overestimates of income, underestimates of hospitalizations, etc.) and to develop strategies for increasing accuracy in self-reports. Unfortunately, although we know a lot more about interaction, response error, and have developed guidelines for "effective" interviewing, we are still without a systematic theoretical framework for understanding how an interaction or interview is regulated, the impact of context and person variables (roles, personality, cognition, etc.) on the process, the influence of interaction process on interview outcome, or the ways in which these factors may combine to affect each other.

INFORMATION ACQUISITION AND INTERACTIONAL
SYNCHRONY

Each interview contains within it a set of implicit guidelines or rules for response. Although the nature of these guidelines vary, they include at a minimum that (a) the interviewee respond, (b) the interviewee's response address the content of the interviewer's questions, and (c) the response be characterized by appropriate elaboration (commentary expanding on the question asked or information associated with the commentary that would be helpful to the interviewer). Successful information acquisition is characterized by the extent to which these guidelines are fulfilled.

A couple of these points may need further delineation. First, the relevance of information content is largely determined by the interviewer, although it should be noted that information initially identified as irrelevant may prove relevant at some later point. The style in which the interviewee provides information should not be seen as especially relevant although his or her manner (friendly, detached, disagreeable) might provide insight into potential problems with the accuracy of the data being collected.

Second, the elaboration of a response is appropriate to the extent that it provides relevant details that the interviewer intended to elicit or needed, to capture a more complete account of some set of events. However, we are often caught between a rock and a hard place in the sense that brief almost monosyllabic (but relevant) responses provide too little information, whereas excessive responses may frustrate the goals (to say nothing of the time limits) of the interview.

In a way, our task as interviewers is to achieve interactional synchrony, that is, we must encourage respondents to participate fully in the task, providing relevant and complete answers to our questions and simultaneously volunteering relevant unsolicited information. Several factors are thought to influence interactional synchrony, including interviewee responsiveness, attention to the other, and personal and situational factors associated with accuracy.

Interviewee Responsiveness

Interviewee responsiveness plays an important part in successful interviewing. Half-hearted responses to questions have obvious detrimental effects on conversational flow. Such responses indicate a disinterest in the conversation that discourages further efforts and should make the interviewer question the quality of the data. Irrelevant responses often constitute efforts to end an interaction (Watzlawick, Beavin, & Jackson, 1967) and certainly have a number of negative effects that make the interview unenjoyable.

Any attempt to maintain responsiveness must involve efforts to involve the interviewee at some level in order to maintain the focus. Involvement will almost certainly achieve an acceptable level of responsiveness, although it does not guarantee that the goals of the interviewer will be achieved. For example, irrelevant answers or overly elaborated responses are unlikely to allow the interviewer to gather all the relevant information that he or she may have hoped for. Hence, involvement and responsiveness from an interviewee is a necessary but not sufficient condition for a successful interview.

Responsiveness does have an impact on conversational accuracy and efficiency. Research in conversation analysis has identified a number of behaviors that indicate when the speaker does not intend to elaborate but desires a response ("Uh Huh," "Yeah," "I see," etc.) or desires the next turn at talk (Duncan & Fiske, 1977; Sacks, Schegloff, & Jefferson, 1978). These brief back-channel responses serve to regulate conversations and failure to respond or utilize them would disrupt the interview in a variety of ways.

Other researchers have pointed out that ordinary conversations, like interviews, are governed by social norms in several ways including norms of relevance (Grice, 1975), and that prior utterances provide a kind of context in which we make sense of current utterances (Bransford, 1977). Planalp and Tracy (1980), for example, have shown that increased cognitive distance between topics of conversation by a speaker tend to lead to judgments of speaker incompetence.

Most individuals who agree to be interviewed will be committed to the implicit norms of relevance and responsiveness. However, on occasion one can expect a certain reluctance to be entirely candid with an interviewer. Obviously, for an interview to succeed, the interviewer will have to attempt to overcome interviewee reluctance. Issues related to trust, confidentiality, and so forth, should be resolved prior to the interview. However, any lingering doubts should be dealt with immediately. During the interview itself, it is vitally important that the participants develop a personal relationship. Research has shown that conversational responsiveness is positively related to perceived acquaintance level and to interviewees' perceptions of the interviewer's attraction to them (Davis & Perkowitz, 1979).

Attention to the Other

Interviewees will be positively affected by the amount, range, and specific content of cues that are attended to by the interviewer. Respondents need to know what kind of information is required. Research has shown that a kind of reciprocity exists in the sense that increased attention leads to attention and perceptual accuracy in processing information (Kahneman, 1975). Furthermore (although covered in more detail later), accuracy in communication increases as channel (verbal, postural, facial) availability increases (Mehrabian & Reed, 1968) provided there is consistency in channel use.

Obviously, the context or situation affects the amount of attention we pay to others. For example, one can devote far more attention to an interview when in a quiet place than on a manufacturing shop floor or during a large family meal. In another case, the situation may affect the range of cues to which an interviewer can attend. For instance, visual channels are unavailable during telephone interviews and other situations that prevent face-to-face interaction.

One's goals, expectations, concerns, and so forth, also may affect what cues are attended. During "an interview" we would expect that such qualities would assist the gathering of relevant information in that the interview situation should guide interactants to schema-relevant (Wyer & Srull, 1980) aspects of their life. However, it is possible that the interviewee may have other goals that are incompatible with the interviewer's goal (e.g., "getting this over with as quickly as possible").

Like divergent goals, interviewees' self-consciousness may influence their ability to attend to the interview (for a review, see Buss, 1980). In general, self-consciousness is said to involve a shift in attention from the external environment to the self (Argyle, 1969). Self-consciousness may involve private or public aspects of self and may be a reaction to situational cues (e.g., cameras, tape recorders, the sound of one's own tape-recorded voice) or to others in the environment. Interviewers should do whatever is necessary to reduce potential interviewee self-consciousness because it is likely to interfere with accurate recall and disrupt the flow of the interview.

Fortunately, to some extent, "an interview" is still a relatively unusual type of interaction—one that is perceived by most as important or novel and as such can be expected to receive more attention than other communicative events (Lanzetta, 1971). Interviewers (including oral historians) are generally regarded as important in that they possess desired resources and are in control of potential rewards (a place in history). As such, interviewers (regardless of their status out of the role) may be perceived as more interesting, having more status, and so forth, and hence receive more attention than other interactants.

Accuracy in Communication

There are two issues concerning accuracy that are dealt with here. One issue concerns the extent to which the interviewee is accurately reporting his or her knowledge of some aspect of the past. This is largely a memory issue (although deception is always a possibility) and is dealt with later in the chapter. A second issue (and one dealt with here) concerns the extent to which communication is accurately expressed (encoded) and received (decoded; e.g., Mehrabian & Reed, 1968). Communication consists not only of information that is deliberately conveyed, but also that which is unintentionally conveyed. In this sense, communication accuracy will be influenced by aspects of the content or situation that facilitate or inhibit encoding, decoding, and individual communication skills in sending and interpreting.

Context Effects on Accuracy. Accuracy may be influenced by the situation in that encoding is affected when either party is distracted or preoccupied. Effective interpersonal communication is heavily reliant on feedback, including facial cues, vocal tones, comments, requests for clarifications, and the like. (Kraut & Lewis, 1984; Street & Brady, 1982). To the extent that the context detracts from our attention to such cues, accuracy is impaired. Accurate communication is also reliant upon our expectations or definition of the situation and related sociolinguistic factors (Ervin-Tripp, 1969; Hymes, 1972). Research in social cognition has also shown that perceptions of the situation including scripts (Schank & Abelson, 1977), schemas (Sypher & Applegate, 1984), and heuristics (Sherman & Corty, 1984) can enhance or hinder accuracy in on-line or memory-based reports.

Contexts also differ with respect to the number of communication channels that are available to interactants. A number of studies have shown that communication accuracy increases as the number of channels increases (Mehrabian & Wiener, 1967; Rosenthal, Hall, DiMatteo, Rogers, & Archer, 1979). Accuracy is also affected by the degree to which feedback is possible

(Kraut & Lewis, 1984). Content as well as channel use can influence accuracy. For example, accuracy decreases as ambiguity increases (Macy, Christie, & Luce, 1953).

Individual Effects on Accuracy.   Individual differences in communication ability also play a role in sending and receiving information. Skill in encoding and receiving information has been related to such characteristics as intelligence, cognitive development, cognitive complexity, self-monitoring ability, and perspective-taking ability (see Burleson, 1984; Hale & Delia, 1976; Neuliep & Hazelton, 1986; O'Keefe & Sypher, 1981; Synder, 1987). Such skills may be the result of socialization, innate abilities, or training.

Just as individual differences, schemas, and so on, may facilitate communication accuracy they may also lead to distortions or systematic inaccuracy in encoding or decoding. Indeed, much of the work in social cognition has focused on distortion in on-line and memory-based reports. As Kihlstrom (1981) pointed out:

> features of personality, including personal constructs, intentions, goals, motives, and emotions, can influence the interpretations given to perceptual events; and that these aspects of the individual's state are themselves features of the experiential context in which the events took place. (p. 127)

Researchers interested in the self and self-schemata have noted that such frameworks naturally direct attention to self-relevant aspects of the environment and that such aspects are probably processed much more thoroughly than is other information (aspects of this related to memory bias are covered later). This research (Greenwald, 1981; Markus & Smith, 1981) suggests that self-involvement can produce predictable information acquisition accuracy and inaccuracy effects. So, we can expect to interpret questions or answers in ways that might be systematically distorted by some aspect of a cognitive framework and respond accordingly.

So, one can expect a number of external and internal variables to influence the interviewing process. Obviously, we could not detail all such influences in this limited review, however, we hope that we have highlighted several important aspects of the process. Good interviews do not just happen. Good interviews require good faith efforts on the part of all parties and good interviewers should take into account context and personal effects in preparing for and conducting oral history interviews.

PERSONAL MEMORY

In a sense, everyone is a historian. We are constantly recalling events that we were told about, or have read about, or have experienced. Indeed, it is natural that our past holds a certain fascination for us that is virtually unlike any other. Our sense of personal identity is wrapped up in this construction and although we see change, we also see constancy rather than continual flux (James, 1890/1950).

Historians are no different from nonhistorians in that they are subject to several kinds of errors and biases in their analyses of the past. Biases and errors in reconstruction and interpretation of historical events have been documented by a variety of researchers (Becker, 1985; Fischoff, 1982; Gallie, 1964; Nowell-Smith, 1970). Historians, like ordinary people, appear susceptible to hindsight bias in that they tend to bestow the appearance of inevitability on known outcomes. However, a rendering of such biases in the writing of history is not the purpose of this section and is best left to others (Nowell-Smith, 1970).

Instead, this section focuses on the kinds of errors interviewees are likely to make in reconstructing their past. An understanding of such errors will hopefully allow interviewers to detect where and when such errors naturally occur. In doing so we depart from earlier views of memory that suggested that memories of the past are safely stored and can be retrieved when necessary minus any trace of decay. We treat long-term memory as selective, in that we tend to recall only a subset of our experiences. We also argue that at any given time we might recall things differently in that we constantly reinterpret our past. Finally, we argue that the latest theory and research shows that we tend to smooth over any gaps in our memories, filling in the blanks through an inference process that involves active reconstruction of the past (Bartlett, 1932; Lindsay & Norman, 1972; Mead, 1934).

ERRORS IN MEMORY AND PERSONAL ORAL HISTORY

Oral history is, if anything, more sensitive to potential cognitive errors in personal memory than other forms of historical information gathering and reporting. It is precisely the collection format of "the personal interview" that makes oral history problematic. In an interview a respondent is asked to report feelings, attitudes, and behavior that occurred 5, 10, and perhaps 20 or more years ago. This poses an incredible memory load that often goes unrecognized by either the interviewee or interviewer. Respondents appear to have little difficulty in directly accessing long-term memory and will often give quick answers to questions about themselves and others. We all recognize that memory is imperfect, yet we tend to forget this, especially when a respondent reports experiences in vivid detail. Many people were amazed, fascinated, and a few were incredulous by the apparent ability of John Dean (former legal advisor to President Richard Nixon) to recall the details of meetings with Nixon. Many rejected his claims outright, whereas others believed that he had a unique ability to recover detailed accounts. However, as Neisser (1981) so persuasively demonstrated, Dean was incredibly *accurate and inaccurate at the same time.*

Neisser (1982), a cognitive psychologist, compared Dean's memory about conversations with Nixon to transcripts of the actual recorded conversations. He concluded that, in many instances, Dean failed to recall accurately both the details and gist of the conversations, yet:

his testimony had much truth in it, but not at the level of "gist." It was true at a deeper level. Nixon was the kind of man Dean described, he had the knowledge Dean attributed to him, there was a cover-up. Dean remembered all of that: he just didn't recall the actual conversation he was testifying about. (p. 151)

Another type of memory inaccuracy has come to be called *telescoping* (Rubin & Baddeley, 1989). This type of memory error refers to the tendency of people to think that events occurred more recently than they actually did. So, even when we can recall events with relative accuracy we are likely to be chronologically inaccurate.

STORING, REMEMBERING, AND FORGETTING INFORMATION

The recognition that respondents make errors in memory construction and recon-struction is not new. Bartlett (1932) is generally credited with first describing this process, and a number of researchers prior to the 1970s undertook research with this focus. In a classic study, Allport and Postman (1958) showed the effects of "constructive" errors caused by stereotypes. This research showed that constructive errors are caused by our tendency to supplement remembered facts with con-structed facts in a process that was referred to as *refabrication.*

Although most cognitive psychologists today accept this reconstructed view of memory, such has not always been the case. A number of researchers have argued that people are fully capable of recovering observational data that have been stored in long-term memory. Such a videotape-recorded model of memory is much like one proposed by Koffka (1935). Other similar viewpoints suggest that memory traces slowly decay over time or submerge themselves into the unconscious (Freud, 1915/1957). Hence, impressions or information were said to be never really forgotten. They were thought to just fade away, to be possibly retrieved through electrical brain stimulation, drugs, or hypnosis (Loftus, 1980). Unfortunately, respondents appear to be susceptible to reconstructive processes even under the influence of hypnosis or so called "truth drugs." As Loftus (1980; Loftus & Loftus, 1980) pointed out, spontaneous memory recovery is only impressive in the absence of independent verification. Loftus (1980) concluded that

> in most cases where there have been attempts to verify a memory, sometimes an actual event matches recollection, but other times the verification reveals that people are generating not memories of the true events but fanciful guesses, fantasies, or plain confabulations. (p. 45)

Although we cannot fully rely on self-reports of the past to be entirely accurate, we do not suggest that they should be abandoned. Under most conditions, they are very valuable and are the mainstay of oral history interviewing. As such, we must understand under what conditions people remember and also forget.

Event Memory: Forgetting

Not all memories can be successfully retrieved and scholars have suggested a number of reasons for forgetting. First, there are times when we simply did not pay enough attention to some incident and it never reaches long-term memory. Perhaps at the time we just did not deem an event important enough to remember.

Another theory suggests that "memory traces," "stored patterns," or later events literally pile up on earlier events hence interfering with recall in a kind of garbage can model of memory. Other theories contend that memory traces decay as they become older and are simply not reactivated, much like radioactive materials. Still others blame memory problems on selective recall that may favor positively valenced material. Research in memory, attribution, and clinical psychology has shown that we tend to recall good times and/or success and repress bad events and failure (Davis, 1987). Of course, any of these processes may lead to forgetting. But we must keep in mind that when we or our respondents tend to recall something vividly, "constructive" processes are probably at work.

Event Memory: Storage

It is not unusual for an interviewer to ask interviewees to recall some conversation they had with someone else. Recall of such an episode in usually referred to as *event memory*. Events may be stored in one of several ways. Hastie and Carlston (1980) suggested four: undifferentiated associative networks, storage bins or stacks, hierarchical networks, and frames or scripts.

The first type of storage structure, or associative network, can be conceived of as an undirected graph where communicative episodes or events are nodes and associative links connect similar nodes. This model has limited utility, however, because some of the earliest work on social learning (Ebbinghaus, 1885/1964) showed these paths to be directional. Wyer and Srull (1980) provided an alternative structuring of memory for communication events. These authors contended that information about episodes or individuals is located in storage "bins" that are connected by associative pathways. Within bins, information is stored according to recency, making new information the most accessible. However, other processes (e.g., rehearsal) can move information to the top of the bin.

Others, including Hastie and Carlston (1980), suggested that hierarchical structures store event data. The assumption here is that entry to the network is limited to higher level points and that the search moves downward. Higher level nodes represent abstract information; lower level nodes represent concrete behavioral events or inferences. Finally, Hastie and Carlston (1980) posited frame or script models (e.g., Schank & Abelson, 1977) of episode memory. A script is said to be "a predetermined, stereotyped sequence of actions that defines a well-known situation" (Schank & Abelson, p. 41). Scripts have been shown to affect not only our expectations for a particular situation, but also our memory for what occurred in that situation (Reisser, Black, & Abelson, 1985). Indeed, Neisser (1982) suggested that some of John Dean's memory errors may have been due to Dean's assuming his conversations with Nixon followed the "script" for meetings. Obviously, these structures are too complex to be represented as associative graph structures.

Event Memory: Retrieval

Regardless of how memory is structured, oral history interviewing and research depends to a great extent on accurate retrieval. Information stored in memory must be retrieved before it can be used. In discussing memory processes and retrieval, researchers make a distinction between accessibility and availability. Although there is some disagreement, one group of researchers believe that once information is understood and stored in long-term memory it is always available (Lewis, 1979). Others of course disagree and stress the constructive and reconstructive aspects of memory (Neisser, 1982).

Research has shown that people do remember some things well. For example, Kintsch and Bates (1977) and Keenan, MacWhinney, and Mayhew (1977) showed that listeners tend to remember a lecturer's irrelevant asides better than his or her text. Of course, this is somewhat discouraging to many teachers who attempt to impart wisdom in their college and high school classes each day. Brown and Kulik (1977) suggested that vivid, self-selected, personally relevant events exist like "flashbulb memories" because a "now print" psychological mechanism exists. Hence, we tend to recall where we were when some historic event occurred. Neisser (1982) suggested that in part it is the frequent rehearsal and discussion that accompanies historical events (e.g., the Challenger explosion) that contribute to our memory of these events, and that these events act as benchmarks in that they link our personal histories to History. Unfortunately, other research still suggests that even flashbulb memories may be misremembered (Loftus, 1980).

Self-Schemas and Memory Processes

As we discussed earlier, self-schemas are cognitive frameworks that we use to process and store information about ourselves (Markus, 1977). Such structures may affect memory storage and retrieval. Interviewees will have different self-schemas based upon their previous experiences and their feelings about these experiences. As Markus, Crane, Bernstein and Siladi (1982) pointed out:

> some individuals may be intensely concerned with their honesty, their masculinity, or their creativity and may develop highly articulated schemas about themselves in these particular domains. In contrast, others may be relatively undifferentiated or *aschematic* in these domains. (p. 39)

The research on self-schemas has shown that we retain more self-schematic information, attend to it more quickly than to information that does not fit into our self-schemas, are unable to accept counterschematic information about ourselves, and see our future behaviors in terms of our self-schemas (Gotlib & McCann, 1984;

Ingram, Smith, & Brehm, 1983; Kuiper & Derry, 1982; Kuiper, McDonald, & Derry, 1983; Markus & Sentis, 1982).

Self-schemas also affect how we process and store information about others. The more important a particular aspect of our self-schema is to us, the more important that aspect is in determining what we perceive and remember about others. Lewicki (1984) termed this the "self-image bias in person perception" (p. 1177). Not only do we attend to and remember more information about others that is consistent with our self-schemas, we fill in missing information about others from our own self-schemas, are more confident in our schematic than nonschematic judgments about others (even when we are incorrect), and are more sensitive to schematic variations in others' behavior than to other types of variations (Lewicki, 1984; Markus & Sentis, 1982; Markus & Smith, 1981).

IMPLICATIONS FOR ORAL HISTORY INTERVIEWING

We can use our knowledge of the structure and nature of personal memory in planning and conducting an oral history interview, as well as in analyzing the information we learn in the interview. One effective strategy is to design questions that elicit memories of intense emotional experiences, particularly positive ones. As we noted, such experiences are easier to recall than less involving events (Holmes, 1970; Robinson, 1980). However, this technique will not help in the recall of those less intense experiences that may provide the context needed for interpreting the emotional events. The research on scripts indicates that by directing interviewees' attention to the activities in which they were engaged, we might facilitate their recall of behaviors, feelings and people with whom they were interacting at a particular time. Reisser et al. (1985) suggested that such a technique can improve individuals' memory for details (what one said and how one behaved) because it taps into the structure of event memory.

An interviewer might even use activities as the framework for constructing an interview protocol. For example, in an investigation of some aspect of a person's life history, an interviewer could direct the person's attention to a particular activity and from there to specific people encountered in the activity, to particular activities with those people, and so on. Such an interviewing strategy would aid the interviewee's directed search of memory, offering the promise of a more successful interview than would the technique of asking general questions about the person's behaviors.

One should be careful about having individuals draw conclusions from memory data. For example, the hindsight research clearly suggests that we are not only quick to find order in events, but we often feel we knew it all the time. Like people in general, historians have tendencies to construct coherent narratives that link series of somewhat independent events. The accuracy of the narrative depends on the accuracy of the links. Generally, the more events that are linked together, the more complex the events, the less likely the story is to be accurate.

Sensitive interviewers can use their awareness of the existence of self-schemas and their experience with psychological aspects of the interaction itself to assist them in the interview process. As an interview proceeds, interviewers should pick up verbal and nonverbal cues associated with communication effectiveness as well as clues to the self-schemas that are important to their respondents. The ability to recognize aspects of self-schemas should not only suggest areas for further questioning, but also provide clues to themes that might be used to characterize interviewees' worlds.

The self-schema research also provided a cautionary message for any interviewer. Our self-schemas obviously affect what we pay attention to about others and what we remember about them. As interviewers, we must attempt to move beyond our own self-schemas, focusing the interview not on what is important to us in our lives, but what is important to our interviewees—regardless of the accuracy with which they actually recall events.

Finally, if the goal of the interview is "accuracy" then total reliance upon individuals' memories of historical events or persons is likely to add only a part of the puzzle. The research clearly shows that people are inaccurate, but in predictable ways. Triangulation of multiple data sources (e.g., archival data, written correspondence), insight, and so on, are needed to accomplish this goal.

SUMMARY

We have attempted to provide a picture of the interviewing process and individual memory processes as selective and constructive. We hope that we have also provided some suggestions on how to employ this information to improve oral history interviewing as a process. The issue of how to interpret the data an interviewer collects in terms of accuracy remains. This is nothing new and interpretation remains a central concern in almost every area of the humanities and social sciences.

We are all captives of our present personal perspective. As interviewers or interviewees, we tend to use analytic categories that bias our recall/reconstruction. We often have our own implicit (and sometimes explicit) agenda in interpreting the past that stamps forever our recall with a value laden perspective. There is no proven technique for obtaining untainted data. As an oral history interviewer one needs to recognize that such biases exist in both the interviewer and the interviewee and do one's best to overcome these tendencies. This is the advice one often finds in basic texts in anthropology of history. This advice remains valid.

We hope that we have not painted too bleak a picture of the many pitfalls confronting the process of oral history interviewing (e.g., scripts, selective forgetting, communicative incompetence, etc.). Most of these potential dangers will not be new to those who have worked in this area.

In addition, we should point out that for many researchers, the primary goal of the enterprise is not "accuracy," but instead is to discover the meaning of events for the participants. Hence, you may not be interested in acquiring some objective account (if such a thing could be obtained anyway!) and will be satisfied with rich, thick description that promotes understanding. This is certainly a goal worth pursuing (see Mishler, 1989).

REFERENCES

Allport, G., & Postman L. (1958). *The psychology of rumor.* New York: Holt.
Argyle, M. (1969). *The psychology of interpersonal behavior.* Harmondsworth: Penguin.
Bartlett, F. A. (1932). *A study in experimental and social psychology.* New York: Cambridge University Press.
Becker, C. (1985). Every man his own historian. *American Historical Review, 40,* 221–236.
Bransford, J. D. (1977). *Human cognition: Learning, understanding and remembering.* Belmont, CA: Wadsworth.
Brown, R., & Kulik, J. (1977). Flashbulb memories. *Cognition, 5,* 73–99.
Burleson, B. R. (1984). Comforting communication. In H.E. Sypher & J.L. Applegate (Eds.), *Communication by children and adults: Social cognitive and strategic processes* (pp. 63–104). Beverly Hills, CA: Sage.
Buss, A.H. (1980). *Self-consciousness and social anxiety.* San Francisco, CA: Freeman.
Davis, D., & Perkowitz, W.T. (1979). Consequences of responsiveness in dyadic interaction: Effects of probability of response and proportion of content-related responses on interpersonal attraction. *Journal of Personality and Social Psychology, 37,* 534–551.
Davis, P. J. (1987). Repression and in inaccessability of affective memories. *Journal of Personality and Social Psychology, 53*(3), 585–593.
Duncan, S., & Fiske, D.W. (1977). *Face-to-face interaction.* Hillsdale, NJ: Lawrence Erlbaum Associates.
Ebbinghaus, H. (1964). *Memory.* New York: Dover. (Original work published 1885).
Ervin-Tripp, S. (1969). Sociolinguistics. In L. Berkowitz (Ed.), *Advances in experimental social psychology* (Vol. 4, pp. 91–166). New York: Academic Press.
Fischoff, B. (1982). For those condemned to study the past: Heuristics and biases in hindsight. In D. Kahneman, P. Slovic, & A. Tversky (Eds.), *Judgement under uncertainty: Heuristics and biases* (pp. 335–354). Cambridge: Cambridge University Press.
Freud, S. (1957). Repression. In J. Strackey (Ed. and Trans.), *The standard edition of the complete psychological works of Sigmund Freud* (Vol. 14, pp. 48–51). London: Hogarth Press. (Original work published 1915)
Gallie, W. B. (1964). *Philosophy and the historical understanding.* London: Chatto & Windus.
Gotlib, I. H., & McCann, D. (1984). Construct accessibility and depression: An examination of cognitive and affective factors. *Journal of Personality and Social Psychology, 47,* 427–439.
Greenwald, A.G. (1981). Self and memory. In G.H. Bower (Eds.), *Psychology of learning and motivation* (Vol. 15, pp. 67–94). New York: Academic Press.
Grice, H.P. (1975). Logic and conversation. In P. Cole & J. L. Morgan (Eds.), *Syntax and semantics speech acts* (Vol. 3, pp. 104–121). New York: Seminar Press.
Hale, C.L., & Delia, J.G. (1976). Cognitive complexity and social perspective-taking. *Communication Monographs, 43,* 195–203.
Hastie, E., & Carlston, D.E. (1980). Theoretical issues in person memory. In R. Hastie, T. Ostrom, E. Ebbesen, R. Wyer, D. Hamilton, & D. Carlston (Eds.), *Person memory: The cognitive basis of social perception* (pp. 179–226). Hillsdale, N.J.: Lawrence Erlbaum Associates.
Holmes, D. S. (1970). Differential change in affective intensity and the forgetting of unpleasant experiences. *Journal of Personality and Social Psychology, 15,* 234–239.

Hymes, D. (1972). Models of the interaction of language and social setting. In J. J. Gumperez & G.D. Hymes (Eds.), *Directions in sociolinguistics: The ethnography of communication.* (pp. 35–71). New York: Holt, Rinehart & Winston.

Ingram, R.D., Smith, T.W., & Brehm, S.S. (1983). Depression and information processing: Self-schemata and the encoding of self-referent information. *Journal of Personality and Social Psychology, 45,* 412–420.

James, W. (1950). *The principles of psychology* (Vol. 1). New York: Dover. (Original work published 1890)

Kahneman, D. (1975). *Attention and effort.* Englewood Cliffs, NJ: Prentice-Hall.

Keenan, J.M., MacWhinney, B., & Mayhew, D. (1977). Pragmatics in memory: A study of natural conversation. *Journal of Verbal learning and Verbal Behavior, 16,* 549–560.

Kihlstrom, J.F. (1981). On personality and memory. In N. Cantor & J. F. Kihlstrom (Eds.), *Personality, cognition and social interaction* (pp. 200–214). Hillsdale, NJ: Lawrence Erlbaum Associates.

Kintsch, W., & Bates, E. (1977). Recognition memory for statements from a classroom lecture. *Journal of Experimental Psychology: Human Learning and Memory, 3,* 150–159.

Koffka, K. (1935). *Principles of gestalt psychology.* New York: Harcourt, Brace.

Kraut, R., & Lewis, S.H. (1984). Some functions of feedback in conversation. In H.E. Sypher & J.L. Applegate (Eds.), *Communication by children and adults* (pp. 231–259). Beverly Hills, CA: Sage.

Kuiper, N.A., & Derry, P.A. (1982). The self as a cognitive prototype: An application to person perception and depression. In N. Cantor & J.F. Kihlstrom (Eds.), *Personality, cognition and social interaction* (pp. 215–232). Hillsdale, NJ: Lawrence Erlbaum Associates.

Kuiper, N.A., McDonald, M.R., & Derry, P.A. (1983). Parameters of a depressive self-schema. In J. Suls (Ed.), *Psychological perspectives on the self* (Vol. 2, pp. 191–219). Hillsdale, NJ: Lawrence Erlbaum Associates.

Lanzetta, J.T. (1971). The motivated properties of uncertainty. In H.I. Day & D.E. Hunt (Eds.), *Intrinsic motivation: New directions in education* (pp. 134–147). Toronto: Holt, Rinehart & Winston of Canada.

Lewicki, P. (1984). Self-schema and social information processing. *Journal of Personality and Social Psychology, 47,* 1177–1190.

Lewis, D.J. (1979). Psychology of active and inactive memory. *Psychology Bulletin, 86,* 1054–1083.

Lindsay, P.H., & Norman, D.A. (1972). *Human information processing: An introduction to psychology.* New York: Academic Press.

Loftus, E. (1980). *Memory.* Reading, MA: Addison-Wesley.

Loftus, E.F., & Loftus, G.R. (1980). On the permanence of stored information in the human brain. *American Psychologist, 35,* 409–420.

Macy, J. Jr., Christie, L.S., & Luce, R.D. (1953). Coding noise in a task-oriented group. *Journal of Abnormal and Social Psychology, 28,* 401–409.

Markus, H. (1977). Self-schemata and processing information about the self. *Journal of Personality and Social Psychology, 35,* 63–78.

Markus, H., Crane, M., Bernstein, S., & Siladi, M. (1982). Self-schemas and gender. *Journal of Personality and Social Psychology, 42,* 38–50.

Markus, H., & Sentis, K. (1982). The self in social information processing. In J. Suls (Ed.), *Psychological perspectives on the self* (Vol. 1, pp. 41–70). Hillsdale, NJ: Lawrence Erlbaum Associates.

Markus, H., & Smith, J. (1981). The influence of self-schema on the perception of others. In N. Cantor & J.F. Kihlstrom (Eds.), *Personality, cognition and social interaction* (pp. 233–262). Hillsdale,NJ: Lawrence Erlbaum Associates.

Mead, G.H. (1934). *Mind, self and society.* Chicago: University of Chicago Press.

Mehrabian, A., & Reed, H. (1968). Some determinants of communication accuracy. *Psychological Bulletin, 70,* 365–381.

Mehrabian, A., & Wiener, M. (1967). Decoding of inconsistent information. *Journal of Personality and Social Psychology, 6,* 109–114.

Mishler, E.G. (1989). *Research interviewing: Context and narrative.* Cambridge, MA: Harvard University Press.

Neisser, U. (1981). John Dean's memory: A case study. *Cognition, 9,* 1–22.

Neisser, U. (1982). *Memory observed.* San Francisco: Freeman.

Neuliep, J.W., & Hazelton, V. (1986). Enhanced conversational recall and reduced conversational inference as a function of cognitive complexity. *Human Communication Research, 13,* 211–224.

Nowell-Smith, P.H. (1970). Historical explanation. In H.E. Kiefer & M.K. Muritz (Eds.), *Mind, science and history* (pp. 213–233). Albany: State University of New York Press.

O'Keefe, D.J., & Sypher, H.E. (1981). Cognitive complexity measures and the relationship of cognitive complexity to communication: A critical review. *Human Communication Research, 8,* 72–92.

Planalp, S., & Tracy, K. (1980). Not to change the topic but...: A cognitive approach to the management of conversation. In D. Nimmo (Ed.), *Communication Yearbook 4* (pp. 237–258. New Brunswick, NJ: Transaction.

Reisser, B.J., Black, J.B., & Abelson, R.P. (1985). Knowledge structures in the organization and retrieval of autobiographical memories. *Cognitive Psychology, 17,* 89–137.

Robinson, J.A. (1980). Affect and retrieval of personal memories. *Motivation and Emotion, 4,* 149–174.

Rosenthal, R., Hall, J.A., DiMatteo, M.R., Rogers, P.L., & Archer, D. (1979). *Sensitivity to nonverbal communication: The PONS test.* Baltimore, MD: Johns Hopkins.

Rubin, D.C., & Baddeley, A.D. (1989). Telescoping is not time compression: A model of the dating of autobiographical events. *Memory and Cognition, 17*(6), 653–661.

Sacks, H., Schegloff, E.A., & Jefferson, G. (1978). A simplest systematics for the organization of turn taking for conversation. In J. Schenkein (Ed.), *Studies in the organization of conversational interaction* (pp. 7–56). New York: Academic Press.

Schank, R., & Abelson, R. (1977). *Scripts, plans, goals and understanding: An inquiry into human knowledge structures.* Hillsdale, NJ: Lawrence Erlbaum Associates.

Sherman, S.J., & Corty, E. (1984). Cognitive heuristics. In R.S. Wyer & T.K. Srull (Eds.), *Handbook of social cognition* (Vol. 1, pp. 189–286). Hillsdale, NJ: Lawrence Erlbaum Associates.

Snyder, M. (1987). *Public appearances, private realities.* New York: Freeman Press.

Street, R.L. Jr., & Brady, R.M. (1982). Speech rate acceptance ranges as a function of evaluative domain, listener speech rate, and communicative context. *Communication Monographs, 49,* 290–308.

Sypher, H.E., & Applegate, J.L. (1984). Organizing communication behavior: The role of schemas and constructs. In R.N. Bostrom (Ed.), *Communication yearbook 8* (pp. 310–328). Beverly Hills, CA: Sage.

Watzlawick, P., Beavin, J.H., & Jackson, D.D. (1967). *Pragmatics of human communication.* New York: Norton.

Wyer, R.S. Jr., & Srull, T.K. (1980). The processing of social stimulus information. In R. Hastie, T. Ostrom, E. Ebbesen, R. Wyer, D. Hamilton, & D. Carlston (Eds.), *Person memory: The cognitive bases of social perception* (pp. 227–300). Hillsdale, NJ: Lawrence Erlbaum Associates.

5

Interpreting the Complexity of Women's Subjectivity

Susan E. Chase
University of Tulsa

Colleen S. Bell
Hamline University

In discussions of how feminist principles influence conventional social science methodology, it has become axiomatic to assert that the subject–object dichotomy between researcher and researched should be challenged. Feminist researchers work at treating others not as objects of research but as subjects of their own experiences. In this chapter we explore one problem that arises in the course of practicing this commitment. We have discovered that what it means to treat interviewees as subjects becomes unclear and problematic when we ask about their experiences of being subject to various forms of inequality.[1] How are we to invite women to speak as subjects when we ask questions that evoke narratives about discrimination, isolation, and exclusion? Drawing examples from our in-depth

---

[1] A note on terminology. Althusser (1972) pointed out that even the everyday use of the term *subject* is ambiguous: It refers at once to "a free subjectivity, a centre of initiatives, author of and responsible for its actions"; and to "a subjected being, who submits to a higher authority, and is therefore stripped of all freedom except that of freely accepting this submission "(p. 182). In the social sciences, however, the word is more often used to refer to an actor's agency (the first meaning) than to an actor's subjection. Throughout the chapter we speak of women as subject and subject to, or as active subjects and subjected in order to make clear that we are pointing to the multiple meanings of the word. However, what we mean by subject to (or subjected or subjection) is different from the meaning outlined by Althusser. Rather than submission to a higher authority, the phenomenon to which we refer is the experience of subjection to inequality embedded in social structure and culture.

interviews with women public school superintendents, we argue that researchers should focus on the complexity of women's subjectivity and how women narrate that complexity within the interactional context of the interview.

TREATING INTERVIEWEES AS SUBJECTS

Among feminist theorists such as Harding (1987), Ferree and Hess (1987), Mies (1983), and Westkott (1979), there is general agreement concerning the impact of feminism on the research relationship. Others would probably consent to Harding's delineation of three features that are characteristic of the best in contemporary feminist research. First, in contrast to much conventional social science research that defines as worthy of study phenomena that appear problematic from men's perspectives, feminist research "generates its problematics from the perspective of women's experiences" (Harding, 1987, p. 7). Second, "the goal of this inquiry is to provide for women explanations of social phenomena that they want and need" rather than answering questions raised by those who have the power to "pacify, control, exploit, or manipulate women" (p. 8). Third:

> The best feminist analysis...insists that the inquirer her/himself be placed in the same critical plane as the overt subject matter, thereby recovering the entire research process for scrutiny in the results of research. That is, the class, race, culture, and gender assumptions, beliefs, and behaviors of the researcher her/himself must be placed within the frame of the picture that she/he attempts to paint. (p. 9)

The first and second features outlined here clearly aim at treating women as subjects of their experiences rather than as objects of research. And accomplishing this aim requires the third feature, including the entire research process—the researchers' assumptions, the research relationship—in the analysis.

Similarly, Westkott articulated the difference between conventional social science and feminist research in this way:

> Th[e] aura of objectivity can be maintained so long as the object of knowledge, the "known," can be an "other," an alien object that does not reflect back on the knower.... It is only where women are also brought in as the *subjects* of knowledge that the separation between subject and object [researcher and researched] breaks down. (p. 425)

According to Westkott, when we treat those we study as subjects—as active knowers and agents—we transform the research relationship. We open ourselves to interaction, to intersubjectivity, to others' understandings of and relations to us as researchers.

Although he did not use the vocabulary of feminism, Briggs' (1986) criticism of conventional research practices resonates with that offered by Harding and Westkott and contributes to our understanding of what it means to treat those we interview as subjects. Briggs argued that interpretation of data gathered from interviews must begin with acknowledgment that the interview is a particular kind of "communicative event," an event structured by norms that do not necessarily operate in everyday interactions. He claimed that because researchers frequently do not understand the native communicative patterns of a community—what should and should not be asked about, in what context, and by whom—"we commonly impose our communicative norms on our consultants. This practice amounts to *communicative hegemony*" (p. 131). And communicative hegemony, he argued, is a "subtle and persistent form of *scientific colonialism*" (1986, p. 121).

We embrace Harding's, Westkott's, and Briggs' ideas about breaking down the subject–object split between researcher and researched and recognizing interviews as particular communicative and interactional events. But what has yet to be articulated is how researchers should practice these commitments in relation to interviewees' experiences of *subjection*. How do we take into account that women experience themselves not only as active subjects but also as subject to inequalities in their social worlds? How do women express and communicate their complex subjectivity in the interview context? Throughout our interviews, women interwove stories about active subjectivity, about making a difference in their social worlds, with stories about subjection to various gendered, racial, and ethnic inequalities. We address issues that arise in the research relationship, issues that are related to complexity in women's subjectivity.

WOMEN IN THE PUBLIC SCHOOL SUPERINTENDENCY

Although women comprise 70% of all public school teachers in the United States (National Center for Education Statistics, 1992), only 5.6% of the nation's K–12 superintendents are women (Bell & Chase, 1993). This asymmetry is particularly striking because teaching experience is a prerequisite for most administrative positions in public education. Furthermore, the superintendency is White- as well as male-dominated. African Americans, Asian Americans, Hispanics, and American Indians comprise 3.4% of superintendents, and of this small number, 12% are women (Jones & Montenegro, 1990). Hence, those few women of any racial or ethnic background who achieve the position of school superintendent are at once powerful leaders in their communities and persons subject to gender, race, and ethnic inequalities in a male- and White-dominated profession.

Between 1986 and 1989 we conducted in-depth interviews with 27 women superintendents of varying racial and ethnic backgrounds in rural, suburban, and urban school districts across the United States. All interviews were conducted jointly by us, tape-recorded, and transcribed. We spent between 2 and 14 hours interviewing each woman, asking questions about the work she does; the educational and political issues she confronts; the local, political, professional, and interpersonal contexts in which she works; her career history; and the relationship between her personal and work lives. In addition, we asked these superintendents to reflect on what difference gender and race or ethnicity have made to their experiences. Our questions were open-ended and unstructured, that is "conducted along thematic lines, rather than according to a prewritten format" (Wiersma, 1988, p. 209).

The kind of interview we sought to conduct was in part a familiar and in part a strange communicative event for women superintendents. These educational leaders are accustomed to speaking publicly to community groups and reporters because establishing and maintaining good public relations in their communities are major aspects of their jobs. In addition, two thirds of the women we interviewed hold doctorates and so have experience as researchers themselves. On the one hand, their familiarity with various kinds of interviews was an advantage for us in that we shared unspoken ground rules for the interaction (e.g., in general, we would ask and they would answer questions). On the other hand, people who are accustomed to being interviewed or publicly describing their experiences sometimes have stock answers and stories that they pull out for those occasions. We attempted to establish an interview situation that was different from TV, radio, newspaper, or other forms of public interviews by creating a safe context for women to reflect on and interpret their experiences, rather than simply report them as they had probably done innumerable times before. The safety of this interview situation as compared to others lay in our promise to protect their identities by using pseudonyms and other forms of disguise in any publication of our research. Thus, what was at stake for the women was for the most part internal to the interview situation. The central project for both them and us was communicating and interpreting their experiences as women who are educational leaders.

Women superintendents consented to in-depth interviews for a variety of reasons and experienced the interviews in different ways. Some enjoyed the opportunity to be listened to and stated explicitly that the interview was therapeutic. Some felt that research on women in their occupation would be of direct help to other women and so viewed their participation as a contribution to that effort. Several women have kept in contact with us, letting us know about changes in their situations or adding new thoughts concerning their experiences. But another more subtle factor was often present: We felt that many women readily agreed to talk with us because of their professional isolation. Many studies have shown that women who work in male-dominated occupations experience isolation from their peers because being one of a few creates performance pressures and difficult interactional dynamics between men and women (Epstein, 1983; Kanter, 1977; Lorber, 1984). Consequently, some women seemed to welcome the chance to talk with us at length about their experiences. Their enjoyment of the interview was enhanced by the fact that Colleen's field is educational administration. Colleen shared with our interviewees a body of knowledge concerning their everyday work experiences, as well as familiarity with persons in the field.

However, even though their professional isolation often facilitated their consent to be interviewed, talking about the gendered character of their experiences was problematic for some superintendents. Our attempts to ask directly how gender shapes their experiences produced some very awkward moments in two of our earliest interviews. These uncomfortable interactions alerted us to the need to think carefully about what it means to treat women as subjects of their experiences, and particularly how we should go about inviting women to reflect on their experiences of subjection. We realized that intending to establish a safe context in which women could interpret their experiences was not sufficient for accomplishing that interactional task. We needed to re-think the interactive aspect of the interview situation, especially how we show our interest in their experiences.

BLUNDERING[2] UPON A COMPLEX NARRATIVE

In the spirit of Briggs'(1986) idea that "some of the most interesting situations emerge when the participants realize that something has gone awry" (p. 110), we examine awkward moments in one of our earliest interviews, an interview that was otherwise interactionally unproblematic.

Elizabeth Swenson[3] is a 50-year-old White superintendent in a small-town school district. We interviewed her twice for a total of 6 hours; the first interview took place in her office, and the second in her home after we had taken Elizabeth and her husband to dinner. During the first interview, Elizabeth described the issues she has faced in her current position and recounted the history of her aspirations and career. Her comments about the hiring process for the superintendency clearly reveal her perception that gender has influenced her experiences. After Elizabeth had been assistant superintendent in Montgomery for several years, the superintendent retired; by her own account, the school board was reluctant to interview her for the superintendency even though she had applied and was qualified. (Note: we present excerpts so that they are both readable and inclusive of significant speech practices: pauses, repetitions, stutters, emphases.)[4]

E: The one guy who is no longer on the school board finally said
   "*I* think we deserve to give Dr. Swenson an *interview* anyway"
   because *some* of them didn't even want to interview me
C: why not?
E: well they I think it was because I was a woman
   I think they knew I was doing a good *job*
   it wasn't that I wasn't *capable* but they just hadn't thought of me in the
   superintendent's position.

---

[2]We have adopted Briggs' (1986) notion of communicative blunders for our own use. Although interactional blunders are part of the folklore of research methodology, researchers rarely expose blunders in their published work (for exceptions, see Corsino, 1987; Mbilinyi, 1989). In this chapter, we risk public examination of portions of an interview that were awkward for us and our interviewee because understanding those interactions was a turning point in our conceptualization of what it means to treat women as subjects.

[3]With the exception of our names, all names of persons and places are pseudonyms.

[4]In our presentation of the excerpts, italics indicate emphasis and dashes show a break-off of speech. Noticeable pauses of less than 3 seconds are identified by [p] and pauses of more than 3 seconds by [P]. We use punctuation sparingly, only when intonation clearly indicates a full stop, question, or exclamation. Quotation marks show that a speaker is reporting someone else's (or her own) speech. We end each line of transcript where there is a rise or a fall in pitch; indentations of subsequent lines signify that speech is continuous. This method of transcription is closest to that developed by Riessman (1990).

Shortly after this, Elizabeth reiterated twice that the source of the school board's hesitance about her candidacy was gender related. For example, when we asked whether the fact that she is a woman was ever addressed directly during the job interview, Elizabeth stated, "Oh yes they talked about that in the interview. Whether I could deal with the male principals and how they would react to me."

At the beginning of our second interview, Elizabeth talked about the traditional gender expectations with which she grew up—"I expected just to get married and have a family and be ambitious through my husband"—and how her own ambition developed despite those expectations. The following exchange occurred shortly after that discussion. Susan intended to invite Elizabeth to reflect on the gendered character of this story and those she had told during the first interview.

S: Thinking back over your over the history of your career
    was there any particular point when *you* realized that being a woman was
        going to make some kind of a difference?
E: [P] gosh [P] uuh [p] negative or positive?
S: yeah hm hmm
E: hm hmm [p] I I really hate to say this in a way but I really
    [P] never really considered that an issue
S: hm hmm [p] ok yeah yea um but—
E: I mean I really didn't
S: yeah well that's another thing I meant to say I didn't say
    when I'm asking about the gender issues
    we *really* want to hear *your* perspective
E: yeah uh you know I *know* it's not [p] a lot of people say
    but yeah but *I'll* tell you the way I feel (S: yeah yeah)
    I don't really (S: hm hmm) I never really considered
    I *always* knew I was capable (S: hm hmm)
    and knew I was as smart as anybody (S: hm hmm)
    and so I just *assumed* that would win out or something maybe I don't know
    but uh in my *career* it never really uh
    I never considered that to be a problem or a either a
    negative or a positive thing (S: hm hmm ok)
    [p] although I want to say realistically I *know* [small laugh]
    I know that it *does* I know that probably it does *matter* in a lot of cases (S:
        hm hmm hm hmm)
    but that's never been my uuuhh a concern to me for some reason.

At the time of the interview, we were puzzled by Elizabeth's qualified and hesitant response to Susan's question and confused by her statement that she "never really considered that an issue." Her response seemed to contradict her preceding stories in which she clearly articulated gender as shaping her experiences. How are we to understand this apparent contradiction within Elizabeth's narrative? Westkott's (1979) criticism of conventional social science research offers us a guide.

Conventional social science research continues to assume a fit between consciousness and activity.... [This] assumption reflects the condition of being a male in patriarchal society, a condition of freedom, which admittedly varies greatly by race and class, to implement consciousness through activity. (p. 428)

Westkott reminded us that we should not expect a fit between parts of a woman's narrative; rather, we should anticipate a complex relationship between her descriptions and interpretations of her experiences. From our analytical and retrospective stance, we suggest that the contradiction within Elizabeth's narrative is related to a certain tension in her experience. On the one hand, she knows that as a woman she is subject to gendered inequalities; on the other hand, she does not want to focus on her lack of control in relation to those inequalities. Once we understand that women often work to achieve control over their lives in social contexts that make their desire for control problematic, such contradictions within a woman's narrative come as no surprise. Because we were not thinking about this tension as central to Elizabeth's narrative, her response simply confused us.

Our failure to understand the complexity of Elizabeth's subjectivity was also implicated in the following exchange—including an obvious blunder—that occurred near the end of the second interview.

S: I just have a couple questions left [p] about um [p]
    well *general* issues about women
E: I don't think I'm very good at this
    I don't I don't really *think* about these things
S: well that's that's ok
E: do you know I really *don't*
C: that's important for us to know though
E: I don't
S: but that's that's fine if that's the way you are
E: so you know I don't really uh I don't spend any time (S: uh huh) thinking
    about all the stuff and I don't really I'm not very good on that.
S: well that's ok [laugh] I mean
C: all we want to do is describe [p] how it *is* for you (E: yeah)
S: how you experience things and (E: ok) what you think about so if if you
    don't think about it that much that's the way it is
E: you really don't have too much time to sit around and think about issues like
    this in this job you know
S: yeah well that's one of the things that people are saying
    it's so [p] women *know* that those issues are *there*
    but it feels like another big *task* to have to *think* about them
E: it's *true* you know it's kind of like *golly* I don't
    it's really not too pleasant even (S: hm hmm) so uh
S: yeah [p] ok but if you were to say [laugh]
C: [laugh] let us just force you into this!
E: all right go ahead

Two interactional features are salient in this excerpt. First, neither we nor Elizabeth simply drop the topic of women's issues when she claims she doesn't think about them. Instead, the fact that Elizabeth doesn't think about women's issues itself becomes the topic of discussion. This subsequent discussion could be interpreted as the result of Elizabeth's sense of obligation to answer our questions. But this discussion could also be related to the particular topic at hand: Unlike other kinds of topics that a woman superintendent might feel she "is not too good at," not thinking about women's issues is something that requires explanation. Together the three of us collude in creating that explanation.

Second, despite the cogent explanation we concoct for why Elizabeth might not think about women's issues, Susan persists in asking the original question anyway, as if she is not convinced by the explanation: "yeah [p] ok but if you were to say." Colleen's exclamation—"let us just force you into this!"—captures succinctly the nature of Susan's blunder. Although we have repeatedly asserted that our interest is to "describe how it *is* for you," Susan's persistence in asking the question *disregards* how it is for Elizabeth. "Forcing" Elizabeth into discussing a topic she does not really think about is obviously an example of what not to do as an interviewer. But for the purposes of this discussion, we are more interested in understanding the meaning of the blunder than we are in speculating about what we could have done differently. Westkott's (1979) notion of intersubjectivity in the research relationship helped us to understand this interaction.

> The questions that the investigator asks of the object of knowledge grow out of her own concerns and experiences. The answers that she may discover emerge not only from the ways that the objects of knowledge confirm and expand these experiences, but also from the ways that they oppose or remain silent about them. (p. 426)

Understanding and articulating how experience is gendered is one of *our* interests as researchers. By asking direct questions about gender we attempted to invite Elizabeth to articulate her gendered subjectivity in her own terms. We did not anticipate that such questions would violate Elizabeth's perspective because her own stories offered evidence of her sense of gender's significance. Nonetheless, the questions we asked about gender made sense from our perspective as researchers but not from Elizabeth's particular perspective as a practicing educational leader. Elizabeth's perspective is that thinking about gender is something she is "not very good at" and that is "really not too pleasant" because it disrupts her concentration on her everyday work. It is also possible that Elizabeth chooses not to reflect directly about gender because it is difficult and painful to sort out the relation between one's active subjectivity and one's subjection. At one point, Elizabeth volunteered an explanation along these lines: "I may deny, that's what I'm using, denial." Denial may be a strategy for limiting one's vulnerability to experiences of subjection that one cannot control.

It is important to stress the specific character of the disjunction between our perspective and Elizabeth's because different perspectives do not always produce awkwardness as they did in this case. The awkwardness represents the problematic nature of inviting women to talk about subjectivity. The awkwardness and blunder occurred because we were not yet conceiving of women as narrators of complex experiences of subjectivity. After our interviews with Elizabeth, we dropped these particular questions because they treat much too literally what it means to invite women to speak about gendered subjectivity.

AWAITING THE DEVELOPMENT OF A COMPLEX NARRATIVE

Now we turn to our interview with Rose Farrell, a 55-year-old Hispanic[5] superintendent in an urban school district. The excerpts we examine show how she develops her narrative about subjectivity over the course of the interview. By looking closely at the interview transcripts, it becomes apparent that we patiently awaited—rather than pushed for or blundered upon—the development of her narrative.

Our single interview with Rose took place in her office and lasted 2½ hours. During the first part of the interview, Rose spoke of the many problems she has faced as the educational leader of a poor, urban, ethnically diverse district. Later, while recounting her work experiences, she described the particular barriers women of color face in educational administration and how she thinks women should respond to them. For example, superintendency search consultants whom Rose trusts have told her that certain districts "aren't ready for an Hispanic," and thus have advised her not to apply there. Rose expressed appreciation of the consultants' forthrightness and has taken their advice seriously because "you can't be fighting and expect to be successful." Rose also spoke about the impact of gender on her relations with colleagues: "women have certainly played an important role in my personal development and my career development. There is *no doubt* about that and no man has done as much for me as the women were able to do. I don't say that men were unwilling but it's very much more awkward it's very difficult."

These few quotations show that Rose conceives of ethnicity and gender as salient aspects of her experiences. The two excerpts presented here enable us to look more closely at how she articulates her subjectivity in the context of the interview interaction. The first is from the middle of the interview; at this point Rose had just finished describing the highlights of her career history. Susan's question intended to evoke general reflection on that history.

S: umm let's see [p] thinking about the work history that you've related to us
the whole thing that you've been talking about would you say that you've
experienced discrimination because of gender or ethnicity?
R: [p] uuh yes but some people either handle it better or get less
and I think both of that is true
both of those things are true for me (S: hm hmm)

---

[5]In order to protect her identity, we do not name Rose Farrell's ethnicity specifically but use the broader term *Hispanic*.

uh [p] I remember when I first went to York as a principal
I needed to call another principal about a teacher who was transferring from
   his school to mine
and I called and we were on the phone and I had identified myself and told
   him what it is I wanted to know
and then *midway* through this conversation or it might have been as we were
   hanging up
he said "tell me your name again?" and I told him
and he said "and what is your position over there?" and I told him
and he said "well I thought they hired a little Hispanic girl over there" (All:
   [laugh])
and I says "well I'll be sure and introduce [laugh] myself when we meet
   when we have the next meeting"
I says "you you you you'll just have to tell by looking I guess I don't know"
   (All: [laugh])
so anyway uh he was *tremendously* embarrassed and uh he said
"I guess I've really gotten off on the wrong foot with you"
and I says "oh forget it who cares?" [laugh] (C: hm hmm)
S: is that an example of what you mean by handling it better?
R: and also getting less I don't consider that a terrible threat (S: yeah) or or uh
      or insult you know (S: uh huh) uh
    but it could be handled differently and made a big horrible case out of but
      it wasn't worth it to me
S: someone could have been angry
R: yeah I just thought it was I think *I've* told the story a million *times* cuz I
      think it's kind of *funny*
    but uh you know but it doesn't *hurt* me and it doesn't and I couldn't care
      less (S: hm hmm)
    and there's always little stuff like that you know
    but I do remember growing up that I I *always* did business first on the *phone*
      because people couldn't *see* me (S: hmm) and uh uh [p] and then I
    and so I have *always* experienced the surprise uh you know uh
    when I finally had to give my name or finally had to show up

In responding to Susan's question, Rose affirms that she has been subject to
discrimination, but she focuses on herself as an active subject in relation to that
problem. As she tells the story about the phone conversation, she emphasizes how
she handled the discriminatory treatment rather than the fact of experiencing it. In
other words, she turns our attention to what she can control—her response—rather
than to what she cannot control—others' discriminatory actions and attitudes.
Furthermore, Rose portrays the man who assumed she couldn't be Hispanic
(because she does not speak with an "accent" and does not have an Hispanic
surname—she uses her husband's name) as the more vulnerable person. He is more
embarrassed by his mistake than she is offended by it. By choosing not to make "a

big horrible case out of it," Rose asserts her control over the situation and sets a
positive tone for her future relationship with her embarrassed colleague.

This story is about how Rose exerts control in response to others' discriminatory
actions and attitudes. Moreover, by choosing to tell this story in response to the
question about discrimination—a story she has told "a million *times*" about an
incident of discrimination that she categorizes as "little stuff"—Rose exerts a
certain kind of control in the interview interaction. She could have chosen other
stories, for example, the one about districts that are "not ready for an Hispanic."
How are we to understand Rose's choice? Briggs (1986) claimed that "if the analyst
pays close attention to how a statement is made, he or she will find clues to the
interpretation the speaker wishes to attach, so to speak, to the words" (p. 106). By
informing us she has told the story a million times, Rose lets us know that this story
belongs to a strategy she has developed for answering questions about discrimination. Perhaps Rose offers this story to those (reporters? acquaintances? colleagues?
interviewers?) who need an easy and upbeat answer to a difficult question.

Indeed, this story is similar to the "press release" that Wiersma (1988) described
as characteristic of women's initial accounts of their career changes. Even though
"these women seemed to be offering me someone else's version of their actions
and feelings," Wiersma argues that the press releases "were actually telling the truth
about something when properly interpreted" (p. 206). The story Rose has told a
million times is like a press release in that it is a prepared story, a ready answer to
a difficult question. In addition, the story is about "little stuff" that she easily resists.
But as Wiersma suggested, the "press release" serves some purpose for the narrator
and reveals as much as it conceals. By choosing to begin with a press release, Rose
controls her response, and that need for control hints at her deeper vulnerability.
Significantly, at the end of the excerpt, Rose goes beyond the often-repeated story
and exposes a deeper sense of her subjection: " but I do remember growing up that
I I *always* did business first on the *phone* because people couldn't *see* me."
Although doing business on the phone is a clever strategy for dealing with others'
prejudices, it also represents Rose's understanding of how vulnerable she is to those
prejudices.

As the interview drew to a close, the following exchange occurred:

S: um one kind of [p] end question here
    a really general question and it's hard to ask because it's general
    but this is the first district that we've been to that really was ethnically diverse
       (R: hm hmm)
    most of the women the White women superintendents well *all* of them work
       in predominantly White districts (R: hm hmm)
    um the Black women superintendents some of them worked in dist work in
       districts where the students are 98% Black (R: hm hmm)
    and one thing that we found is that for the *White* women [p]
    race and ethnicity are really not dominant features of their experience
    uh for the *Black* women it's it's *really* a major
R: it's *prominent*

S: prominent
R: yes it's prominent
S: in their experiences and in *your* talk today it's it's been prominent there too
    (R: hm hmm)
    talking about it a *lot* in in various kinds of ways (R: hm hmm) in different
    kinds of situations and contexts
    um so the question is very general but do you [p]
    how do you *see* or how do you *think* of the role of ethnicity in *your* work
    and life experiences?
R: I think it's more prominent than I usually [p]
    uh when *you* say it's a lot there was a lot in my conversation
    uh [p] I'm thinking uh my first reaction was [p]
    "but I'm not thinking about that all day"
    and that (S: hm hmm) and but that lasted about two seconds
    and then I thought "yes I am I'm thinking about it *all* the time" (S: hm hmm)
    (C: yeah)
    I'm thinking about the the reaction of the various board members who
    represent different constituencies
    uh so when you live in a diverse area you *are* uh uh *conscious* of those
    sensitivities
    and so and so if I have an issue to bring to the *board*
    I have to think about how they're going to take it from their from where they
    are and from *who* they are and who they represent
    and and so it *does* play a major role but it's a *political* role (S: hm hmm)
    uh I think it's a it's a big role too for for minority women because that's
    where you *identify*
    and that's where you are likely to have your closest friends
    it's g it's gonna be that's probably gonna be the most people around you
    know
    because we don't get *hired* in White districts (S: hm hmm)
    and so we don't have that kind of an experience.

In this excerpt, unlike the previous one, it is clear that Rose answers spontaneously. By reflecting out loud about her initial and second responses, Rose shows
that she is thinking about what she is saying as she speaks rather than offering
another press release. This spontaneity signifies a change in the interaction as well
as a change in the context of her talk about subjectivity.

After describing how ethnicity plays a major political role in her work, Rose
recounts the significance of ethnicity for minority women. She suggests that
minority women tend to identify and develop friendships with each other, in part
because they often end up in the same places. At this point, Rose states bluntly that
women of color are subject to discrimination: "We don't get *hired* in White
districts." Unlike the earlier story she has told a million times, this experience of
subjection is hardly "little stuff." But even as she acknowledges this form of
subjection, Rose's manner of speaking shows the complexity of her subjectivity.

By using "we"—"we don't get *hired* in White districts"—Rose reiterates her statement of identification and friendship with other women of color. Friendship and identification are sites in which a strong sense of self develops. Thus, Rose interweaves her experience of discrimination as an Hispanic woman with her experience of friendship and identification with other minority women. Although the story Rose has told a million times suppressed her experience of subjection, here Rose articulates her subjectivity in a way that reveals its complexity.

Examining these two excerpts in relation to each other helps us to see that interpreting a woman's subjectivity is not just a matter of understanding her answers to specific questions. As Briggs (1986) stated, "If one considers each 'answer' only in the context of the preceding question, then a great deal of meaning will be lost" (p. 103). If we had interpreted the story Rose has told a million times in isolation, we might have concluded that Rose believes she has suffered little subjection and that it is up to an individual to deflect discrimination. By hearing that story *as a press release*, we take into account the interactional context in which she speaks, we well as how she develops and changes her narrative over the course of the interview. By listening to the two excerpts in relation to each other, we can offer a less literal interpretation of what she means by some people "handle [discrimination] better." With the support of friendship and identification with other women of color, we can imagine that Rose might handle it better than those who lack such support. Rather than an individualistic ideology, then, Rose may be invoking the social connections that make it possible for her to handle it better and to distinguish between discriminatory incidents that she will treat lightly and those that have greater consequences.

Close attention to the interaction in this interview reveals that Rose develops a complex narrative about her subjectivity over the course of the interview, and that we patiently await that development. In the context of the first exchange, some interviewers might have pressed Rose for an answer she has not told a million times. By the end of the interview, however, Rose has moved away from the press release by spontaneously discussing the part ethnicity plays in her work as well as the relation between ethnicity and her subjectivity.

CONSTRUCTING A COMPLEX NARRATIVE

Our last example reveals a different kind of interactional dynamic. Rather than blundering upon or awaiting the development of a complex narrative, we are more active participants in the construction of Diane Turner's narrative about subjectivity.

Diane is a 45-year-old White superintendent in a suburban school district. We conducted the first interview in her office and the second in her home; together the interviews produced 6 hours of tape. During the first interview, Diane described the problems she has faced in a district that has been plagued by quick turnover of both superintendents and board members, lack of trust between the community and schools, and financial problems. Throughout both interviews, Diane spoke directly about how gender has influenced her work experiences. She related various incidents that she defined as either subtle or blatant discrimination: graduate school advisors directing her away from administration and toward counseling; school boards asking during job interviews what she does for a social life as a single woman; a powerful administrator jeopardizing her candidacy for a superintendency by starting a rumor that she is a lesbian; community leaders failing to make lunch invitations (when she moved to town as superintendent) because of the awkwardness of male–female interaction. Diane has responded to the barriers women face in her occupation by helping to found a statewide professional organization for women who are practicing or aspiring educational administrators, an organization that claims a membership of several hundred. In addition, she has initiated informal monthly meetings among the small group of women superintendents in her state.

In the following excerpt from the first interview, Diane discussed the statewide professional organization for women in educational administration.

> D: So there are special *needs* that aren't always *addressed* at the administrators'
>   meetings
>   and we get right down and *address* some of them at the *women*
>   administrators' meetings.
>   and the women who don't care to be *honest* probably don't get a lot out of
>   it
> S: who don't care to be honest about how they have different needs?
> D: hm hmm or that uh [p] it is different that the job is different because they
>   are women
>   I believe the job is different because I'm a woman
>   because of people's *perception* of women in the job
>   and because of how people *react* to women as how people react to the one
>   they expect to be there.

According to Diane, the professional organization of women administrators provides an opportunity for women to address needs that arise from the fact that the job is different for men and women because of people's gendered perceptions. What remains unarticulated here is why some women would not want to be honest about the fact that the job is different for women. Diane may mean that honesty is difficult because it requires women to acknowledge subjection to gendered inequalities that they cannot control.

Halfway through our second interview with Diane, the discussion picked up where the above left off. A note of clarification: Although she previously stated that the women administrators' meetings address women's particular needs, in what follows she argues that those meetings do not serve the needs of women superintendents, those few women who have achieved the highest position in the educational hierarchy at the level of the local school district. Although women teachers who aspire to administrative positions and women who hold jobs at various points on the administrative hierarchy need the professional organization for women in order to become part of a broader network, those few women, like Diane, who have already become superintendents, have a different set of concerns. In Diane's state, only 8 out of approximately 500 K–12 superintendents are women.

D: I don't think the women superintendents learn that much from what happens at [the statewide professional organization for women administrators] (C: hm hmm S: yeah)
but we *need* a place to share and to learn (C: hm hmm)
and it's not going to be *there* (C: right)
so I think it's going to be with each other
C: you create your own
D: yea *exactly* and it's not going to be with with *too* many of the men although we learn some things there
but *because* it's *different*
I think I have an opportunity to *learn more* from those women than I do from—see even I said it "those women" from the *women* who are superintendents than I do from the *men* who are superintendents
uh I can learn the *factual* things as well
I can learn some *strategies* from the men
but I think that it's different for them
C: [p] so *what* they deal with is different because they're men not women and maybe *some* of the things that they *do* are different because they face a different set of *perceptions* from other people
D: that's right exactly exactly
S: [P] so there's a kind of [p] common
with with the women superintendents you *share* some maybe even *unspoken* ideas about what you have in common
there's a certain level of knowing what you all have to deal with but you don't even have to talk about it
D: yea I think yea I think we respect each other and know what we're going through to the point that we have that understanding
S: yeah but um [p] I take it I don't really know I'm asking
for the most part what you talk about are the problems from your work?
D: we have um [p] it varies
last time we talked about the State Secondary Schools Association...
and *Beth* took an hour and a half or so at our meeting in Rochester last week to share that information and...
Anne is kind of our resident expert on AIDS education
so she brings us along on that
I'm kind of our legal person and you know
it just kind of moves around on what we need to hear about

In this discussion, we actively participate in constructing the meaning for Diane of the informal meetings of women superintendents. Drawing on what Diane had said earlier about how the job is different for men and women because of people's perceptions of women in the job, we seek clarification and suggest interpretations or elaborations of Diane's statements. Her affirmative responses to our statements tell us that we have understood and have further articulated what she is trying to say.

For Diane, the informal meetings of women superintendents in her state provide an answer to problems they face because there are so few of them. The informal meetings of women superintendents fulfill the need for collegiality, "a place to share and to learn." Although the content of their meetings may be similar to the content of meetings among any group of superintendents—statewide education issues, AIDS education, legal issues—the need for meetings among the women superintendents lies in what they can take for granted among themselves: "We respect each other and know what we're going through to the point that we have that understanding." In other words, they don't necessarily spend their time together discussing gender-related issues, but it is because of gender-related issues that they turn to each other for support in doing their work.

In these passages, Diane narrates the complex relationship between being subject to gender inequality and being an active subject in response to that inequality. She does not hesitate to articulate how the job is different for men and women and she is not reluctant to speak of how she is subject to gendered perceptions and expectations. Her response to this problem is an active one: Because she does not get the support she needs from either the men administrators' meetings or the women administrators' meetings, she and the other women superintendents in her state have created their own support system.

The interaction in these exchanges with Diane was influenced by our mutual assumptions that gender shapes women's experiences and that gender issues are worth talking about directly. These shared assumptions facilitated our participation in the construction of Diane's narrative. It was obvious to us that Diane had already devoted much energy to thinking and talking about women's experiences. She was well aware of the problems produced by women superintendents' professional isolation and had acted on that problem. Interestingly, in her case, we did not feel that professional isolation played much of a part in her consent to be interviewed. Because she has worked so hard at creating opportunities for women's professional relationships to develop, her own isolation was not an issue in our interview relationship.

CONCLUSION: TREATING INTERVIEWEES
AS *NARRATORS*

We have argued that the feminist commitment to treating women as subjects of their experiences must take into account that women's subjectivity is complex: Women experience themselves both as active subjects who make a difference in their social worlds and as subject to gendered and ethnic or racial inequalities. We describe women's subjectivity as complex not only because of its multiplicity, but also because our interviews show that experiencing oneself simultaneously as subject and subjected is oftentimes confusing and sometimes painful. It is not always easy for a woman to determine the boundary between her active subjectivity and her subjection. Is subjection constituted by the situation itself or by one's orientation to the situation? Can one decide not to conceive of oneself as subjected? That women experience the boundary as shifting and as something they must make decisions about is evidenced by their accounts. For example, Rose Farrell distinguished between those discriminatory actions that do not hurt her ("little stuff") and those that are harmful. And Diane (in a story not cited) spoke of the method she has devised for limiting her vulnerability to others' discriminatory attitudes: For any particular situation she decides "whose problem it is, if it's not mine I'm not going to worry about it." By drawing a distinction between "their problems" and hers, Diane extricates herself emotionally from what she cannot control—others' attitudes and actions—in order to concentrate on those aspects of her experience that she can control.

Given the complexity of women's subjectivity, then, how do we understand the commitment to treating women as subjects of their experiences? In our view, the strongest version of that commitment requires a focus on women as *narrators* of their experiences. This subtle conceptual switch—from thinking about women as subjects of their experiences, to thinking about women as narrators of their experiences—preserves the feminist interest in empowerment that underlies the injunction to treat women as subjects. As a narrator, a woman has the power to speak as she chooses; she controls the telling of her experiences. At the same time, this conceptual switch makes room for women's experiences of subjection. By conceiving of women as narrators, we treat them as active subjects in the telling and interpreting of their stories, even when the narrative itself includes experiences of subjection.

Thinking of interviewees as narrators guides our understanding of the interview situation in several ways. First, it helps us to remember that we only have access to women's narratives about their experiences, rather than to their actual life experiences in any direct sense. As our examples show and as others have argued (Briggs, 1986; DeVault, 1990; Mishler, 1986; Riessman, 1990; Wiersma, 1988), understanding what is being said about experience requires interpretation of the telling itself. For example, Wiersma (1988, p. 233) cogently criticized researchers who have accepted as unproblematic "returning women's" very positive reports on their experiences. Wiersma's analysis of the press release demonstrates the importance of interpreting self-report statements in the context of their telling. Similarly, we have argued that Elizabeth's statement that she "never really considered [gender] an issue," and Rose's claim that "some people either handle [discrimination] better or get less," are not self-evident but gather meaning within the context of their broader narratives.

Second, thinking of women as narrators requires that we take into account the interview interaction, particularly how our research interests shape the other's narrative. Shostak (1989) wrote of her interviews with Nisa, a !Kung woman, that "there was also no doubt that Marjorie Shostak, aged twenty-four, recently married, a product of the American 1960s, asked questions relevant to a specific phase of her [Shostak's] life. I asked Nisa to tell me what it meant to be a woman; her answer was her narrative..." (p. 232). Likewise, our interest in how gender, race, and ethnicity shape women's experiences provided a vague outline for the narratives women related to us. It was in the context of *our* interest that women's narratives about their complex experiences of subjectivity became audible.

Recall Harding's (1987) argument that "the best feminist analysis...insists that the inquirer her/himself be placed in the same critical plane as the overt subject matter" (p. 9). For Harding this means that "the class, race, culture, and gender assumptions, beliefs, and behaviors of the researcher her/himself must be placed within the frame of the picture that she/he attempts to paint" (p. 9). In our view, this notion needs to be amended to include the fact that it is often in the process of conducting interviews that researchers discover some of their most taken-for-granted assumptions. Thus, it is not enough for researchers to preface interpretations of data with descriptions of their assumptions and beliefs, as if their meanings were self-evident outside of the interview context itself. For example, the awkward moments in Elizabeth's interviews clearly revealed our assumption that a successful woman in a male-dominated occupation would be interested in thinking about how gender shapes her experiences. This kind of assumption surfaces only during such an interaction; it is an assumption we could articulate only after the fact. As soon as we acknowledged that assumption, the meaning of our research question changed. We expanded the question of how Elizabeth interprets the gendered character of her experiences to include how she decides such interpretive work is not worth doing. Hence, just as treating women as narrators requires interpreting the telling itself, understanding how the researcher's interests and assumptions shape the narrative requires interpreting the interaction itself.

Analysis of interview interaction allows us to consider how our own interests and assumptions hinder or encourage the other's narration, and how we should alter our interviewing practices and interview questions. But the goal of such analysis is not simply to figure out how to produce the smoothest possible interview. Rather, focusing on interaction of whatever kind—awkwardness, blunders, patience, mutual participation—makes it possible to interpret how individual women communicate their complex subjectivity. By examining our interviews with Elizabeth Swenson, Rose Farrell, and Diane Turner, we have shown that narrating subjectivity is a complex interactional process and that interpreting women's subjectivity is a matter of embracing that complexity.

REFERENCES

Althusser, L. (1972). *Lenin and philosophy and other essays.* New York: Monthly Review Press.

Bell, C. S., & Chase, S. E. (1993). The underrepresentation of women in school leadership. In C. Marshall (Ed.), *The new politics of race and gender* (pp. 141–154). London: Falmer Press.

Briggs, C. L. (1986). *Learning how to ask: A sociolinguistic appraisal of the role of the interview in social science research.* Cambridge: Cambridge University Press.

Corsino, L. (1987). Fieldworker blues: Emotional stress and research under involvement in fieldwork settings. *The Social Science Journal, 24*(3), 275—285.

DeVault, M. L. (1990). Talking and listening from women's standpoint: Feminist strategies for interviewing and analysis. *Social Problems, 37*(1), 96—116.

Epstein, C. F. (1983). *Women in law*. Garden City, NY: Anchor Books.

Ferree, M. M., & Hess, B. B. (1987). Introduction. In B. B. Hess & M. M. Ferree (Eds.), *Analyzing gender: A handbook of social science research* (pp. 9–30). Newbury Park, CA: Sage.

Harding, S. (1987). Introduction: Is there a feminist method? In S. Harding (Ed.), *Feminism and methodology* (pp. 1–14). Bloomington: Indiana University Press.

Jones, E. H., & Montenegro, X. P. (1990). *Women and minorities in school administration: Facts and figures 1989–1990*. Arlington, VA: Office of Minority Affairs, American Association of School Administrators.

Kanter, R. M. (1977). *Men and women of the corporation*. New York: Basic Books.

Lorber, J. (1984). *Women physicians: Careers, status, and power*. New York: Tavistock.

Mbilinyi, M. (1989). "I'd have been a man": Politics and the labor process in producing personal narratives. In Personal Narratives Group (Ed.), *Interpreting women's lives: Feminist theory and personal narratives* (pp. 204–227). Bloomington: Indiana University Press.

Mies, M. (1983). Towards a methodology for feminist research. In G. Bowles & R. D. Klein (Eds.), *Theories of women's studies* (pp. 117–139). London: Routledge & Kegan Paul.

Mishler, E. G. (1986). The analysis of interview-narratives. In T. R. Sarbin (Ed.), *Narrative psychology: The storied nature of human conduct* (pp. 233–255). New York: Praeger.

National Center for Education Statistics. (1992). *American education at a glance*. Washington, DC: U.S. Department of Education.

Riessman, C. K. (1990). *Divorce talk: Women and men make sense of personal relationships*. New Brunswick, NJ: Rutgers University Press.

Shostak, M. (1989). "What the wind won't take away": The genesis of *Nisa—The life and words of a !Kung woman*. In Personal Narratives Group (Ed.), *Interpreting women's lives: Feminist theory and personal narratives* (pp. 228–240). Bloomington: Indiana University Press.

Westkott, M. (1979). Feminist criticism of the social sciences. *Harvard Educational Review, 49*(4), 422–430.

Wiersma, J. (1988). The press release: Symbolic communication in life history interviewing. *Journal of Personality, 56*(1), 205—238.

6

Intersubjectivity and Interviewing

Allan W. Futrell
Charles A. Willard
University of Louisville

Intersubjectivity is an often-discussed phenomenon, but the ways that relationships between interviewers and informants create reality are less well understood. One reason for this lack of understanding is that overpsychologized views of interviewing obscure the communication processes by which interactants create joint reality.

Our point is not that personal psychologies or narrator's first-person accounts are useless. Utterances often reflect private cognitive processes, so interpretation requires imputing intentions (meanings, motive, and goals) to speakers. An exclusively psychologistic stance toward oral history, however, misleads in an important way. Oral historians who seek to understand their narrators' psychologies—whether for meanings or for facts—may unreflectively adopt a misleading picture of communication as exclusively a process of revealing private thoughts.

We view expression as the developmentally simplest mode of communication, one that competent speakers often find inadequate to meet the demands of conventional—etiquette-based, rule-governed—public life. When purely conventional methods prove inadequate, speakers may exploit rhetorical communication by negotiating identities, roles, and definitions of situation so as to create new, more manageable realities. Because public life demands conventional competence and frequently rewards rhetorical competence, communication-as-expression betrays a kind of incompetence, and serves as a poor basis for understanding intersubjectivity. Intersubjectivity is a distinctively public achievement. It consists of the cooperative invention of a shared context to which speakers' utterances are indexical. It is the process of interviewers and interviewees negotiating meanings and jointly creating and maintaining a relationship, albeit sometimes only for the length of the interview.

The oral history interview, like other forms of social discourse, may be the scene of a multitude of diverse communication strategies. Oral historians need to appreciate the differences. Although psychological imputations may sometimes be appropriate, often they obscure more sophisticated happenings. We want to emphasize the emerging relationship between the interviewer and the interviewee as the key component in understanding the meaning created during the interview.

The Overpsychologized View

The oral history movement has long accepted the methodological thrust of interpretive approaches. Conventional wisdom now holds that interviewees schematize their testimony to fit cognitive constructions of reality. Thompson (1988) cautioned, "Remembering in an interview is a mutual process, which requires understanding on both sides. The historian always needs to sense how a question is being answered from *another* person's perspective" (p. 135).

This interpretive turn counters the naive realism that infused early oral histories. The idea that the interviewer passively records the reality pouring from the mouths of neutral dispensers was, for a time, reinforced by logical positivism. If one believes an objective social reality exists, and thus an objective history, then social science inquiry becomes a quest to discover that reality. Interviewing, so viewed, is a process of recording the reality the narrator reveals.

The implausibility of this picture, combined with the decay of logical positivism as a philosophy of science, led many oral historians to the psychological, interpretive stance. Bertaux-Wiame (1985) suggested that two main orientations delimit the use of oral sources to develop social history: "One looks for 'facts,' and the other focuses on mentalities" (p. 25). She pointed out, however, that the two need not be mutually exclusive. Hareven and Langenbach (1978) represented a meshing of these two orientations in their oral history, *Amoskeag*:

> What is important in oral history is not merely the facts that people remember but how they remember them and why they remember them in the way they do. For example, a number of interviewees, when asked when they finished working in the Amoskeag, replied 1922. The work records of many of these people show, however, that they continued working into the 1930s and sometimes until the shutdown. This discrepancy comes from the fact that the strike of 1922 was such a shattering experience that the world they had known seemed to end with it. (p. 32)

The mistaken "facts" in this case gave the oral historians insight into the mentalities of the interviewees, and thus a deeper understanding of the meaning of the 1922 strike for those involved. This insight emerges, as Rosaldo (1980) suggested all insight should, by using convergent lines of evidence, and not through internal criticism of single testimonies. In general, Bertaux-Wiame said that scholars focusing on mentalities "will consider them as texts and proceed to analyze them as such, using techniques which may be derived from linguistics or hermeneutics" (p. 26).

Scholars interested in oral history narratives as a source of information about social features of situations will be more interested in viewing oral history interviews for this literal accuracy. Irrespective of the oral historian's immediate use for an interview, the defining characteristic of oral history is that the interviewer taps the memory of a narrator to obtain testimony about a memorable lived-through experience (McMahan, 1989).

Interviewing and Interpretation

Oral histories invariably focus on texts. A narrator's story is recorded and transcribed. The result is an objectified entity, a *text*. This text may be subjected to standard textual scrutiny with the results comprising the narrative that becomes the oral history, or segments of it may be inserted into the researcher's narrative to add spice or legitimacy. Focusing on text succeeds in getting transcriptions analyzed and in generating narratives (more texts), but it also abridges the researcher's insight. It obscures the communication practices that make up the interview. Seeing texts solely as the creations of narrators (and seeing interviewers as passive recorders) is untenable in the context of viewing interviews as social interactions.

The oral history interview may more precisely be viewed as a dialogue between interviewer and narrator—a mutual construction of reality in which participants exchange messages, negotiate meanings, and try to achieve a degree of agreement on what they are doing and why.

This approach makes the interview itself problematic. Viewed as an active participant in the creation of dialogue, the researcher emerges as an instrument in the data-gathering phase of the research—one to be treated with the same caution social scientists apply to any research instrument. The researcher's psychology and performance are as important as the narrator's. The wise researcher will thus emphasize prior planning and reflexive self-monitoring during and after the interview.

The switch in perspective from text to dialogue has been discussed by interpretive anthropologists (Marcus & Fischer, 1986). The traditional goal of seeking the native's point of view has not been replaced; it has been recast in communicative terms. Originally, the Dilthey/Weber *Verstehen* view stressed empathy as the necessary precondition of understanding (Weber, 1947). Although empathy may be a useful device, communication cannot thrive on empathy alone: "In ordinary conversation, there is a redundancy of messages and mutual correction of understanding until agreement or meaning is mutually established" (Marcus & Fischer, 1986, p. 31). Understanding, as Geertz (1973) pointed out, is essential if members of one culture or societal group are to communicate with members of another, but it requires negotiation.

"Redundancy" does not signify that the interactants achieve *shared* meaning—that they hold identical beliefs. Although communicators often believe that they share identical beliefs with others, or act as if they do, communication does not require identical beliefs. It requires a sufficiently agreed-upon working consensus to make cooperative activity possible (Cicourel, 1974).

In addition to making the interview itself problematic, the dialogue focus emphasizes the importance of the researcher's translation. In perusing notes and composing a narrative, the researcher makes the interviewee's language meaningful for a reading audience. Geertz (1979) specified the dynamic involved as a juxtaposition of *experience-near* terms and *experience-distant* terms. The researcher must fashion the interviewee's terms to make sense to people unfamiliar with the interviewee's "distant" world. This translation puts a creative burden on the researcher who must recast the narrator's experience-near terms in the audience's vernacular.

The first juxtapositioning occurs during the interview. The researcher must make sense of the interviewee's world as the interaction proceeds. Interpretation is not put off until the interview becomes a transcribed text. It guides the researcher's performance during the interview, continues throughout the collecting and transcribing processes, and thus becomes part of the analysis.

Two orders of translation exist in composing the oral history—an in situ performance and a post-facto performance. Translation involves distortion and imprecision because it loses detail and background awarenesses from one language and substitutes (possibly inappropriate) detail and background awarenesses in the other. These problems are so enormous that they merit attention from the beginning. The researcher's responsibilities include devising a theoretical framework to guide communicative activity before, during, and after the interview.

Systematic analysis, in other words, requires a blueprint for interpreting communicative actions. The blueprint used here draws upon O'Keefe's (1988, 1990) scheme of message design logics, adapted to accommodate the dynamics of the research interview.

O'KEEFE'S MESSAGE DESIGN LOGICS

Much communication scholarship involves the analysis of discourse systems. One prevalent interest in these systems is the fit between messages and intentions. The underlying assumption of this research is that speakers design messages systematically to achieve desired effects. Messages are adapted to fit the contexts of their production, and their content and structure reflect this adaptation.

One way of analyzing this adaptation process is to develop a typology of message strategies used in various contexts to accomplish a particular goal. Scholars have developed lists of comforting strategies, compliance-gaining strategies, identity management strategies, and so on. In developing these lists scholars try to isolate sets of message types produced in a given situation. For example, in a compliance-gaining situation a speaker might choose an altruistic strategy ("Please give a donation for the good of humankind"), a promise ("I'll be glad to give you a tax receipt for your donation"), a threat ("I'll burn your house down if you do not donate"), or a variety of other strategies. The presumption is that the speaker's choice of strategy will have an effect on whether the audience complies with the request. The analysis in this scheme involves the researcher examining the consequences of the chosen strategies; altruism might work better in charity drives, but threats might work better when trying to get children to go to bed at night. Thus, researchers guided by a message strategies typology attempt to locate factors that influence the speaker's strategy choice (context, age, gender, background of situation, etc.) and then examine the consequences of those choices.

Other researchers working on functional communication focus on speakers' abilities to create messages in the pursuit of goals rather than on the types of messages themselves. These scholars define and order message types along abstract, often ambiguous dimensions, such as "cognitive complexity," "listener adaptation," "construct integration," "mechanistic stereotype," "reaction subjectivism," and so on. For example, Delia, Kline, and Burleson (1979) found that "construct abstractness" differed with age; older children could give more reasons for rejecting requests than younger children. Kline's (n.d.) summary of this research expands the point:

> as children grow older they...perceive persuasive situations in more complex ways, they develop more complex goal sets, they develop a more differentiated strategy repertoire, which they successfully use to create persuasive messages that are tailored to their message recipients' goals and desires. (p. 11)

The researcher's goal in this type of analysis is to assess a speaker's communication competence, and ultimately to find factors that influence competence. That is, the researcher wants to determine how proficient someone is at using communication to achieve goals, and how that efficiency is obtained.

Both the typology and the abstract dimension approaches involve exploring message types and goals by accounting for message variations in terms of goal variation. This approach assumes a universal sense of relevance or rationality that underscores all communication processes. This model anticipates that speakers with similar goals and similar communication competencies create similar messages. O'Keefe's research, however, indicates that speakers with similar goals and competencies often create very different messages. To explain these differences, O'Keefe focused not on the message goal or the speaker's competency but on how people reason from goals to messages. Her analyses are two dimensional: (a) analyze speakers' goals, (b) analyze speakers' beliefs about what is relevant to the communication situation.

The device O'Keefe used to accomplish these analyses is a system of *message design logics* (MDLs). An MDL is a constellation of related beliefs and operations about communication messages and their functions. O'Keefe posited three MDLs that people employ when reasoning from goals to messages: expressive, conventional, and rhetorical. These methods of reasoning influence the structures of the messages people create.

Expressive Messages

Expressive MDL reflects a view of communication as a process in which "language is a medium for expressing thoughts and feelings" (O'Keefe, 1988, p. 84). A speaker using this logic makes no distinction between thought and expression; the contents of the speaker's mind are simply "dumped" into the discussion. Expressive messages are rather literal in their creation: Their originators do not see that expression can be made to serve multiple goals, and "they interpret messages as independent units rather than as threads in an interactional fabric, and so seem to disregard context" (p. 84).

Being biographical and idiosyncratic, expressive messages relate more about speakers' psychologies than to intersubjective agreements with others. As O'Keefe said:

> There are two (and only two) possible relations between speaker intentions and messages: the message can express the speaker's current mental state fully and honestly, or the message can convey some kind of distortion of the speaker's current state—a lie or an edited version of the whole truth. This limited view of communicative purpose gives rise to a desire to conduct communication as full and open disclosure of current thoughts and feelings, to concern for the fidelity of messages, and to anxiety about deceptive communication. (p. 85)

Successful communication is clear expression—messages being repositories for meaning independent of context. Further, expressive message producers assume their dyad partners view communication in a similar vein.

The rhetorical possibility—the idea that messages can be designed to cause particular reactions—is outlandish to a communicator using an expressive MDL. Expressive messages lack the proactive rhetorical possibilities for strategically affecting others. An expressive message is a "response" to an idiosyncratic and subjective "situation," not to a conventional and intersubjective situation, or to a negotiated reality. For an expressive communicator, adaption to situation is thus either a tautology or a kind of dishonesty.

The symptomology diagnostic of expressiveness includes "pragmatically pointless content": lengthy expressions of the speakers' wants—even if the listener has already heard them or can do nothing about them—redundancies, noncontingent threats, and insults. Complaints often follow this pattern. Imagine, for instance, a disgruntled student saying, "I studied my butt off to pass this damn exam and I think it sucks the way you aren't willing to cut anybody any slack!" Utterances of this sort display a simple expression of feelings. The speaker observes no proprieties governing student–teacher interaction, no adaptation to the teacher's perspective, and makes no effort to edit the message. The message, in fact, is context-free.

Conventional Messages

Conventional MDL assumes that "communication is a game played cooperatively, according to socially conventional rules and procedures" (O'Keefe, 1988, p. 86). Thought and expression are less isomorphic than in the expressive MDL because the speaker can subordinate expression to achieve desired effects. "Language is a means of expressing propositions, but the propositions one expresses are specified by the social effect one wants to achieve rather than the thoughts one happens to have" (p. 86). One accommodates to conventional methods, cooperates, plays the game, obeys the rules, and fulfills obligations.

> Conventional messages generally have some clearly identifiable core action being performed that is easily characterizable as a speech act; the elements of such messages are generally mentions of felicity conditions on the core speech act, the structure of rights and obligations that give force to the speech act being performed, or the mitigating circumstances or conditions that would bear on the structure of rights and obligations within the situation (e.g., excuses). Just as the connections among message elements involve classic pragmatic coherence relations, the connections between messages and their contexts display a conventional basis for coherence. (O'Keefe, 1988, p. 87)

Competence is thus a matter of appropriateness: One succeeds insofar as one occupies the correct position in a situation, and uses one's conventional resources for obligating the interlocutor, behaves competently as a communicator, and is dealing with an equally competent and cooperative interlocutor.

Message content "counts" as performing an action associated with an effect the speaker wants to achieve. For example, under certain circumstances a particular message will count as a request, and performing a request will help obtain goals by exploiting conventional social obligations. Communication contexts, however, are treated as having fixed parameters, so choices of actions are limited. The situation constrains the speaker, who basically responds to it. That is, the conventional message producer responds to the game being played using the orthodox etiquette and methods suggested by the context.

The disgruntled student mentioned earlier might phrase the complaint differently using a conventional MDL: "I realize that you have to make a cut-off for Ds and Fs somewhere, but I really don't understand why you made the decision you did. Should I expect that same type of curve on the next exam?" In this case, the student plays the role of "student" in the student–teacher interaction, being appropriately demure, recognizing the subordinate status of the role, accepting the hegemony of the role of teacher, and so on—responding to a pre-established situation in a conventional fashion.

Rhetorical Messages

Rhetorical MDL reflects the view of communication as the creation and negotiation of social selves and situations. A speaker using this logic sees social structure as flexible and created through communication. Neither words, contexts, roles, nor norms are fixed; rather, dramaturgical enactment and social negotiation dominate. Social reality emerges from interaction; messages are interpreted as being designed to portray a certain perspective. Rhetorical messages solve the problems posed by complex situations by redefining situations and selves, rules and roles, so as to create a mutually acceptable—and workable—cooperative plan.

Rhetoric is *proactive* not reactive. Knowledge of how communication strategies convey character, attitude, and definitions of situation allows one to create social reality and to create deep interpretations of others' actions. Thus, context operates not as an anchor for meaning but as a resource to be negotiated and strategically exploited (O'Keefe, 1988, p. 88). Rhetorical messages display a typical pattern of content and structure.

> [They] contain elaborating and contextualizing clauses and phrases that provide explicit definitions of the context. They convey a definite sense of role and character through manipulation of stylistic elements in a marked and coherent way. (p. 88)

The function of such messages is negotiation. Different speakers can adopt different voices and thereby talk different realities. The whole point is thus to achieve consensus on a definition of situation—finding an agreeable narrative or a common drama.

Rhetorical MDL puts a premium on interpersonal harmony and consensus. It values careful listening, psychological analysis, and adaptation to others in the creation of intersubjective understandings. One is concerned with the goals one wants to achieve, so one designs communication to achieve desired effects rather than simply to respond to others. One's communication strategies are:

> steps in a plan or as moments in a coherent narrative or as displays in a consistent character (and usually all of these). In short, the internal coherence of rhetorical messages derives from the elements being related by intersubjectively available, goal-oriented schemes. (O'Keefe, 1988, p. 88)

In this case, the disgruntled student may use a different tactic to negotiate a different self: "This exam sure was a tough one, and I want to do better on the next one. Have you got any suggestions as to how I might better prepare for the next exam. I mean, I really am not used to flunking tests." The student's ploy here is to plant in the instructor's mind that this exam is not representative of who the student is. The student recognizes the situation as a "student–teacher" interaction, but instead of submitting to the authority of the teacher to give a failing grade, the student uses the situation as an opportunity to solicit help, thus making the student's failing problem both the student's and the teacher's. The student is managing multiple goals—saving face, negotiating a new self, getting help.

The three logics are developmentally different: A speaker progresses from using an expressive logic to a conventional one to a rhetorical one. Not all speakers can employ all three logics, and situation constraints—language, knowledge, or otherwise—may force someone capable of using a rhetorical logic in one instance from using it in another. Each move up the developmental hierarchy offers new possibilities for language use. For example, acquiring a conventional level of functioning provides an option of choosing expression as a goal rather than having it act as a principle for message production. Likewise, rhetorical functioning makes confirming existing roles a choice rather than a necessary foundation from which all meaning derives.

Functional development is not a simple matter of cognitive development or style. It results from exercising control over verbal communication by extending and integrating the functional use of communication concepts. O'Keefe's is not a personality *type* or *trait* theory: A speaker's MDL-in-use may not be an enduring personal characteristic. A person's reliance on or ability to exploit an MDL is a matter of that person's communication competence. As systematic individual differences in communication competence exist, we find some individuals unusually reliant on the expressive MDL, yet others who are more flexible. The latter may use an expressive MDL here, a conventional MDL there, and a rhetorical MDL at still another point, depending on the situation. This system emphasizes the particular message or messages, and not the creator of the message(s).

The chief differences between the three MDLs become apparent when people need to manage multiple, even conflicting goals (e.g., cases where one wants to criticize yet offer face protections to another person). The expressive logic holds that the purpose of communication is the clear expression of thoughts, so the practice is be tactful—edit the message or be less than frank. The conventional logic reasons that communication is guided by external rules and the rule here is be polite by using off-the-record communications and conventional politeness forms such as apologies, hedges, excuses, and compliments (Brown & Levinson, 1978). The rhetorical logic assumes that communication creates situations and selves; the solution: be someone else, by transforming one's social self or identity, by taking on a different character in social interaction. The rhetorical solution is create a new drama, or new characters, so as to minimize the conflict of interest (O'Keefe, 1988, p. 91).

O'Keefe and her associates have empirically tested this three-tiered taxonomy and found a positive correlation between the use of these MDLs and accomplishing communication goals (O'Keefe, 1988; O'Keefe & McCornack, 1987; O'Keefe & Shepherd, 1987). In short, as speakers move from expressive to conventional to rhetorical design logics, they are able to pursue, manage, and achieve more communication goals within a given situation. This research has been largely experimental in nature, and has therefore not involved the researcher in actual interaction with research subjects.

MESSAGE DESIGN LOGICS, INTERVIEWING, AND INTERSUBJECTIVITY

To expand upon and further illustrate O'Keefe's scheme, we use sequences of interviews conducted by the senior author with prisoners. The corpus from which these examples are drawn consists of over 300 hours of ethnographic interviews conducted in nine different maximum security prisons across the United States.

O'Keefe's approach helps explain how interviewers and interviewees attain intersubjectivity. O'Keefe's research has primarily focused on group interaction, and her research protocol typically involves providing subjects with hypothetical situations and asking subjects to respond as if they were in that situation. A typical hypothetical scenario is to have a group of students working on a problem be confronted with a recalcitrant student who does less than a fair share of the work. The experimental subject is supposed to provide a solution to the problem by asserting what should be said to get the student to do a fair share. This style of research is consistent with O'Keefe's concern with explaining how people reason from goal (get the student to do a fair share) to message (what should be said).

Our empirical examples, however, suggest that sometimes the MDL can determine the goal structure and not the other way around. Speakers, in other words, sometimes start talking and then create a goal for the talk. Intuitively, this makes little sense, and in many communicative situations it would make no sense, but an interview situation presents a special problem vis-à-vis goal structure.

In much interactive fieldwork—oral history, folklore, ethnography, and so on—researchers are concerned about the social effects of contacting people to interview. The interviewer is never quite sure why the narrator has agreed to be part of the project. Jackson (1987) made the point well:

> The informants...have agreed to be interviewed by you because they like you and want to help, because they owe you a favor, because they think the information you collect and transmit will do them some good, because they think the information you collect and pass along with help someone or some cause they want helped, because they are bored and therefore happy for the opportunity to talk to someone not noticeably bored by their rambling, because you are paying them for their time and talk—or for other reasons buried so deep in the mind neither of you will ever know what they were. By the time you sit down to talk, the decision to help you has been made. They want to give you what you want and what you need, at least insofar as giving you those things is consonant with their own wants and needs. (p. 90)

The interviewer can never be certain of the goals the narrator wants to accomplish in the interaction. Usually, of course, the interviewer has a goal in mind for choosing to interview a particular narrator. Ideally, an interview would progress with the interviewer asking questions and the narrator responding in such a way that the interviewer's goal is accomplished.

In practice, what happens in an interview is that the communicative definition of the situation must be negotiated by the interviewer and the narrator. Although being the person who called for the interview often gives the interviewer an edge in controlling the flow of the interview, the interviewer cannot ignore the goals, ideas, or other cognitive contributions that the narrator brings to the interaction. The interviewer may have conducted many interviews and thus have long experience to draw upon, but the narrator may find the situation uncertain and confusing. That is, the interviewee may not know what to expect and thus may not develop any communicative goals until the interaction is in progress. Likewise, the various turns that the interview takes may result in the interviewer changing goals in midstream as well.

O'Keefe's MDL system helps to direct the cognitive traffic—whether from goals to messages or vice-versa—in the interview so the interactants can reach some mutual understanding of what they are talking about and where they are going. The system does so by addressing two problems of intersubjectivity that complicate interviews. First, her system addresses the issue of how a situationally relevant goal from one person's perspective may be irrelevant from another's perspective. For example, narrators often wonder "Why do you want to know about me?" because they do not understand the research process or the underlying assumptions that motivate the researcher to learn about history or life from the narrator's perspective. An anecdote about Uncle Joe falling into the creek may seem unimportant to the narrator, but it may be the heart and soul of the interview from the interviewer's perspective.

Second, O'Keefe's system can account for how people can agree on the desired outcomes or goals of an interview even when their understandings of situational constraints differ. That is, even when a narrator does not know, from the interviewer's point of view, how to play the role of narrator the two can agree on why they are involved in an interaction. For example, while talking about the 1937 flood the narrator may think that only the "facts" are relevant when the interviewer is interested in what aspects of the event are recalled by the narrator, empirically verifiable or not.

The interviewer must be able to adapt goals to fit the abilities and understandings of the narrator. This puts a premium on the interviewer's abilities to construct rhetorical messages, to recognize when the narrator does so, and to recognize expressive and conventional messages. Recognizing types of messages enables the interviewer to stay in synch with the narrator and thus develop and maintain some degree of intersubjectivity of thought and purpose.

Here we offer our examples of how these MDLs can be used to help establish intersubjectivity and to help the flow of an interview. We preface each example with our view of how each logic works, using O'Keefe's system as our blueprint, but deviating from it when we see fit.

Expressive Discourse

In an interview, expressive messages can either be a blessing or a curse. The interviewer will get the narrator's view on the topic at hand, but the risk is that the narrator will take charge of the interview. The expressive communicator, remember, is dumping mental contents, and may want to continue until all thoughts and feelings on a topic have been expunged.

In the following excerpt the narrator has been asked to describe how prisoners talk about their sentences. Instead, he has been talking for several minutes about how the system has "violated" him personally. The interviewer perceives this extended response to his question as an expressive message because most of what he is talking about is irrelevant to the interviewer's immediate goal in this interaction—to talk about the narrator's view of prison sentences. When asked to talk about prison sentences, the narrator chose to respond to the word "sentence" rather than "talk." Perhaps Al did not make the question clear in the first place, or perhaps the prisoner simply wanted to talk about his sentence. At any rate, in 001, Al makes a move to change the topic and reinforce that this situation is a question and answer session. He wants to get the narrator to play the role of answerer; that is, he wants to get the narrator to switch from using an expressive logic to using a conventional one:

001—Al: Okay, so what I'm trying to figure out is that if you're 32 years old now how old...what's the youngest you could be to get out?
002—Pr: You know, I didn't even figure that out. I figure around 37.
003—Al: That's right. That's what that would be, 37. Okay, what about getting back to talking about the way guys talk. When guys talk do they talk about their sentences or do they, most guys, try to put that out of their minds?
004—Pr: I think most guys don't need to be reminded of that constantly. I don't talk to nobody about mine. Although I'm sorry, you know, I work on my case a lot, too. Right?
005—Al: Yeah? When you say you work on your case, what do you do when you work on your case? What does that mean exactly?
006—Pr: I go up and look over the law books, you know, to find out where I was violated. What did they do to me, you know, to put me in here that was illegal, right? Stuff like that [10 minutes passes].... At the preliminary hearing he mentioned the knife, but he couldn't describe it and at the trial...[Tape ends].

In 001 Al attempts to close the topic by summarizing all that has come before by determining how old the narrator will be when he gets out of prison, and in 003 Al says that he wants to return the conversation "to how guys talk." In 004 the narrator tacitly agrees and even apologizes for getting off the topic. He mentions that he works on his "case." In seeking clarification for what it means to work on one's "case," Al, seeking clarification for the phrase "working on my case" unwittingly gives the narrator an opening to return to the previous matter of his own case, a topic about which the narrator is clearly obsessed and that he wants to talk about. The fact that the formal context of the interaction is an interview about prison life and language, complete with a running tape recorder and a university professor as interviewer, seems irrelevant to the narrator. He continues to relate the details of his case as if he were involved in a confessional and must purge all thoughts from his mind. His diatribe continues for 10 minutes of recorded interview and another 5 minutes after that. The interviewer allowed the tape to run out and did not restart it until the narrator was through with his confessional. Once these contents were expunged from the narrator's mind the interview continued.

In this situation the problem Al encountered was the second of the two O'Keefe deals with. Both the narrator and the interviewer agreed to talk about prison life and, in this immediate context, about prison sentences; thus, they shared an understanding of what the goals of the situation were. However, they differed in what situational constraints were appropriate. Al's interpretation was that the narrator was ignoring convention by not answering the question even though the two of them were in a "research interview" situation. Presumably, and we can never be certain of this, the narrator attempted to answer the question in what he thought was an appropriate fashion. The fact that he continued talking about the same topic after he had been asked other questions, however, provides ample empirical evidence that the narrator was employing an expressive logic—dumping what was on his mind—rather than a conventional logic. He was not addressing the context of the interview situation; rather, he appeared to be responding to a single word in a stream-of-consciousness fashion that appeared, from Al's perspective, to have little to do with the present context.

Of course, in any interview situation the experienced interviewer is likely to encounter a narrator who has never been in this context previously. The problem is that the narrator has no rules to follow because he does not know how to act in the situation. Some narrators, of course, have more communication competence than others, and thus are able to adapt to the interview situation much more quickly. The interviewer must be aware of this possibility and call upon his own communication competence to move the interview in the desired direction. Sometimes moving it in the desired direction means having to allow irrelevant talk to flow so that the narrator can get used to the situation and, eventually, reveal the competence to produce conventional messages.

Conventional Discourse

Conventional messages often dominate interviews because conventions are dependable methods for negotiating interaction among strangers. Even inexperienced narrators understand conversational structure. They abide by the rules of turn-taking, speaking pertinently, answering questions, and responding to requests. They also understand the conventions of interviewing, though prisoner narrators are most accustomed to caseworker–counselor interviews. And these narrators are also aware of the institutions of prisoner life—and the tensions between prisoner conventions and conversational rules such as truthfulness and sincerity.

The narrator's turns at talk may mimic those of the interviewer; for example, when the interviewer tells a story about another prison the prisoner counters by telling a story in kind. After a while the narrator might even interrupt the flow of the interview so he can comment on something the interviewer has just said or so he can clarify something said earlier. The upshot is that a set of rules, derived either tacitly or explicitly, emerges; they are rules negotiated within the immediate context that are salient for both participants.

The following excerpt is dominated by a conventional MDL. The topic of discussion is the various *hustles* prisoners use to scrape up extra money, to survive, or to help pass the time. The procedure in this interview has been for the narrator to introduce new topics, for he and the interviewer agreed before starting that the narrator would not have to answer any questions that he felt might jeopardize him or any of his fellow prisoners. The interviewer, however, maintains control of the interview by deciding which topics will be explored more fully. In the following excerpt, the interviewer has just reviewed what has been discussed up to this point. The two have been discussing how loan sharks operate in the prison. The interviewer feels this topic has been exhausted, so he is trying to get the narrator to discuss another hustle. The narrator obliges him by throwing out a couple of ideas that are fair game for discussion. The interviewer then seizes the opportunity to explore the hustle of running a card game:

001—Al: Okay. So, how about, what other types of hustles can a guy operate? I'm talking about, you know, he can run a gambling operation, he can do drugs, he can do, you've talked about, you know, like running a store [being a loan shark]. Is there anything else that a guy can do to pick up extra money?

002—Pr: Not really. I mean, you got little hustles around here, like if you need some browns [work clothes]. You know, like when you come in the institution they give you browns with all these black spots where numbers is covered up. If you want them, why you pay them a pack [of cigarettes], you get you a pair of pants. You pay them another pack, we'll get you a shirt. If you want something out of arts and crafts, like a piece of leather or something.

003—Al: Oh, you just swipe garments back there you mean?

004—Pr: Yeah, they just steal it. That's their little hustle, you know, for a pack here and a pack there. But there isn't a whole lot around here that you can make money off of. If you work in the kitchen, right, you could bring sandwiches back; people be paying him a pack a piece for a sandwich, you know, but there's, you know, there's nothing that you can make a lot of money on in here unless you're running a card game, right? Or drugs, or a store, right? Those are the three main things.

005—Al: How much does a, I don't know what you call it—we call it vig—I don't know what you call it here, the money that if you run a card game, how much does the guy running it take?

006—Pr: He takes 10¢ on every 80¢ bet. Every 80¢ that's in the pot he takes 10¢ out of it. Sometimes there's 30 some cuts on one pot, so he's making three packs [of cigarettes] on just that one hand.

007—Al: How does he keep track of that? Does he write it out?

008—Pr: No. We use chips.

009—Al: Oh, okay. I see, so that's easy for him to pull it out.

010—Pr: Yeah. They make a killing.

011—Al: If you use chips, what do you do when you get the chips out? [When you start the game] Do you go and buy the chips from somebody?

012—Pr: No. You can cut them down out of old cards, you know, what I mean? Put a mark on them or something so they're, you know, they're yours, right?

013—Al: Okay, so they're like IOU's basically.

014—Pr: Like I would take these out and give four packs to the guy right? Say he'd give me chips; he would give me eight 40¢ pieces and four 10¢ pieces—90¢ to a pack, right? And that's how they do it. They take the cigarettes and put it in a bag and tell you, you know, either you lose, or you cash in.

015—Al: I see. And what do you do? Do they...it's obvious if you get enough guys around you've got all this stuff going on, the guards are obviously going to see what's happening.

016—Pr: Well, you're not allowed to use chips, right? So what we do is we put somebody out in the yard, man, as a watchout. Whenever a guard comes close we take the chips off the table. They can't do nothing if there ain't no chips on the table. The only time they can do something is if there's chips on them tables.

017—Al: Okay. So, you call the guy who does the watchout? What do you call him, the "watchout?"

018—Pr: Yeah, that's all. The "lookout," you know. We call him somebody hard up for a pack of cigarettes, right? That's what we call him.

The narrator [Pr] clearly sees this situation as one in which he is to react to questions and answer them in what he feels is an appropriate manner. In 001, the interviewer [Al] seems to be asking permission to continue this line of discussion and in 002 Pr gives him permission, but focuses on the hustle of stealing browns. Al is uninterested in this topic, so when Pr mentions running a card game in 004, Al jumps at the opportunity to discuss gambling.

In a prison context some narrator responses are informed by a set of rules—for example, that a prisoner is never to wise up an outsider. The interviewer may or may not know these rules. In 005 Al hedges his question about how the man running a game makes money by inserting "we call it vig." This insertion is an attempt to inform Pr that Al is not naive on the subject. Al uses a similar ploy in 015 when he asks what the prisoners do to keep from getting caught. Pr's response is interesting, but difficult to interpret. He says they take the chips off the table because "they can't do nothing if there ain't no chips on the table." This phrase might mean that the prisoners are putting something over on the guards, a common prisoner pastime, but it might instead (or also) mean that Pr is exonerating the guards from wrong doing. If "the only time they can do something is if there's chips on the tables" then the guards are simply doing their job. Pr is either being clever not to tip his hand to an outsider, not to implicate the guards, or both. However, in every interaction in this segment Pr is simply responding to Al's questions. Never does he offer anything other than the answer to the previously asked question. Al, too, engages in conventional message logic by simply asking questions. This appears to be one of the rules the two have negotiated: The interviewer asks questions and the narrator answers them. Because of Pr's insistence on following the rules, his responses appear to all be conventional messages.

This last point cannot be taken lightly. Because we use the narrator's messages as an index to how he interprets the situation and ultimately as a guide to the types of messages interviewers should construct, it is imperative that the interviewer not be hasty in interpreting the narrator's definition of the situation by classifying his message production too quickly. For this reason, the analysis of the interview must take several turns at talk into consideration and not simply evaluate the type of message being uttered by the content of a single utterance. Otherwise, what might be part of an expressive or a rhetorical message sequence may be misconstrued, and thereby the intended meaning lost. The following excerpt indicates how a single narrator might use both expressive and conventional messages in close proximity:

001—Al: I had some guys at other places that had female guards tell me they don't like it because they [the female guards] take away, you know, it's like the guys...

002—Pr: Beats the hell out of me, man. You know, I was thinking the same thing when they first started coming in here. What would make.... And then there's, like, I've never talked to any of them, rather than, "Hey," and they say "You're in the wrong place." And then "Fuck you, I am not." That's about as far as it goes, me talking to them, because, you know, they're like the rest of them. Boy, the wrong place! What the fuck is the wrong place? Yeah, I'm in the wrong place! I don't belong here, you know? (pause) They're fun to look at and that's about it.

The narrator in 002 seems to be responding to the stimulus of female guards mentioned in 001. But then, out of the blue: "Boy, the wrong place!" He shifts MDLs and topics: It occurs to him that being in prison is being in "the wrong place," so he goes expressive. O'Keefe's model is developmental in the sense that a person using conventional MDL might also use expressive MDL at times. Pr knows he is in an interview and for the most part he plays the game. But suddenly, irrespective of context, he dumps mental contents. Al notices this lapse into expressiveness and instead of interrupting he allowed the prisoner, who had just produced a series of conventional messages, to sort of "snap" back into context. Pr returns to the subject of female guards and the interview progresses in a conventional fashion.

Rhetorical Discourse

A rhetorical narrator may be aware that the interviewer wants something from him. The narrator can decide to give the interviewer the information he wants but at the same time fulfill some other objective for himself. In prisons, the narrator often pursues this dual agenda by cooperating with the interviewer in such a way as to present a self-serving persona. A segment of an interview (the topic is ways of handling conflict in prison) illustrates the point:

001—Pr: Like the other day a fella come down the steps and knocked a man's coffee out of his hand. Didn't apologize, didn't say nothing. He said, "Yo, man, you knocked my coffee out of my hand. What you gonna do?" "I ain't doing a motherfucking thing!" We were drinking wine; we were drunk, right? so the dude jumped on his ass, right? So they got into a fight and the officers took them down to the shack [security office]. So the dude that got the coffee knocked out of his hand pulled his ass in there and said, "Man, what you gonna do about it?" He said, "I ain't gonna do a damn thing if this man'll get me a cup of coffee." He said. "If he don't get me coffee, I'm gonna get back on his ass again." So I went and bought the man the coffee. I had a dollar in my pocket, right? I said, "Come on, man, I'll buy you a cup of coffee." But the other dude was wrong for knocking the man's coffee over. And the boy was right, you know. But they don't necessarily make them right to keep this thing stirred up. Do you see what I'm saying? So, if a cup of coffee is what can keep you from getting upset or hurting somebody else, then I'll get you a cup of coffee. Because he wouldn't have got his coffee.... I mean, by law he was right. You know sometimes when you see things like that. I've been through a lot, man. You know what I mean? And if I can see the little things that can be avoided before getting out of proportion and I have a certain amount of communication with these people, then I'll approach them. But if I don't know them and don't know how they're gonna react, I leave them the hell alone.... See they ain't looking at the value of the outcome of what they do when they do it. They're just doing it because they feel it's hip to be aggressive. It's hip to move like that.... If somebody disrespects you, you supposed to disrespect them right back. It ain't like that. I don't see it like that. Some are disrespectful because they're ignorant. They don't know no better.

One interesting, and typical, aspect of this narrative is that the narrator depicts other prisoners as using expressive messages while he uses rhetorical messages himself. The self-serving effect is that the narrator places himself in an elevated status vis-à-vis the other prisoners simply by the way he ascribes messages to them. Clearly, in addition to telling the story of this conflict he is also negotiating a self for the benefit of the interviewer. In the narrative, he plays the role of the peace keeper: he calms everyone down by buying the man a cup of coffee and by telling what the proper conduct is. The narrator is no simple conveyer of prison activity; he becomes a teacher of how one should live life in prison. He pronounces rule after rule so the interviewer will know that this prisoner knows how one is supposed to live. He thus accomplishes the goal of telling the interviewer how conflicts are handled—so the interviewer should be satisfied—and he also presents himself in a favorable way. In this interview the interviewer noted these accomplishments and the presentation of self and used this knowledge in forming later questions and broaching other topics.

Prison narrators often come to interviews with an ulterior motive—to "check out" the interviewer, to see whether the interviewer will pass some test. The chief test is whether the interviewer is genuine because it is always possible that the interviewer is a police agent investigating prison happenings. Because the prison researcher often uses a snowball method of acquiring his narrators (he relies on one prisoner to refer other prisoners for interviews) passing muster from a testing narrator is crucial to the research. The narrator may go along with the interview and will touch upon things to try to trip up the interviewer. He may make false statements to see whether the interviewer is well versed enough to catch him. This situation may seem to be one in which conventional messages dominate, but in fact the narrator is using a sequence of rhetorical messages. Sometimes, the interviewer is doing the same thing, which makes for an interesting rhetorical jockeying for position. The following segment, for instance, is a case in which a conventional move by an interviewer has a rhetorical effect—and decisively changes an ongoing negotiation of meaning. The discussion is about whether guards use illegal force in order to keep the prisoners in line:

001—Al: Okay. Is there very much of that where a guard just sort of decides they're going to use some of their authority over inmates and rough them up?
002—Pr: You have a few. You have a few. I'm not going to say rough em up, right?
003—Al: Yeah.
004—Pr: Because, eh...
005—Al: In the can I guess that's not—they wouldn't rough em up. They'd get in too much trouble.
006—Pr: Now wait—they rough your ass up if they get you in one of them tight spots. They'll beat your goddamn ass.
007—Al: Uh-huh.
008—Pr: Yeah. I know this. I know this for a fact.

The prisoner's remark at 002 is a standard conventional move: You could say that guards rough up prisoners, but *I'm* not going to say it. 002 ends with a question— "right?"—to ensure that the speaker is understood as saying it but doesn't want to be held accountable for saying it. At 005, however, Al gives a conventional but different reading of 002—namely a literal interpretation: The guards do not actually rough up prisoners because they would get into trouble for it. Notice that the text does not betray whether this is a rhetorical move (to elicit what in fact happens at 006) or a simple but mistaken conventional move. Pragmatically it doesn't matter: The prisoner realizes that he is being misunderstood. Functionally, the overt agreement in 005 is a disagreement. Willfully or innocently, Al has misunderstood a conventional hedge, so 006 is an expressive correction and 008 an even stronger expression (*I* know—meaning it has happened to me). If 005 is an intentional rhetorical move, it illustrates an interviewer strategy for eliciting clarification—in cases, for example, where conventional hedges are more ambiguous than the one in 002. One violates Grician (Grice, 1975) cooperation by failing to lock onto the conventionally standard implicit meaning of a conversational move. This violation is on a par with interrupting Brutus' announcement that he has come to praise Caesar with literal-minded felicitations.

Sometimes the interviewer is able to get the prisoner to switch from one MDL to another, and thereby improve upon the quality of the interview.

001—Al: What do they call guys when they're brand new in the institution?

002—Pr: I don't know. When I first came here no one told me anything. I had to find out for myself.

003—Al: Tell me about when you first came here. What was it like when you first came here?

004—Pr: When I first came here they sent me to TCU. I stayed up there for about a week or two weeks. And then I was put in the population. . .

When I came down to ward 3 so many things that shouldn't be happening. The main thing was the case workers, you go to them with a problem, and whenever I went to them with a problem the first thing I hear is "I got no control over that. There's nothing I can do about that." They don't even want to try, so I decided that if I want anything done I go to the deputy warden or the assistant deputy warden. I guess they just didn't like that idea too much. I had a slang threw at me once that I needed to use the phone to call home long distance because I couldn't call collect because everyone was working at that time. I asked the case worker if it would be all right if I use the phone to call home because my mother had her phone blocked off and the only way I could get hold of my mother was to call my sister and she would dial my mother on the other line and all three of use would talk. Only way I could get through to my mother's line if someone would pay for the call on the other line. So I asked one of the case workers if I could use the phone and he said, "No, why don't you go ask Mr._____? Aren't you and him good buddies?" He is our ROC representative of our unit. And he let me use the phone. It wasn't that long a call at that time. That's when I had, um, a case worker is supposed to work with an inmate. Not only just tell him when he's getting out, when he's eligible for A-custody and stuff like that. I thought a case worker is whenever you have a problem to try to work it out. I went through quite a few of them. I had a problem about 8 or 9 months ago with an inmate that had moved next to me in my ward. He was sort of unstable at the time and he would get up and, when I'm sleeping, he'd kick my bed over—kick it or push it over, whichever, and say "Stay over on that side." Now I'm in my area where I'm supposed to be at and I went to the case worker about it. Told me "I can't do nothing about it." Went to the security officer and she told me she couldn't do nothing about it without he had to be willing to go up to TCU. Understand me? So I went over to Deputy Warden H____ office and talked with Deputy Warden H____ and I got the best results from him that I got from any of the others. He told me that the best thing he could do was to move me on the other side of the room where they had just moved someone out to another institution. And he just moved me on the other side of the room and after that I was fine. I get along with everyone. I try my best to.

005—Al: Well, how long do you plan on being in here?

006—Pr: I have quite a long sentence. I have a life sentence. I'm eligible for parole in 20 years. Hopefully, within 10 between 7 and 10 years I may be able to get out in that time. My crime was a violent crime, but it was a domestic violent crime. Two concurrent life sentences. I'm eligible for parole in 20 years cause I caught my wife and another guy in bed and I shot both of them and killed them.

[5-second silence]

007—Al: Have you heard the term "fire in the hole"?

008—Pr: Fire in the hole! Yeah, I hear that a lot. That means any time a correctional officer walks in the ward anyone who's doing anything wrong that alerts them to stop doing it—get rid of the drugs, marijuana, whatever, or cut down the music because they got a rule that if your music boxes or television are playing too loud they can confiscate it for 30 to 60 days depending on how many times they confiscate it. The first time is 30 days, the second time is 60 days and the third time they send it home and you're not allowed to have any at all. Because the noise level. They try to keep the noise level down. And whenever an officer walks in the ward usually in the afternoons, after, on the second shift, and they walk around—they have a tendency to walk around once and a while see if everything is ok—and whenever they walk in someone will yell out "Fire in the hole."

This interview shows a change in context induced by the interviewer. Initially, the interviewer attempted to engage this narrator in a dialogue dominated by rhetorical messages, but after several turns at talk the interviewer's goal switched to checking the validity of some lexicon collected from other prisoners. The interviewer decided that the narrator was incapable of producing rhetorical messages, so the interviewer decided to switch the level of message production to conventional messages. As this excerpt begins, the interviewer is trying to reinforce, for the benefit of the narrator, that the two of them are involved in an interview, and that an interview proceeds with the interviewer asking questions and the narrator answering them. As the interview progresses, the interviewer senses that the narrator is uncomfortable. He in fact seems uncooperative: He answers questions hesitantly; he either gives terse, spotty, unexpected answers, or he gives no answer at all. The interviewer assumes that the narrator either does not want to answer these questions or that he does not know the answers. In this case, paralinguistic cues indicate the former rather than the latter: The man is staring at the floor with something of a glazed look in his eyes, an indication that he is otherwise preoccupied. Whatever the reason for this narrator numbness, the interviewer decides that a conventional MDL is inappropriate. Therefore, the interviewer attempts to redefine the situation by putting the onus of talking more on the narrator. In 003 the interviewer says, "Tell me about when you first came here." The narrator starts slowly but nevertheless gives an answer. The interviewer regulates the flow of talk by nodding his head. The narrator continues to talk for several minutes, but after the first few phrases he is no longer answering the question. Rather, he is telling about the troubles he has had in prison, about the role caseworkers should play in prison, and finally about how he was once able to get satisfaction in a situation by confronting a caseworker. In other words, he tells the story of his life as a prisoner, lapsing into private matters, ultimately confessing that he killed his wife and her boyfriend. In detailing his woes, the narrator may be conforming to a rational, and thoroughly conventional picture of the function of interviews; prison life accustoms one to being interviewed by counselors or caseworkers. The narrator has dealt with these interviews by dumping mental contents—in the vernacular, spilling his guts. He does the same thing here. He views the situation as one in which he is supposed to empty the contents of his mind, and until his mind is emptied he will be struggling to interpret the interviewer's questions. Apparently, the narrator believes self-disclosure to be the appropriate behavior here. The interviewer tries to impose his definition of situation, but the prisoner clearly does not understand the proposed context. However, given a free hand to determine what function his messages are to play in this interview, the narrator moves right along emptying the unedited contents of his mind. Once the interviewer realizes this, he allows the conversation to flow, asking in 005, "how long do you plan on being in here?" The narrator not only tells how long his sentence is, he embellishes it with his life story.

At this point, the interviewer realizes the conversation has strayed, so, after a pause, he abruptly changes the subject back to his original goal—verifying lexicon. Now, as he asks the narrator what "fire in the hole" means he is greeted with an enthusiastic response, one in which the narrator expands upon the topic as if to make certain the interviewer gets all the needed information. The interviewer, trying to switch to a conventional logic gets more than he bargained for. Now (in 008), the narrator seems to have switched into delivering rhetorical messages. He is making the interviewer's quest for information his own problem and is visibly straining his mind for more information. He goes out of his way to answer the question. No more simple answers or "I don't know," now he seems to embrace every question and think about it earnestly and answer it accordingly.

SUMMARY

The argument of this chapter has been that overpsychologized models of interviewing obscure communication processes. Interviewing, we have argued, is an emergent, intersubjective process in which the interviewer's strategies and performances are as important as the narrator's. The private meanings individuals hold may be important in some cases, but communication is a distinctively public process in which interactants exploit agreements to facilitate cooperative action. The working consensus jointly achieved by the interviewer and narrator has decisive influence on the translations every interviewer must make. These translations of meaning during the interview affect the strategic adjustments made during the ongoing dialogue, as well as the interpretations created after the interview during text analysis. Because important differences between private and public meanings of agreements obtain, the interviewer must be sensitive to and cognizant of the difference.

We have used O'Keefe's MDL as a systematic technique for aiding the interviewer in making interpretations. Her scheme places interpretative prominence on the dialogue between the two parties creating discourse in which one party (in this case, the interviewer) attempts to regulate the flow of the messages. Moreover, the scheme allows for analysis at two points in the interpretive process: during the interview, and during the analysis of transcriptions.

However, in implementing O'Keefe's taxonomy to interpret interviews, we are using it here in a fashion for which it was not originally intended. Previous research using these logics has employed different types of data, specifically self-report or behavioral observation. By applying it to the interview domain of discourse, we seek both to bolster immediate understanding of interactive discourse as well as provide fodder for future expansion of the theory. The idea of evaluating a narrator's definition of the situation by focusing on his use of different design logics seems quite beneficial in helping the interviewer move the interview along as well as in comprehending why a narrator may be speaking as he is.

Three logics, however, may be too few for the interviewer to fully appreciate the narrator's communicative definition of the situation. The three discussed here seem to provide a substantial base—O'Keefe called them "premises"—from which to develop more logics. As we have indicated, at times it is difficult for the interviewer to be certain of which logic is being used. We also must wrestle with the difficulties such as that encountered in one prison interview in which, after approximately a half hour of spewing out conventional messages, one narrator quickly rose to his feet, slammed his hand on the table in front of him and demanded in a fit of rage, "I been listening to you for half an hour, man, and I can't tell what it is your trying to get out of me. What is it?" The narrator, clearly capable of producing rhetorical messages, but choosing to define the situation in a conventional fashion, used an expressive message to make a point. This type of situation is roughly explicable by the MDLs, but examples of this sort may require finer-grained distinctions (e.g., multiple kinds of conventional messages). For example, in some situations a narrator might begin his reasoning with a conventional logic by responding to the a priori situation in which he has been cast. The interviewer might then successfully rearrange the narrator's definition of the situation by presenting information or cues that alter the narrator's view of the situation—the interviewer gets the narrator to view the situation not as a formal interview but as a bull session. The narrator may be able to adapt to the new context but may simply respond to the context and not generate any rhetorical messages; he may have enough communication competence to shift contexts but then be unable to shift to a higher order design logic within the new context. He will still create conventional messages, but he is following different conventions. In other words, the distance between a conventional design logic and a rhetorical one may be greater than the distance between an expressive design logic and a conventional one. More categories between the latter two categories might make the distinctions between different messages more specific, and in so doing enhance the interviewer's understanding of the narrator's messages.

REFERENCES

Bertaux-Wiame, I. (1985). Between social scientists: Responses to Louise A. Tilly. *International Journal of Oral History, 6*, 21–31.

Brown, P., & Levinson, S. (1978). Universals in language usage: Politeness phenomena. In E. Goody (Ed.), *Questions and politeness* (pp. 56–311). Cambridge: Cambridge University Press.

Cicourel, A. V. (1974). *Cognitive sociology.* New York: The Free Press.

Delia, J., Kline, S., & Burleson, B. (1979). The development of persuasive communication strategies in kindergartners through twelfth-graders. *Communication Monographs, 46*, 241–256.

Geertz, C. (1973). *Interpretation of cultures.* New York: Basic Books.

Geertz, C. (1979). From the native's point of view: On the nature of anthropological understanding. In P. Rabinow & W. M. Sullivan (Eds.), *Interpretive social science: A reader* (pp. 225–241) Berkeley: University of California Press.

Grice, H. P. (1975) Logic and conversation. In P. Cole & J. L. Morgan (Eds.), *Syntax and semantics, Vol. 3: Speech acts* (pp. 41–58). New York: Academic Press.

Hareven, T. K., & Langenbach, R. (1978). *Amoskeag: Life and work in an American factory city.* New York: Pantheon Books.

Jackson, B. (1987). *Fieldwork.* Urbana: University of Illinois Press.

Kline, S. (n.d.). *Developing rhetorical skill.* Unpublished manuscript, University of Washington, Seattle.

Marcus, G. E., & Fischer, M. J. J. (1986). *Anthropology as cultural critique: An experimental moment in the human science.* Chicago: University of Chicago Press.

McMahan, E. M. (1989, April). *Displaying insiderness and unity in oral history interviews through placement, timing, intonation and pitch.* Paper presented at the meeting of the Southern States Communication Association, Louisville, KY.

O'Keefe, B. J. (1988). The logic of message design: Individual differences in reasoning about communication. *Communication Monographs, 55*, 80–103.

O'Keefe, B. J. (1990). The logic of regulative communication: Understanding the rationality of message designs. In J. P. Dillard (Ed.), *Seeking compliance: The production of interpersonal influence messages* (pp. 87–104). Scottsdale, AZ: Gorsuch, Scarisbrick.

O'Keefe, B. J., & McCornack, S. A. (1987). Message design logic and message goal structure: Effects on perception of message quality in regulative communication situations. *Human Communication Research, 14*, 68–92.

O'Keefe, B. J., & Shepherd, G. J. (1987). The pursuit of multiple objectives in face-to-face persuasive interactions: Effects of construct differentiation on message organization. *Communication Monographs, 54*, 396–419.

Rosaldo, R. (1980). *Ilongot headhunting, 1883–1974: A study in society and history.* Stanford: Stanford University Press.

Thompson, P. R. (1988). *The voice of the past: Oral history* (2nd ed.). New York: Oxford University Press.

Weber, M. (1947). *The theory of social and economic organization* (A.M. Henderson & T. Parsons, Trans.). New York: Oxford University Press.

7

A Riot of Voices: Racial and Ethnic Variables in Interactive Oral History Interviewing

Arthur A. Hansen
California State University, Fullerton

The truth of objectivism—absolute, universal, and timeless—has lost its monopoly status. It now competes, on more nearly equal terms, with the truths of case studies that are embedded in local contexts, shaped by local interests, and colored by local perceptions.

—Rosaldo (1989)

When invited to write this chapter exploring how race and ethnicity intertwine the relationship between oral history interviewers and narrators, I was delighted yet unnerved. Having transacted interviews for nearly two decades within one racial-ethnic group, Japanese Americans, I naturally was pleased to reflect upon that experience. I found daunting, however, the prospect of extrapolating generic truths about the interviewer–narrator relationship in cross-cultural interviews from my particular interactions with Nikkei (Americans of Japanese ancestry).

Reading the Chicano anthropologist Rosaldo's recent manifesto for interpretive sociocultural studies, from which my epigraph is taken, had deepened my conviction that the quest for "laws" in the human sciences, although a powerful intellectual prod for gaining knowledge, tends to ignore the changing nature of human facts and to obscure existential truth embedded in meaning and interpretation. In what follows, therefore, I have paid preponderant attention to my own fieldwork encounters with Japanese Americans, specifically those among the Nisei (second-generation Japanese Americans) generation, while consigning generalizations about racial and ethnic variables to a subordinate status. As with Rosaldo and his

107

108   Hansen

counterparts in cognate disciplines, my approach is relativist, eclectic, subjective, perspectival, and empirical.

In fall 1987, I attended a conference on the University of California, Berkeley (UCB), campus that was devoted to re-evaluating the documentary contribution of those social scientists who, during World War II, had compiled extensive fieldnotes, journals, and reports for the UCB-sponsored (Japanese American) Evacuation and Resettlement Study. My responsibility was to critique a revisionist interpretation of two spectacular acts of resistance—a strike and a riot—that had occurred in late 1942 at, respectively, the Poston (Arizona) and Manzanar (California) concentration camps.[1] My concern here is not with the content of that paper. Rather, it is with a trio of Nisei—Harry Ueno, Karl Yoneda, and Togo Tanaka—who were in the audience to hear the paper presented by its Sansei (third-generation Japanese American) author. All three had figured prominently in the Manzanar Riot of December 6, 1942, which culminated in military police gunfire that left two internees dead and nine others wounded. All, too, were men I had interviewed years before, when researching that episode (Tanaka, 1973b; K. Yoneda, 1974; Ueno, 1976).[2]

During the paper's oral presentation, I glanced, intermittently, at each of my former narrators who had not been together since their common incarceration, along with 10,000 other Nikkei, in the mile-square area constituting the Manzanar War Relocation Center in eastern California. I thought of the traumatic conditions under which, during a 5-day span in early December 1942, these men had been spirited out of the Owens Valley camp: Yoneda, on December 2, to enlist in the Military Intelligence Service Language School; Ueno, on December 6, to be confined in a neighboring Inyo County town jail; and Tanaka, also on December 6, to be placed under protective custody at the adjacent military police compound. Seeing them now, 45 years after the riot, I was struck by how contrasting, even conflicting, their lifestyles and philosophical outlooks had been back then as comparatively young men behind barbed wire and how divergent these had remained ever since (Hacker & Hansen, 1974; Hansen & Mitson, 1974; Raineri, 1991; Tachibana, 1980; Tanaka, 1973a; Tateishi, 1984; K. Yoneda, 1983).

In this chapter, I examine the context of my interview with only one of these three Nisei, Togo Tanaka, as well as another Manzanarian of their generation, Sue Kunitomi Embrey (1973a,1973b; Hansen, 1991; Hansen & Mitson, 1974), my very first Japanese American interviewee. Even though this scaled-down approach reduces the interviews with Harry Ueno and Karl Yoneda to comparative and

---

[1]The Berkeley conference, "Views From Within: The Japanese American Wartime Internment Experience," was organized by Professor Yuji Ichioka of the Asian American Studies Center at the University of California, Los Angeles, who later edited an anthology based on papers presented there (Ichioka, 1989).

[2]These interviews and others cited in this chapter are housed in the Japanese American Project collection in the Oral History Program at California State University, Fullerton. See Stephenson (1985). The Ueno interview has been published in part and in full (Embrey et al., 1985, 1986).

illustrative purposes, it simultaneously points up, as we see here, the necessity for interviewers within racial and ethnic populations to be acutely sensitive to the operations of intracultural variation.

Prior to the summer of 1973, when I interviewed both Embrey and Tanaka, I was painfully uninformed about Japanese and Japanese American people, their culture and history, the specific topic of the Japanese American Evacuation, and the research method of oral history. What scanty knowledge I possessed of Japanese people as a preadolescent in New Jersey had been filtered through the demonic representation of them in wartime Hollywood propaganda films as cunning, immoral, ruthless, and practically inhuman (Ogawa, 1971). After moving to southern California in 1949 and forging multiplex peer relationships with Nisei and Sansei through school, athletics, and social organizations, this image was sharply recast. Although I never fully subscribed to the then emergent public stereotype of them as a "model minority," my perception did entail such descriptors for this stereotype as "quiet," "studious," "polite," and "family centered" (Peterson, 1970, 1971).

Although I had become conscious of the importance of the Evacuation in Japanese American history while an undergraduate at the University of California, Santa Barbara, it was not until 1972 that I focused serious attention on it. During a research seminar offered to seniors at California State University, Fullerton (CSUF), a student affiliated with the CSUF Oral History Program asked to conduct interviews with several Nikkei about their wartime lives. She had me listen to several of the dozen interviews with Japanese Americans already housed in the program's archives. At her urging, I persuaded the oral history program to launch a Japanese American project under our joint direction (Hansen, 1991).

The next year I taught several research seminars on the Evacuation. For background reading, I assigned Kitano's (1969) *Japanese Americans: Evolution of a Subculture* and Daniels' (1971) *Concentration Camps, U.S.A.: Japanese Americans and World War II*. A Nisei sociologist who had attended high school in wartime Utah at the Topaz War Relocation Center, Kitano adroitly combined *emic* (actor-perceived) and *etic* (investigator-perceived) approaches in his treatment of the history, social structure, and cultural values of the Japanese American community. Daniels' book, on the other hand, represented the first comprehensive study of the Evacuation by an academic historian (Daniels, 1971; Kitano, 1969). Additionally, I led class excursions to the Little Tokyo district of Los Angeles, the cultural and commercial center of the southern California Nikkei community, accompanied by a Nisei colleague/friend (who had been raised there before the war and returned to live there after Manzanar's closing in 1945). This same year I began to research the Manzanar Riot, prompting my immersion in the secondary literature inspired by the Evacuation, as well as the primary source material on the Manzanar center archived at the University of California campuses in Los Angeles and Berkeley. Finally, I coordinated a lecture series that relied mainly on ex-internees and others from the Nikkei community as speakers and explored Japanese American life from the late-19th-century immigration experience through the contemporary Asian American consciousness movement.

Because two of the series' lecturers, Sue Kunitomi Embrey and Togo Tanaka, had experienced the Manzanar Riot, I decided to make them my first interviewees. From their presentations, I had discovered that both had been employed at Manzanar in news-gathering positions—Embrey as an editor of the *Manzanar Free Press*, the misnamed camp newspaper, and Tanaka as a documentary historian— and so were accustomed to interviewing.

Immediately before interviewing these Nisei in August 1973, I came across two new books that, in tandem, conditioned my approach to and conduct of the interviews. The first, Wise's (1973) *American Historical Explanations: A Strategy for Grounded Inquiry*, juxtaposed an alternative model of historical inquiry, the "perspectivist" model, against the model then paradigmatic for the discipline, the "ideal-observer" model. At bottom, these models predisposed historians to ask different questions of sources. The ideal-observer model, because it was preoccupied with *what happened* in the past, urged a line of questioning designed to disentangle the objective truth of history from the snares and delusions of assorted interpreters. The perspectivist model, because it discounted *what happened* as its sole or even fundamental concern, called for querying sources in quite another manner. In the words of Wise, historians under the sway of this model were concerned primarily "with the question, 'How do particular people *experience* what happened?' And further, 'How do they *put form* on their experience?' And yet further, 'How do these forms connect into their particular locations in time and place?'" (p. 34)

The second book was Hilary Conroy and T. Scott Miyakawa's (1972) *East Across the Pacific: Historical and Sociological Studies of Japanese Immigration and Assimilation*, an anthology containing two essays, S. Miyamoto's "An Immigrant Community in America" and, most especially, Lyman's "Generation and Character: The Case of Japanese-Americans," that afforded me insight into the Nisei interpersonal style.

The main thrust of the selection by Miyamoto, a Nisei sociologist at the University of Washington who not only had been born, in 1912, and bred within but also written a classic study about the prewar Japanese American community in Seattle (F. Miyamoto, 1984), is to account for the greater socioeconomic status and degree of cultural and civic assimilation achieved by Japanese Americans relative to other racial-ethnic minorities in the United States. What chiefly interested me, however, was his claim that the foremost normative value instilled in Nisei via parental training had been etiquette. Allowing for distinct family deviations from community norms, this value, according to Miyamoto, had mandated an implicit regard for status. Thus, teachers and other authority figures were to be addressed and otherwise treated with respect, even deference. Moreover, the training Nisei had received in etiquette undergirded other, more nuanced aspects of socialization.

> Etiquette requires a regard for others, and a sensitivity for the feeling and attitudes of others. In turn, sensitivity for others induces a coordinate self-awareness and self-control. Although the Nisei, trained and socialized in the direct and informal patterns of America, were by Issei standards lacking finesse in social relations, they nevertheless

acquired some basic Japanese features in their habits of interpersonal relations. (F. Miyamoto, 1972, p. 229)

Lyman, a sociologist at the New School for Social Research, was born in 1933 to immigrant eastern European Jewish parents and grew up during the Depression and prewar period amid African Americans and Nisei in San Francisco's "Western Addition" ghetto. After matriculating at Cal-Berkeley, he became the only non-Nikkei in a club comprised of recent Nisei returnees from the wartime camps. Like Miyamoto, then, Lyman's assessment of the social and personal relations of Nisei was rooted in protracted and intensive peer interaction (Lyman, 1988a, 1988b, 1988c).[3]

After substantiating Miyamoto's claim that Japanese Americans had "outstripped all other 'colored' groups in America in occupational achievement and education," Lyman's (1972, pp. 280–281)[4] article considers whether a unique Japanese American character structure might account for the cluster of stereotypical traits attributed to members of this "model minority." That nearly identical traits had been applied but a few years earlier to serve racist evaluations and policies actually enhanced their validity for Lyman and recommended their analytical utility to him.

> What was once caricature is now recognized as character.... The existence of a correspondence between racist stereotype and culturally-created character should not cause great concern. A stereotype survives through time and other changes by distorting a kernel of fundamental truth.... Progress in the social analyses of culture and personality might be enhanced by assuming for the sake of research that the worst statements made about a people have their origins in some fundamental truth which needs first to be abstracted from its pejorative context and then subjected to behavioral and cultural analysis. (pp. 281–282)

Guided by a conceptual framework devised by sociological phenomenologist Alfred Schutz and refined by symbolic anthropologist Clifford Geertz, Lyman constructed a characterological topology for comprehending the Nisei personality. According to Lyman (1972):

> In every culture and in many subcultures a predominant time-person perspective organizes the relevant temporal and personal categories in order to structure priorities with respect to past, present, and future and to structure orientations with respect to intimacy or impersonality. (p. 282)

Nikkei perceived time and person relative to geographical and generational distance from Japan; thus to them, perspective is geogenerational. Indeed, they are the sole U.S. immigrant group to employ distinct terms (Issei, Nisei, Sansei, etc.) to signify each generation's respective spatiotemporal position and the presumably

---

[3]See the recently published (and, at times, choleric) exchange over the Nisei interpersonal style between Lyman (1988a, 1988b) and Miyamoto (S. Miyamoto 1986/1987, 1988).

[4]Although subsequent references to this luminous essay pertain only to direct quotations, my indebtedness to Lyman extends to his entire analysis.

singular personality corresponding to it. The singularity of generational personality, moreover, is intensified by the subcultural proclivity for simultaneously accentuating contemporaries and downplaying predecessors and successors. Thus, both Issei, who migrated here from Japan between 1885 and 1924, and Sansei, whose maturity is mostly a postwar phenomenon, are perceived by the intervening Nisei geogeneration as inhabiting quite separate, albeit shadowy, time and space spheres and possessing profoundly different social and personal orientations from their own.

It is, of course, the personality of the Nisei that Lyman analyzed. Born between 1910 and 1940 but bunched in their late teens on the eve of the Evacuation (Kitano, 1969),[5] their collective identity is compounded, in its formulation, of a perfervid belief in their objective existence as a unique, time-bounded generational group and the subjective meanings attendant upon group membership. Paradoxically, their identity comforted and distressed Nisei. If their community and generation mitigated the turbulence of mainstream society, they were nonetheless

> threatened by both centripetal and centrifugal forces, by individual withdrawal [i.e., through establishing intimate associations in the Nikkei community below and outside the generational level] and acculturative transcendence [i.e., by befriending non-Nikkei peers]. (Lyman, 1972, p. 284)

Phrased in group parlance, what was at risk was "Nisei character," a perfect, if precarious, combination of Japanese and American traits. It was precisely to salvage this vaunted character, proclaimed Lyman, that a Nisei style of interaction distinguished by social distance and personal formalism had evolved—to such an extent, in fact, that generational "contemporaries" only rarely were converted to "consociates," whereas virtually all others were denied admittance into the charmed circle of Nisei friendship.

As children of immigrants from late-Victorian Japan, Nisei had been nurtured in a familial–communal context wherein Japanese language was pervasive and Japanese culture paramount. Put more pointedly, their primary socialization had transpired via a linguistic medium whose forms promoted indirection, circumlocution, and politesse, and within a cultural milieu that, to quote Lyman (1972), "served the goal of anonymization of persons and immobilization of individual time through its emphasis on etiquette, ceremony, and rigid status deference" (p. 285). Clearly, this socialization process predisposed Nisei toward and deepened their generational style of associational management and emotional control.

Because, as disclosed earlier, I had read Lyman's analysis as I was preparing to interview two Nisei, the most germane section to me was that delineating how

---

[5]In the words of one authoritative source:

> The Nisei generation ranges over a wide span of years and their experiences differ substantially as a result of changing times and different customs in varied locales. There were Nisei among the children whom the San Francisco School Board segregated for a time in 1906. Yet in 1942, at the time of the relocation, the median age of the Nisei was only seventeen. Thus, many of them reached maturity in the postwar years when the social climate was quite different from the prewar period. (Wilson & Hosokawa, 1982, p. 163)

conversational discourse inscribed the Nisei personality. Not content with simply echoing Miyamoto's observation as to the ubiquity of etiquette in Nisei deportment, Lyman explained the functional bases for this state of affairs—to conceal genuine feelings from others and to regularize behavior so as to avert unpleasant surprises—and even to emphasize the ways in which etiquette patterns the conversations among Nisei and with non-Nisei.

Lyman suggested that etiquette is embedded in Nisei speech through tonal control, as evidenced by a pervasive flatness of tone and equality of conversational meter. Although this talking style causes little difficulty for those like Miyamoto and Lyman who are intimately familiar with it, those who are not find verbal exchanges with Nisei perplexing, primarily because they cannot readily differentiate important from insignificant items. Moreover, Nisei tonality frequently causes the uninitiated to doubt what is being said to them and, further, to suspect that Nisei conversations often conceal ulterior motives.

Another distinguishing feature of Nisei speech that was traceable to their universal regard for etiquette was to lapse into euphemistic language when touching upon topics considered unseemly or uncomfortable for those with whom they were talking. Lyman explained:

> When there is no English euphemism or the use of one is so awkward it could be embarrassing, a Japanese term may be employed. This is especially the case in using nouns to designate racial or ethnic groups. (p. 286)

Aware that race and ethnicity are sensitive, supercharged subjects in this country, Nisei tend to resort to substitute Japanese terms: *hakujin* or *keto* for Caucasians; *kuron-bo* for African Americans; *pake* for Chinese; and *ku-ichi* for Jews.

The use of indirect speech and circumlocutions found in the Japanese language have been imprinted so powerfully upon the Nisei psyche as to be reproduced in a transmuted form in their English-language conversations. Because propriety requires that the private feelings of both parties in a conversation be respected, Nisei regularly resort to "abstract nouns, noncommittal statements and inferential hints at essential meanings"(p. 288). Projective tests done with Nisei confirm that, when confronted by issues laden with moral or emotional ambiguity, they often take refuge in confabulatory responses. Nor do they come to grips right away with the gist of a given conversation. According to Lyman:

> Indeed, conversations among Nisei almost always are an information game between persons who maintain decorum by seemingly mystifying one another. It is the duty of the listener to ascertain the important point from the context and his knowledge of the speaker. (p. 288)

Those attuned to this rhetorical mandate, particularly generational peers, adroitly negotiate conversations with Nisei. It poses a nettlesome problem, however, for "outsiders" or *gaijin*:

Exasperation with the apparent pointlessness, frustration with vain attempts to gauge
the meaning of sequential utterances, and the desire to reach a conclusion often lead
non-Nisei to ask a pointed question directed at the heart of the matter. (p. 288)

This tactic, in turn, is so uncomfortable for Nisei respondents that they respond
with rhetorical management: "They may refuse to answer, change the subject,...subtly redirect the conversation back to its concentric form [or bury] potentially affective subjects...beneath a verbal avalanche of trivia" (p. 288).

The Nisei concern for etiquette surfaced in their conversations in still other
ways. There was, for example, their tendency to subordinate content to performa-
tory considerations, so that discussions involving vital, sometimes controversial
issues often got sacrificed to innocuous yet elegant disquisitions about technical,
tertiary, or tangential matters. Another way was through the insistent Nisei emphasis upon democratic speech participation, so that neither party in a conversation
became dominant and threatened the parity of expression. Still another was in the
deployment of dissimulation, so that Nisei, as ascribed by Lyman (1972), "tended
not to volunteer any more information about themselves than they had to...some-
times would not talk about an important event or suggest by style and tone that it
was not important at all," or even retreated into obdurate silence (p. 291).

For Lyman, the manifestations of etiquette found in Nisei conversation were
functionally related; all represented linguistic responses to a psychosocial imperative for emotional management. According to Lyman, this imperative became
abundantly evident when one heeded paralinguistic forms of Nisei communication.
A prime example was how Nisei set their faces so as to achieve an expressionless
countenance, thereby discouraging access by others to their inner selves. "An
uncontrolled expression met by the searching gaze of another," remarked Lyman,
"may lock two people into a consociative relationship from which [extraction]
would be both difficult and embarrassing." Fear of disclosure, moreover, even led
some Nisei to "avoid facing others for any length of time or [to]...erect barriers to
shield them from involvement with another's gaze" (Lyman, 1972, pp. 290–291).

On August 24, 1973, I interviewed Sue Kunitomi Embrey, then employed by
UCLA's Asian American Studies Program in a liaison capacity with Los Angeles's
large Japanese American population. During the drive to the interview site, I
meditated on my two prior meetings with Embrey, a 50-year-old native daughter
of Los Angeles, the past spring. Although I had telephoned her in January to
confirm her participation in my lecture series, actual contact was not made until 2
months before her June presentation.

The day of that encounter, April 14, 1973, marked the fourth annual Manzanar
Pilgrimage. It was a particularly significant day both for Embrey and the Nikkei
community. At the entrance to the old Manzanar War Relocation Center, Embrey,
the Manzanar Committee's founding co-chair, had presided over a dedication
ceremony designating the site as a state historical landmark. First, a bronze plaque
was cemented into a sentry house by an octogenarian Issei stone mason who, 40
years earlier, had built it. Thereafter, Embrey instructed the 1,000 plus "pilgrims"—
a large throng of former internees and/or their offspring, a small contingent of

government officials, and a sprinkling of interested spectators—to assemble inside the camp (proximate to where the Manzanar Riot had been staged) to hear commemorative addresses from Manzanar Committee representatives from America's major metropolitan centers. Embrey then directed the participants to gather around one of the 10 raised placards bearing the place names of the War Relocation Authority detention centers and to weigh the words inscribed upon the plaque.

In the early part of World War II, 110,000 persons of Japanese ancestry were interned in relocation centers by Executive Order 9066, issued on February 19, 1942. Manzanar, the first of ten such concentration camps, was bounded by barbed wire and guard towers, confining 10,000 persons, the majority being American citizens. May the injustices and humiliation suffered here as a result of hysteria, racism and economic exploitation never emerge again.

Because Embrey was preoccupied that day with coordinating the program and responding to media requests for interviews and background information, I was only able to observe her as a public speaker. To be sure, the customary Nisei attention to etiquette was firmly in place, particularly in the deference Embrey extended to politicians and the press. But her impassioned address, which assailed American racism and imperialism and recounted the struggle the Manzanar Committee and its allies had waged against recalcitrant state bureaucrats to gain the controversial plaque wording, betrayed few of the telltale traits mentioned by Lyman. Embrey's voice, facial expressions, and gestures were suitably varied to emphasize her unvarnished message. She gazed directly at the assembled crowd and spoke directly to us about unpleasant, and for some perhaps, unpalatable truths. Although comporting herself with decorum, her vigorous oratorical style implicitly mocked the title of Bill Hosokawa's recent book about her ethnic generation, *Nisei: The Quiet Americans* (Hirabayashi, 1975; Hosokawa, 1969).

My next meeting with Embrey took place on June 5, 1973, after she had lectured about the symbolic meaning of the wartime concentration camp experience for Asian Americans. Following her lecture she, along with another Nisei woman from the Manzanar Committee, joined me and my aforementioned Nisei colleague/friend for food, drinks, and conversation. All three Nisei had been born in the 1920s, grown up in the Los Angeles Nikkei community, and shared many acquaintances and memories. Although Embrey and my colleague had not met previously, they had lived in adjacent "blocks" at Manzanar and each knew of the other's family. Because of their enmeshed pasts, it took only minutes for us to fall into enraptured talk about the prewar and wartime Nisei world. When, several months later, I reflected upon that evening's conversation through the screen of Lyman's article, it dawned on me just how large a quotient of our talk had been expended upon trivia like sports, movies, music, and sheer nostalgia. However, I could not, in truth, recall that my Nisei conversants, particularly the two women, had used the circumlocutions, euphemisms, confabulations, silences, or any other mechanisms of emotional management mentioned by Lyman. If anything, my recollection of their conversation ran in the opposite direction, toward openness, intimacy, frankness, expressiveness, and subjectivity.

Because of my first meetings with Embrey, I approached our interview from the angle that her personality contradicted Lyman's ideal type. I deduced from Lyman's example that his construct had been based almost exclusively upon conversations with Nisei men. At one point, he even stated explicitly that "the primary concern of a *Nisei male* is the economical management and control of his emotions" (Lyman, 1972, p. 286, italics added). Furthermore, I took seriously the caveat he had entered and then reiterated about ideal types—that because they were mental constructions designed to represent rather than describe reality, which was both messier and more complicated, they did not apply in every aspect to any individual. "No particular Nisei incorporates all the traits described and the typology may also be less applicable to the Nisei who grew up outside the Japanese communities or who associated primarily with non-Nisei peer groups" (Lyman, 1972, p. 282). I learned from our postlecture conversation that Embrey had grown up within the Nikkei community, but I knew also, as her surname clearly denoted, that she had married exogamously. Moreover, her "performance" at the Manzanar Pilgrimage had made me realize that, although her past associations might have been chiefly intragenerational, her Manzanar Committee involvement meant that her primary interactions of late were likely with activist college-age Sansei. Indeed, several of them had urged me to include her in the lecture series so as to voice *their* perspective on the Evacuation.

Even before I turned on the tape recorder, Embrey's behavior afforded proof that my approach to our interview was appropriate. Whereas Lyman had portrayed Nisei interactions with colleagues and friends as episodic rather than developmental (Lyman, 1972),[6] Embrey greeted me as a new friend and fondly recalled our previous conversation. Once the interview got underway, her generational "deviance" was registered both by the content and the style of her discourse. Instead of being reticent to explore her roots as the sixth of eight children of Issei parents from the same hamlet in Okayama Prefecture, she eagerly related her family's history. Similarly, she responded with alacrity and detail to my questions about her childhood in the Little Tokyo district (*Nihonmachi*) of Los Angeles and the inner workings of the prewar Nikkei community there. The following exchange, which occurred early in our interview, illustrates her departure from normative Nisei comportment.

AAH: Did you resent going to it [the Japanese language school] like some Nisei?
SKE: Well, I went all the way through, almost to the twelfth grade. My mother says I was the only one who seemed to have any interest in the school.... But I had a teacher who was bilingual...and he said to me that he thought that my direction in life was going different from the others, that he didn't think I would be too happy within the Japanese community. Now where he got this impression, I don't know. But he said to me, "I don't think that you are intellectually tuned in with these kids in this school." (Hansen, 1991, pp. 103–111)

---

[6]This observation proved a bone of contention in the exchange between Lyman and Miyamoto cited in footnote 3.

Embrey's plain speaking persisted throughout the interview. When, for instance, the conversation turned to the various political factions at Manzanar, notably the Japanese American Citizens League (JACL) "para-administrators" and the leftist "progressives" who dominated the camp newspaper's editorial staff, Embrey's message and manner of speaking again demonstrated her generational marginality.

AAH: What's the name of the woman who was the first editor of the *Manzanar Free Press*?

SKE: Chiye Mori. She was quite active in the Democratic Club [Nisei Young Democrats][7] before the war, I think. I don't know whether she was active in JACL or not.

AAH: About how old was she at the time of the evacuation? Was she a contemporary of yours?

SKE: No, I would say she was older than I. I used to watch her, because to me she was a very unusual Nisei. I never had come across anyone who could talk about politics and who damned the leaders of our country like she did; I had never heard such talk before! And she had some very liberal ideas which I had never come across, and I used to listen to her a lot.

AAH: [Aside from Chiye Mori] can you think of specific individuals in the left-of-center group [at Manzanar]?

SKE: Yes. There was Koji Ariyoshi, who lives in Honolulu now, and Karl Yoneda. And let's see, who were some of the others?

AAH: Would they be part of the group you would have described as "Red" prior to the war?

SKE: I guess the people considered them that way. I don't know how active they were. I know that both Karl and Koji were very active in labor unions before the war, trying to get labor unions opened up to minority groups. And I think their ideology was based on the thought that they had to fight Fascism first, and they went along with the evacuation as just one of the minor things that had to happen during a war.

AAH: Would you say they were equally as detested by the Japanese community at Manzanar as the JACL faction?

SKE: I think so. Yes, because I think some of them were also victims of beatings as well as those who were connected with JACL. But I think that they were not doing anything that was out of line with what they'd been doing before the war. (Hansen, 1991, pp. 110–111)

It was not until my second taping session with Embrey, 4 months later, that I was exposed to the full extent of her variance from the conventional behavior of her generation and made privy to the reasons precipitating her postwar transfor-

---

[7]The progressive character of the Nisei Young Democrats within the context of the competing prewar political styles of the Nisei generation has been clarified by Jere Takahashi (1982).

mation from a relatively quiet Nisei to a clamorous advocate for civil rights and human justice.

In the meantime, however, I capitalized upon the information she had supplied me about the Manzanar Riot in our initial session to schedule an interview on that topic with Togo Tanaka. Tanaka had been the English language editor of the *Rafu Shimpo* (Los Angeles Daily Japanese Newspaper) between 1936 and 1942. He had graduated from UCLA in the mid-1930s with Phi Beta Kappa status and was an accomplished orator whose skill had been honed during a lifetime of making public addresses. He had also been one of the most influential Nisei leaders in the prewar Los Angeles Nikkei community and had held important JACL offices. During the war, he had been employed by both the War Relocation Authority (WRA) and the UC-Berkeley-sponsored Evacuation and Resettlement Study to produce social-scientific reports. Tanaka had been one of the key persons in the Manzanar Riot and could discuss that event from the perspective of someone who just barely had escaped being murdered by the "rioters."

During his April 1973 presentation in my lecture series, Tanaka's style was urbane, professorial, and direct. By the time that I reviewed a transcript of that lecture, however, I had become acquainted with Lyman's analysis of Nisei character and therefore was sensitized to previously overlooked communicative subtleties. I now noticed, for example, how Tanaka's prefatory comments illustrated what Lyman had observed about the Nisei propensity for masking stage fright in potentially embarrassing social situations. To lessen accountability for his address, Tanaka explained at the outset that while he was out of the country, his daughter had accepted the invitation for him to speak because "she felt that there might be some purpose in my doing this." He then further reduced his culpability by declaring: "I find myself somewhat at a handicap here, however, because it has been some three decades since I have had occasion to do anything like this." Finally, having divested himself, at least partially, of the psychological burdens of egoism and personal responsibility, Tanaka segued with consummate humility into his speech proper by entreating his audience to permit him "to start off with some biographical information" (Tanaka, 1974, p. 84).

Tanaka's discussion of his family life and upbringing in the Hollywood area resonated with Lyman and Miyamoto's characterization of the typical Nisei experience as a hybridized one. On the one hand, Tanaka's parents, particularly his father, had transmitted traditional Japanese family and community values to him, thereby preserving and reinforcing a sense of Japanese identity. Upon entering Tanaka in public school at the age of 6, his father, "who was proud of his race and of his samurai heritage," deposited him at the classroom door, and directed him to "Honor and respect your teachers." Up to this point, Tanaka's only language was Japanese, which his father, "a self-taught Confucian scholar," continued to urge upon him because "he disdained the English language as a means of communication for the white man." Moreover, it was in his native language that his father instructed Tanaka in "*Shushin*, the Japanese code of ethics, and...the values of honor, loyalty, service, and obligation that had been taught to him by his forebears in Japan" (Tanaka, 1974, p. 85).

On the other hand, a competing set of values were being instilled in Tanaka through his participation in mainstream American institutions. Instead of being raised in the Buddhist religion of his parents, Tanaka was sent by his mother to worship at a Christian Sunday school. Whereas his father had taught him to "challenge and correct anyone calling me a Jap," Christian teaching admonished him to turn the other cheek when "the outrageous slings of racism struck." Then, too, until he matriculated at UCLA in 1932, Tanaka attended schools where "it was usually ninety-nine percent white, one percent yellow, and there were neither red nor black." By junior high school, his "Americanization" had become so pronounced as to provoke his chauvinistic father, set on a career for his son in Japan's diplomatic service, into caustic rebuke: "You are beginning to think and talk like the enemy." At Hollywood High School, in spite of domestic pressure to "deliberately conspire to achieve every scholastic award in sight," Tanaka so immersed himself in school and extracurricular activities that he experienced "a growing estrangement from the long held ideals and objectives" of his father (Tanaka, 1974, p. 87).

In the balance of his speech, Tanaka discussed his undergraduate years as a UCLA political science major amidst escalating international and racial hostility, his successive journalistic stints with Los Angeles's two leading Japanese vernacular newspapers, the *Kashu Mainichi* (California Daily News) and the *Rafu Shimpo*, his establishment of the Nisei Business Bureau and its unsuccessful campaign to develop a subdivision where Nisei could obtain housing unfettered by racial restrictions, and his immediate pre- and post-Pearl Harbor encounters with municipal, state, and national officials, including being apprehended by the FBI on December 8, 1941, and held incommunicado in three different Los Angeles jails for 11 days.

In relating this information, Tanaka's communicative style—or so it seemed to me when studying the text of his talk—contrasted noticeably with certain Nisei norms for social interaction that my reading had impressed upon me. I recalled, for example, something that Harry Kitano, himself a highly successful Nisei scholar, had observed in his earlier noted influential treatment of Japanese American life—that is, that although normal for Japanese Americans to be competitive, especially with others of their subculture, it was deemed deviant for them to flaunt their successes. "It is important to be a winner," wrote Kitano (1969), "but equally important that the winner be humble, modest, and self-deprecating" (p. 110). I therefore thought it curious that Tanaka, while suffusing his commentary with a self-effacing tone, should also stud it with references to prominent personalities (e.g., William Randolph Hearst, Eleanor Roosevelt, U. S. Attorney General Francis Biddle, and California Governor Culbert Olsen) whose paths he had crossed. I was initially puzzled and slightly put off by this affectation. Eventually, however, I realized that Tanaka was not name dropping. It was merely that he, unlike the "typical" Nisei, did not feel impelled to purge the names of celebrities from his narrative, especially if censorship of this stripe diminished its veracity or vividness.

Tanaka's departure from Nisei behavioral norms was most blatant, however, during the audience participation period. Instead of skirting unpleasant facts and taking cover in circumlocutions, Tanaka responded freely and frankly to his questioners, most of whom were Sansei activists critical of the role played by Tanaka and other JACL leaders during the Evacuation. As shown in the following excerpt:

Student: I was wondering if you plan to tell us about your experiences in camp?
Tanaka: Yes, I'd be glad to. My family was evacuated to Manzanar.... We were there from April 23 until December 6, 1942.... We went on the assumption that they would give us jobs for which we thought we had some experience, but the experience of evacuation had made those of us identified with the "Establishment" within the Japanese American community somewhat unpopular. And Joe [Grant] Masaoka and I, who had applied for work on the staff of the *Manzanar Free Press*, were told that we could do two things: either sweep the floor or deliver the papers. So we opted for delivering the papers, and we did so for two months. Then the War Relocation Authority offered the job of becoming "documentary historians," and this was a job that they said would entail writing daily reports about camp activities and turning them over to a gentleman in Washington by the name of Solon Kimball, who headed up, I think, a department called Community Services for the WRA. It was explained to us that it was really a part of a research project inspired by Dr. Robert Redfield from the University of Chicago, an anthropologist, and therefore Joe and I had an opportunity to continue our education. What we didn't realize at the time was that we would soon be identified as informers, spies, and dogs, people who were abusing or invading the privacy of the evacuees. As a consequence, when the riot broke out on the eve of the anniversary of Pearl Harbor, both he and I were on the death list—not at the top of the list but about in the middle—and we were removed for our safety and placed in protective custody at an abandoned CCC camp in Death Valley. (Tanaka, 1974, p. 96)

Reading the transcript of Tanaka's life history transacted by two Japanese American Project colleagues a month after his Irvine lecture offered me more evidence of Tanaka's marginality within his generation. As mentioned earlier, his perceived deviancy at Manzanar almost led to his death, as the following dialogue illuminates.

Interviewer: What were your circumstances at the time of the riot itself?
Tanaka: Oh, I was in camp, and we lived in Block 36. On the day of the riot, I was notified by several people that the rioters were going to be going after the people on their various death lists, and that it would be advisable for me not to be in my own barracks at a given time that evening, but to probably be at some other location.... So I had dinner in a mess hall in another block, then spent that evening with my brother and people in his barrack when the rioting had broken out. Out of concern for what might be happening to my family, I joined the mob—I guess, the rioters—as they went by the block

where I was staying and went to Block 36. So I was there when they tried to find me.... It was a very dark night, and we were all dressed alike in these Navy issue peacoats. It was a cold night. Most people were rather warmly dressed. So I saw much of the moving about, but I saw no actual violence. (Tanaka, 1973a)

When I interviewed Tanaka on August 30, 1973 (Tanaka, 1973b) in Los Angeles at the real estate development and investments company he owned, only a week had elapsed since my taping session with Sue Embrey. I was familiar with the analysis of the Manzanar Riot that Tanaka had prepared in early 1943 for the Evacuation and Resettlement Study while holed up in Death Valley. It centered on three internee factions in the disturbance: Group I—the JACL; Group II—the anti-JACL group; and Group III—the anti-administration, anti-JACL group (Tanaka, 1942, 1943).[8] Because Embrey had not been enmeshed in these Manzanarian cohort groups, she was unable to provide me with authoritative information about their personnel or posture. Everything I had heard from and about Tanaka convinced me that he possessed this vital information. Accordingly, I pivoted my interview with him on his riot report.

In interviewing Tanaka, as I had Embrey, I tried to implement Gene Wise's aforementioned perspectival mode of historical inquiry, whereby I was less attentive to finding out precisely what had transpired at the Manzanar center and during the riot there, than in how this period and event had been experienced (and continued to be re-experienced) by the historical actors.

I began by exploring the perspective of Tanaka's own JACL group. I wanted to determine whether all the JACL leaders occupied a marginal position within their ethnic generation, and perhaps even within their subculture, and whether this marginality was the root cause of their ostracism by the Manzanar community.

Aside from Tanaka himself, three other JACLers whose names had been placed on the death list circulated in the camp at the time of the riot were Fred Tayama, Joe Grant Masaoka, and Tokie Slocum. All of them were viewed widely by the camp population as being collaborators and paid intelligence agency informers. My interview with Sue Embrey had sensitized me to this situation from the perspective of an "outsider." What I sought from Tanaka, however, was an *emic* perspective on these individuals.

Tanaka left no doubt that he regarded Tayama and Masaoka as intimate Manzanar consociates. I knew already that some unidentified masked internees had brutally beaten Tayama on the night of December 5, 1942, following his return from an all-center JACL-WRA conference in Salt Lake City. I knew, too, that the assault on Tayama had precipitated Harry Ueno's arrest and removal from camp and that these actions, in turn, had set in motion the riotous violence that erupted the following evening (Hacker & Hansen, 1974). I furthermore knew that at the time of the evacuation Tayama had been a Little Tokyo restaurateur and a JACL leader. Because I knew very little of

---

[8]Both of Tanaka's contemporary treatments of the Manazanar Riot are archived within the Japanese Evacuation and Resettlement Study at the Bancroft Library of the University of California, Berkeley (Barnhart, 1958).

122   Hansen

a personal nature about Tayama and virtually nothing about his relationship with
Tanaka, I asked for help:

AH: Maybe you could tell us...about Tayama's character and what connection you
     had with him prior to the war.
TT: Well, I knew him as the president of the Los Angeles chapter of the JACL as
     well as chairman of the Southwest District Council; he was also a member
     of our editorial advisory board of the English Section of the *Rafu Shimpo*. I
     found myself meeting with him frequently both in connection with the work
     of the JACL and in writing about him and the JACL in the *Rafu Shimpo*
     English Section. Personally, I liked him very much and agreed with many of
     the things he was advocating at our English Section editorial board meet-
     ings.... He was...very close to his father and mother, who were Issei—I knew
     his parents. He had many brothers and sisters; they were a very close family
     and successful in business. I looked up to him because of his leadership in
     the community. I regretted very much what happened to him—his beating on
     the night prior to the riot—in Manzanar; he was a decent person in my book.
     (Tanaka, 1973b)

Because Tayama was one of the few recognized Nisei leaders in the prewar Japanese
American community, explained Tanaka, he had participated, along with a cadre of
other JACL officials (including Tanaka himself) in negotiations with government
officials such as California Governor Culbert Olson during the several-month interval
between Pearl Harbor and the issuance of evacuation orders. According to Tanaka, it
was Tayama's involvement in these unsuccessful negotiations that had brought the
community wrath down upon his head, both literally and figuratively: "He was the
number one JACL figure, so naturally he was going to be the target of most of the
animosity" (Tanaka, 1973b). Because this explanation fell into the area of conventional
wisdom, I tried to prod Tanaka out of his explanatory groove with my line of questioning.

AH: What about rumors concerning Tayama's economic activities?
TT: He and his brothers ran a chain of restaurants on Main Street. There was this
     local bilingual weekly Japanese paper, the *Doho* (Brotherhood), edited by
     Shuji Fujii; it was a small paper, and Communist.... If you refer to Tayama's
     economic posture, he was fighting a labor union. There was an effort to
     organize his workers and he said: "To hell with it!" and he fired them. The
     Doho took up the cudgel for the workers, and Fred was identified as "a
     goddamned, dirty, stinking capitalist who exploited his workers." I think this
     had some carryover into the camp. Anything he did do or didn't do, he drew
     attacks in *Doho*'s columns.[9]
AH: So it was a combination of that reputation as an "exploitive capitalist" and
     his visibility as a JACL leader?

---

[9]A 1943 report, "Doho," by Togo Tanaka is housed with the Manzanar material at U. C. Berkeley, as
cited in footnote 8. This publication has also been discussed in the autobiographical writings of its former
staff members (K. Yoneda, 1983, pp. 98–99, 112–114, 117–119, 122; Oda, 1980, pp. 258–265) and a
historian (Larson, 1975).

TT: Right. Also the fact that we consorted with members of the United States
      Naval Intelligence at dinners, before Pearl Harbor, in an effort to secure
      the JACL's position with the federal government agency. This didn't help
      our image once we were behind barbed wire. I think this led to the
      accusation that we were a bunch of dogs or *inu*, informers. (Tanaka,
      1973b)

I knew even less about Joe Grant Masaoka than Fred Tayama. I was aware that
a younger brother, Mike, was the JACL's controversial executive secretary, that he
had been raised in Utah where the Japanese American population was meager, that
in prewar Los Angeles he had achieved success as a businessman and JACL leader,
that he had worked with Tanaka as a documentary historian at Manzanar, and that
his name had appeared during the riot on various internee black and death lists
(Hacker & Hansen, 1974). Again, I turned to Tanaka to socially situate Masaoka.
    It was true, said Tanaka, that Joe Grant Masaoka had been raised in Salt Lake
City, but his birthplace was southern California and "he was very much a fixture
in Los Angeles before the war and had almost as high a profile as Fred Tayama."
At Manzanar, Masaoka was Tanaka's closest friend along with Tad Uyeno, a
JACLer who "operated and owned a plant nursery in the San Gabriel (Los Angeles
suburb) area before the war...(and) wrote a column called "The Lancer" for the
Rafu Shimpo...expressing a JACL point of view—in terms of our citizenship
obligations." All three had earned a place on the camp administrators' "shit list"
for going over their heads to contact officials in Washington or elsewhere. "Tad
never did that," Tanaka explained, "but he encouraged us. The three of us shared a
great deal in the seven months we were in there. As a result, when Joe and I were
on the death list, Tad was also on the death list. He had to be removed from camp
to Death Valley like us" (Tanaka, 1973b).
    As for Tokatura (Tokie) Nishimura Slocum, Tanaka stressed their differences
instead of their similarities. Slocum had been born in Japan and, after his family's
immigration to the United States, had been adopted and brought up by the Slocum
family in Minot, North Dakota. After serving in the U. S. Army, he successfully
lobbied, in the 1930s, for congressional legislation conferring citizenship upon
veterans who, like himself, were aliens otherwise ineligible for naturalization. At
this same time, he was appointed to the editorial board of the *Rafu Shimpo*, a
position he retained during Tanaka's editorial tenure. "So I had occasion to know
his views," explained Tanaka.

I liked what he stood for. I agreed with the substance of what he believed in, but I
couldn't stand his methods or his *style*. He was an extremist in so many ways. He was
dogmatic, very assertive, and not very cordial or polite.... To me he epitomized.... the
people who wear their flag on their sleeve. You never know...the kind of people they
really are, and they're often personally obnoxious. Slocum was one of these people.
So I didn't like him, personally, that much.... He was kind of an oddball in my
estimation, because our backgrounds were different. He came from a community
where there were no other Japanese. (Tanaka, 1973a, italics added)

In our interview, Tanaka took pains to distance himself, along with the rest of the JACL leadership at Manzanar, from Slocum. He did not "think it would be too accurate to identify Slocum as JACL," for his "extremism" made him a "loner." Even prior to Pearl Harbor, he was vociferously superpatriotic, "to the extent of offending most Issei and Nisei by his loud and outspoken manner," and proclaimed that "it was his duty and everybody else's to not only inform on but 'turn in' people." So conspicuous a target was Slocum at Manzanar, that "anyone who identified...with him immediately became suspect in the eyes of most people." Even after the riot, when the JACLers and their families were held in protective custody in the military police compound next to Manzanar, "whenever Slocum appeared on the scene, the conversation died." And when this contingent was sent to Death Valley, Slocum "was removed elsewhere simply because he didn't fit in with the group, even though in the riot most of the people in Manzanar identified him with us."

AH: Would you say, then, that he [Slocum] was almost *persona non grata* among the JACL people?

TT: Personally, I had neither any feeling of affection, warmth, or trust for the guy.... All of us had parents who were "aliens ineligible for U. S. citizenship," who were technically "enemies of this country"—in wartime—and they were our parents. He was raised by a farm family in the Midwest, the Slocums. His wife was a girl from Texas, and she was different too—that is, his second wife, Sally. See, he didn't have much in common with us to begin with.

AH: Was his wife Caucasian?

TT: His first wife was Caucasian. He was married to her for about ten years. Then he married a girl named Sally Yabumoto, of Japanese descent. They had their circle of friends, but I never regarded myself as belonging to it. I used to feel uncomfortable about being identified with him.... There were some old-time JACL people...[who] recognized his contributions; he was JACL in that sense. I think in terms of their feelings and affinity for him personally, I always figured they felt they had a bull by the tail—you couldn't control him and he was a self-styled spokesman for everybody, in his own estimation, but really only for himself. (Tanaka, 1973b)

If the JACL group denoted in Tanaka's riot report could embrace "Nisei" personalities so diverse as Tad Uyeno "rather forthright and very clear-cut...[but not] a troublemaker" and Tokie Slocum "[an] extremist...dogmatic...oddball," its analytical utility seemed to me exceedingly limited. My attitude in this regard underwent a transformation, however, once our conversation turned to the other two Manzanarian groups depicted in Tanaka's report.

I was especially interested in hearing what Tanaka would say about the anti-JACL group composed of political progressives, since in his report he had not cited particular individuals belonging to it. When I reminded him of this fact, he did provide names of people in this group—Chiye Mori, Tomomasa and Ruth Kurata Yamazaki, and Karl and Elaine Yoneda—but confessed that he did not know them well and that his "anti-JACL" label for them was perhaps not altogether accurate. In interviewing Sue Embrey, 7 years Tanaka's junior, the previous week, I had tried to comprehend what Tanaka might have meant by the term anti-JACL to define Karl Yoneda and his consociates at Manzanar. But all she could recollect was that this group "wanted an increase in monthly wages...fought to try to get some kind of a citizens' council going...were all anti-JACL...[and] were quite left of center in terms of the JACL (Hansen, 1991, p. 110). I therefore pressed Tanaka with the same concern.

AH: From what I can gather from analyzing relevant documentary materials, this designation does indeed seem to be unsatisfactory. For example, when the Manzanar Citizens Federation was established in camp to carry out the work done in the prewar years by the JACL, the person you selected to head this group was Koji Ariyoshi—a close associate of Karl Yoneda's and others in the reputed anti-JACL group. And there are many other examples of close cooperation between the members of the JACL and the anti-JACL groups. In what sense, then, were those in Group II actually anti-JACL?

TT: So long as the adversary was the "pro-Japan" rioters in the camp, the JACLers were one—the prewar JACL leadership group and the liberal left group that I refer to as "anti-JACL." Once removed from the ideological and physical battleground at Manzanar, the so-called "pro-American" coalition came apart at Death Valley. The JACLers, like the Tayamas, Masaokas, Tanakas, and Uyenos, looked to the JACL headquarters at Salt Lake City for leadership. The "anti-JACL" Group like Mori, Yamazaki, and Yoneda looked elsewhere. There was close cooperation within Manzanar. I'm not aware that it survived at all outside that camp. You mentioned Koji Ariyoshi, I didn't know him too well. I remember him as an articulate spokesman at some of the meetings and that he was JACL. I think he would be closer to Karl Yoneda than to Fred Tayama, that's just my observation. (Tanaka, 1973b)

At this point, I was reminded of what Lyman had explained about Nisei "regularly resorting to...inferential hints at essential meanings" in their conversations. Although Tanaka was providing me with some useful contextual information about Yoneda's group, he was not directly answering my question as to why in his report he had labeled this group anti-JACL. It was incumbent upon me, therefore, to steer—but not veer—our conversation into a somewhat different course of development.

AH: How did this group function prior to the war? You call them something of an *aka* group. Could you describe what *aka* means: does it mean precisely Communist or what?

TT: In the prewar establishment press, the *Rafu Shimpo* being an example, the so-called anti-JACL group was referred to as being sympathetic to the Communist Party and its ideals. "*Aka*" was a term used loosely. It was also a broad brush used to smear the liberal left.

AH: The label might apply to Karl Yoneda, for example?

TT: Right, Karl and Koji Ariyoshi—I understood they were labor organizers.

AH: Other than simply commingling with this so-called anti-JACL group for political reasons, did you have much to do with them at Manzanar otherwise, or was it a clear sort of expedient cooperation?

TT: There was probably none at all, except that we might pass each other along the so-called streets of Manzanar or at some meeting. We greeted one another and recognized each other, but beyond that I can't remember ever socializing with them or spending any time with them at all. There was no closeness.

AH: You mentioned in your...report...that Group I, the JACL people, almost without exception arrived later at Manzanar than the Group II [anti-JACL] personalities. Do you recall why that was?

TT: I think we had less mobility because most of the people in Group I owned their own homes and had businesses, so it took longer to wind up. (Tanaka, 1973b)

Based on Tanaka's responses, I was beginning to fathom why those encompassed by his Group II category might be viewed, for ideological and class reasons, as being both apart from and at odds with him and his JACL cohorts. But if, from Tanaka's perspective, there was "no closeness" between Group I and Group II, it soon became clear from our conversation that Group III, "the anti-administration, anti-JACL" group, was practically a pure analytical invention of his, one largely devoid of specificity or palpability. This was the group, comprised mostly of Issei and Kibei (Nisei educated in Japan), that spearheaded the resistance to the rabid pro-Americanism of the other two groups and pressured the camp administration for greater recognition and rights. Before the riot they had drawn up the black and death lists featuring Group I and Group II leaders; after the riot they were arrested on suspicion of having fomented the troubles in camp and then clamped in surrounding Owens Valley town jails.

I queried Tanaka largely about the three men in this group who loomed most notoriously in the reports on the riot I had read: Ben Kishi, a 23-year-old Kibei; Harry Ueno, a 35-year-old Hawaiian Kibei; and Joe Kurihara, a 47-year-old Hawaiian Nisei (Embrey, Hansen, & Mitson, 1986).

Because Kishi was alleged by camp authorities to have been the head of a vocal and violent band of fellow Kibei men who had terrorized otherwise minded inmates during the half year prior to the riot as well as on the night of the riot itself, I was surprised that Tanaka had not mentioned him either in his lecture or his life-history interview. So, in our focused interview, I put the matter to him directly in personal terms.

AH: What about people.... regarded as potential troublemakers who had records before leaving Manzanar? I'm talking about people like Ben Kishi.

TT: I know of him, but I never met or recall him at all.

AH: Some people claim in reports that Kishi—during the time the crowd was looking for you on the night of the riot and you were standing with the crowd outside the door of your apartment—was the one who led the crowd that sought to murder you. But these reports also maintain that he was the one who directed the crowd away from any beating of your family.

TT: Yes, I heard that, too. I really wouldn't know if he was the person who said, "Leave them alone." I didn't know him at all in camp. (Tanaka, 1973b)

I asked Tanaka, too, about Harry Ueno, the head of Manzanar's Kitchen Workers' Union. His arrest and off-site jailing for the ostensible beating of Fred Tayama had led Group III leaders to charge that Ueno was really being punished for accusing two WRA staffers of having appropriated rationed internee mess supplies for sale on the black market, demand that he be returned at once to the Manzanar center, and insist that, following his return, he be released from the camp jail and exonerated of all charges connected with the Tayama assault. Tanaka's response echoed what he had said about Kishi.

AH: What about the popularity of Harry Ueno. Did you know Ueno prior to the evacuation?

TT: I don't ever remember meeting him in camp. I might have heard him speak once, I don't know. During the riot, I wouldn't have been able to identify him; he was just a name. (Tanaka, 1973b)

If Kishi and Ueno were near abstractions for Tanaka, I knew from reviewing the transcripts of his lecture and life-history interview that Joe Kurihara was to him a corporeal being. Following the lecture, one student had asked Tanaka to amplify upon the causes of the Manzanar Riot. After discussing psychological, climatological, and political forces, Tanaka enlarged upon what he believed to be a more potent cause.

When you had an active JACL group telling the young men in the camp, "You are American citizens, and you owe it to your government to fight for the United States and to volunteer for armed service,..." this was not a popular thing to propose. I know that in the three months before we were driven out of the camp, Joe [Masaoka] and I made it a point to speak at mess halls...throughout the camp...urging young men to volunteer, because this had been the policy of the JACL in Salt Lake City. I had a prewar friend, Joe Kurihara, who was convinced that Joe Masaoka and I were out of our minds, and he felt very deeply about this. He would follow us and, after we had made our presentations and told the audience, "The only way out of this place is to...go the second mile and prove that we belong here [in the United States], and we must identify ourselves as Americans," this man...would say, "I served my country, the United States of America, in World War I. I fought and bled on the battlefields of France, and I know what it means to sacrifice one's life and be willing to give my life to this country. But since this government, out of its lack of wisdom, has seen fit to regard me as a 'Jap,' by God, I'm going to be a good Jap, 100 percent! I will never do anything to fight for the United States. I am going to return to Japan.... I've never been there, but I'm going to go to Japan, and if you listen to these young idiots who have just preceded me you're going to find yourselves in other camps like this because there are people in Washington today...who have proposed bills in the Congress of the United States to exclude forever any person of Japanese descent from American citizenship." (Tanaka, 1974, p. 98)

A follow-up student questioner noted that he understood one of Kurihara's complaints to be that Tanaka and Masaoka's documentary reports had been passed along to the FBI, "perhaps through the naiveness of the reporters," who then used the information to intimidate protesting camp groups, especially the Kibei. "His apprehensions," replied Tanaka,

> were justified. We used to meet with Joe Kurihara, and he would say, "Why don't you and Joe quit writing these damn reports, because they're going to use them in kinds of ways that will be detrimental to us." At the time, we couldn't see it. We said, "Well, you know, we have an obligation here to show our best face to the public because we have a public relations function. If we say we have a camouflage factory or we're growing, whatever, rubber plants, guayule, for the war effort, these facts ought to get out, and the fact that we're chronicling these events in no way hurts us in this camp." (Tanaka, 1974, pp. 99–100)

What caught my attention when reading Tanaka's life-history interview was a passage discussing Kurihara in juxtaposition to another World War I veteran, JACLer Tokie Slocum, and the interviewee's transformed relationship to these men as a consequence of their wartime experience.

Interviewer: You mentioned Joe Kurihara and Tokie Slocum before in your lecture. I wonder if you could expand on that?

Tanaka: Well, you know, I had regarded both Kurihara and Slocum as personal friends before World War II. Kurihara, because he was a very pleasant, congenial, friendly and outgoing man who used to visit me at the *Rafu Shimpo*. He was an older Nisei and I always enjoyed talking with people who could give me the benefit of their experiences. I knew he was active in the Commodore Perry Post of the American Legion...I liked Kuihara as a human being much more than [Slocum]. But in camp, the views Slocum expressed— by a stroke of irony—represented what Joe Masaoka and I believed in: in this war, we were Americans; we were not Japanese; and, when we had to make the choice, this was where we belonged. Kurihara took the other view. In camp, Kurihara never personally or openly expressed to me a dislike for me to the extent that I should arm myself or be equipped to defend myself against his wanting to have us put away. So this, I think was a surprise. Before Joe Masaoka died [in 1970], he and I were involved in a number of things. One was a business venture here. We used to think back and say, "You know, life is funny. Joe Kurihara was one of the last people in the world we thought would want to get us knocked off whereas we wouldn't have put it beyond Slocum."... So Manzanar was a puzzle to us. (Tanaka, 1973a)

A puzzle indeed, a place where former friends, like Joe Kurihara, became murderous foes and prewar ideological deviants, like Karl Yoneda, were deemed camp comrades. "If there were a line with Joe Kurihara on one side and some of us on the other," explained Tanaka, "Karl was friendly with us" (Tanaka, 1973a). Because I possessed the ample biographical information on Kurihara, in my interview with Tanaka I limited myself to questioning him about Group III's leadership and Kurihara's role within it.

AH: Who do you think of as leaders in the third group? Kurihara doesn't emerge as much of a leader—precisely speaking, with a following. In fact, he's rather atypical in that he was the only Nisei sent to Moab [a WRA isolation center established in Utah after the Manzanar Riot]. All the rest were Issei and Kibei.

TT: A man named Shigetoshi Tateishi was outspoken. After one of my appearances at a mess hall to explain the desirability of joining the armed services, he was rather conspicuous by saying, in Japanese, what a stupid idea this was.... But Kurihara stands out mostly because I could have a dialogue with him; with the others, it was Japanese coming out of their mouths and English out of mine, so we never met. (Tanaka, 1973b)

On the strength of what I found out from Tanaka, augmented by my interview with Sue Embrey and research into relevant archival and secondary sources, I was able in fall 1973 to offer a preliminary re-evaluation of the Manzanar Riot. Still, I was disturbed by my overreliance upon Tanaka's perspective and voice. Before I could submit my interpretation of the riot for publication, I had to extend my documentary investigation and secure interviews with some surviving leaders of Tanaka's three Manzanarian groups.

Because Tanaka had alluded to "Point of No Return," Tad Uyeno's just-published account of the post-Manzanar stay of the JACL and anti-JACL groups' families at the Cow Creek camp in Death Valley National Monument (Merritt, 1987; Uyeno, 1973), I turned to it immediately after our interview. Upon the exiled party's arrival in Death Valley, recalled JACLer Uyeno, he had been apprehensive lest "a long confinement (would)...result in a clash of personalities, a division of attitudes, jealousies, and struggle for leadership" (Uyeno, 1973, p. 20). Although the "clash" and "struggle" never occurred, probably because the tenure of residence lasted only 2 months, Uyeno depicted an attitudinal division between the "death list members" (Tanaka's JACLers) and the "black list members" (Tanaka's anti-JACLers). According to Uyeno, these two groups of "like-minded persons" found quarters on opposite sides of the camp, carried out segregated social activities, and responded differently to work assignments suggested by the camp director (Uyeno, 1973). "We tolerated each other, true," wrote Uyeno, "but we never got to know each other as well as we should have since we had been thrown together for basically the same reason" (p. 20).

I next read a response to "Point of No Return" by Karl and Elaine Yoneda, which was based on their respective wartime diaries (K. Yoneda & E. Yoneda, 1973). "Although it is an important Evacuation story," wrote the Yonedas, "it is too heavily centered around JACLers and omits many significant events...and contributions (at Manzanar) made by non-JACLers.... We would like, therefore, to outline some of the untold aspects of the Manzanar story."

Clearly, Uenyo's Manzanar (and Death Valley) tale had revolved around JACLer efforts to cooperate with WRA officials, sell the Nisei cause through public relations, protect Japanese American citizenship and property rights, and gain speedy clearance from concentration camp life so as to renew the JACL's prewar campaign for assimilation into mainstream America. In sharp contrast, the Yonedas pivoted their story on their commitment, as well as that of their leftist cohorts, to improve camp conditions, promote the war against the fascist Axis powers, and help prepare for a postwar international order free of racism, sexism, militarism, and capitalist imperialism.

Reading the Yonedas' account was the precise catalyst I required for arranging interviews with them on March 2–3, 1974, at their San Francisco home, to which I traveled with two other Japanese American Project members. The first day I interviewed Elaine (E. Yoneda, 1974), while my colleagues interviewed Karl about his pre-and immediate post-Manzanar life; the next day, I joined one of them for a conversation Karl centered on his months at Manzanar (K. Yoneda, 1974).

Before interviewing Karl Yoneda, I asked my associates to brief me about the facts of his life. Karl Yoneda was born in 1906 in Glendale, California. He was later taken to Hiroshima, Japan, where he lived, attended schools, and became involved in the student and labor movements. After high school, he became a typesetter and was jailed for participating in strikes and then expelled from Hiroshima. In an outlying village, he began issuing a radical publication in 1926, for which he was arrested. That same year, he was drafted into the Japanese Imperial Army but ran away and returned to California. Joining the American Communist Party in 1927, Yoneda assumed the name of Karl Hama, and between then and the outbreak of World War II, was involved in countless strikes, civil rights demonstrations, labor organizing efforts, and radical leftist organizations. During this interval (in 1933), too, he married another Communist activist, Elaine Black, ran for the California State Assembly on the Communist ticket in 1934, became a Bay Area longshore-man in 1936, and in 1939 fathered a son, Thomas Culbert Yoneda. On the day after Pearl Harbor, FBI agents arrested Karl Yoneda on the waterfront and locked him up for 3 days in the Immigration Detention Center. After his stormy Manzanar stint, he undertook courageous wartime service in India, Burma, and China for the Psychological Warfare Team of the Office of War Information (Raineri, 1991; K. Yoneda, 1983).

Subsequent to our taping sessions with the Yonedas, my associates and I discussed what we had witnessed, both inside and outside of the interviewing context, about the contrasting interpersonal communication styles of Karl and Elaine. We agreed that, although their marriage was companionate and comradely, it was also a profoundly cross-cultural union. Consonant with her background as the oldest child of turn-of-the-century Russian-Jewish immigrants in New York City, Elaine's conversation, whether for the benefit of the tape recorder or not, was animated, extremely fast-paced, assertive, disputatious, uncensored, warm, shrill, and punctuated by overtalking, abrupt corrections, and histrionic body language.[10]

When not being interviewed, Karl came across as "typically" Nisei, but once the tape recorder was turned on his interpersonal manner became suddenly transformed. Consistent with other Kibei-Nisei who had been returned[11] to Japan as youths and both educated and partially enculturated there, Karl spoke in a thickly Japanese-accented English conveyed by a singsong cadence. This outward linguistic difference was more than matched by other deviations from the Nisei interactional style. Although always polite in his responses, he was never deferential. Although sometimes judiciously qualifying his remarks, he rarely resorted to indirection or circumlocution. Although good-humored and congenial, his conversation was innocent of both trivia and confabulation. The Nisei preoccupation with emotional management, which Lyman's analysis had adumbrated and Tanaka's lecture faintly evidenced, seemed altogether absent from Yoneda's communicative repertoire. Instead, his conversational style was reminiscent of what I had encountered during my earlier interviews with Tanaka and Embrey: frank, expressive, exploratory, and forthcoming. Like Tanaka, Yoneda peppered his talk with colorful anecdotes and terms, and like Embrey, he occasionally flared up in anger or spoke in contemporary "Youth Movement" argot (e.g., "blow your mind"). However, unlike Tanaka and Embrey (and in common with his Caucasian wife, although less flamboyantly), Yoneda's conversation was ideologically constrained (K. Yoneda, 1973). Yoneda, leastwise to our Orange County-conditioned ears, communicated as much, if not more, through his political subculture as he did his ethnic generation.

By the time that Embrey informed me that Harry Ueno was alive and willing to be interviewed by the two of us, my assessment of the Manzanar Riot had been published (Hacker & Hansen, 1974). Nonetheless, believing Ueno's testimony to be of historical significance, we traveled to his San Jose, California, home in fall 1976 to tape his recollections (Ueno, 1976).

I already knew fragments of Ueno's life at Manzanar and during the balance of World War II, but he told us the details of his pre-Evacuation life and fleshed out the facts of his wartime experiences after the Manzanar Riot. Born in 1907 at a sugar plantation on the island of Hawaii from parents who had emigrated there as

---

[10]I am greatly indebted to a perceptive article by William E. Mitchell (1988) about the Jewish American communicative style.

[11]This terminology, although frequently employed inside and out of the Japanese American community, is technically incorrect because Kibei-Nisei were born in the United States, not Japan.

laborers from Hiroshima, Ueno was sent to Japan at 8 years old to live with his grandparents in Hiroshima and attend school. At 16, he took a job on a ship bound for the United States, where upon arrival in the port of Tacoma, Washington, he jumped ship. Unable to speak English fluently, he worked for several years in a Tacoma lumber mill, then lived briefly with a brother in Milwaukee, Wisconsin, and returned in 1927 to the Northwest. Banned from lumbering work by anti-Japanese sawmill workers' unions, Ueno moved first to northern California, where he was married to an Issei woman, and then to Los Angeles. There, from 1930 until he, his wife Yasu, and three boys were consigned to Manzanar in May 1942, Ueno worked at a fruit stand and several Jewish-run markets, lived away from other Japanese Americans, and stayed aloof from Nikkei organizations.

In the aftermath of the riot, which Ueno observed from inside the Manzanar jail (Embrey, Hansen, & Mitson, 1985), he was taken out of camp and put behind bars for a month in two nearby Owens Valley jails. At the second of these, where he occupied a small cell with 15 other allegedly pro-Japan dissidents responsible for the riot, the military police "sometimes got drunk [at night] and shot the [cell] door with a rifle" (Embrey et al., 1986, p. 65). There, also, he got into a near-violent row with two other prisoners (the aforementioned Ben Kishi and another 23-year-old Kibei) when they overheard him telling Joe Kurihara that they were untrustworthy "two-timers." On January 9, 1943, Ueno and his other cellmates, without being granted a hearing or given a specific reason for their arrest, were transferred to an abandoned CCC camp in Moab, Utah, that served as a temporary isolation center for internee "troublemakers" in all the WRA centers. During his 4-month stay at Moab, Ueno refused to work because of his unclarified prisoner status, mail censorship, and harsh regulations. He also purportedly headed a gang of former Manzanarians who physically threatened those who did work, was placed in a special isolation barracks, attempted to renounce his U.S. citizenship, and was thrown into the county jail in Moab for his resistance to authority. (Embrey et al., 1986) After a brutal 13-hour truck ride, Ueno passed several days in the Winslow, Arizona, town jail and then, on April 28, 1943, was transported to the Leupp Isolation Center, located in a one-time Indian Bureau school on the adjacent Navajo reservation and guarded by military police. There, he cooperated with the camp administration until his transfer to the Tule Lake (California) Segregation Center on December 4, 1943. Rejoined with his family, he stayed clear of the turbulent politics in that camp for presumed "disloyals," established a model record as a maintenance worker, changed his mind about giving up his American citizenship, and was finally released from Tule Lake in March 1946 (Embrey et al., 1986).

Since my interview with Karl Yoneda 2½ years earlier, I had taped numerous oral histories with Nikkei, including four former Manzanarians: the male Issei head of dental services; a Kibei woman elementary school teacher; and two male Nisei, the director of the camp hospital and a member of its internal security force (Chuman, 1975; Fukasawa, 1974; Ishida, 1974; Kikuchi, 1974). Of these, both the Kibei teacher and the Nisei policeman were congruent in most respects with the normative Nisei interpersonal style depicted by Lyman, whereas the Issei dentist (who characterized himself as "very different") and the Nisei medical administrator comported themselves more in the fashion of Togo Tanaka. By the time of the interview with Harry Ueno, then, I remained attentive to Lyman's paradigm but was far less constrained by it than I had been during my interviews with Embrey, Tanaka, and Yoneda.

Ueno was a Kibei who, like Yoneda, had spent part of his developmental years in Japan's Hiroshima Prefecture. Both spoke in Japanized English, but this communicative aspect was positively more pronounced in Ueno than Yoneda. This was no doubt because, as their respective interviews certify, they had moved in exceedingly different social and domestic spheres. For example, whereas before and during World War II Yoneda had enjoyed regular contacts with a multicultural array of political progressives and was married to a Caucasian American woman, Ueno's "few friends were mostly Kibei" and his slightly older wife a native of Japan who came to the United States when she was 19 years old (Embrey et al., 1986). Their intonation pattern was comparable, although the rise and fall in pitch of Ueno's speaking voice, again, was far more conspicuous.

Nonetheless, the interactional styles of these two Kibei men were noticeably similar. If Yoneda, as mentioned earlier, deviated from the model Nisei style in terms of greater spontaneity, intimacy, directness, excitability, and emotional range, so too did Ueno (whose deviation, arguably, was magnified by having spent his early childhood in Hawaii rather than on the mainland). Indeed, Embrey had barely opened the interview with Ueno when, in response to a question about his early stay in Japan, his effervescent mien metamorphosed into tearful melancholy: "The thing is, you know, to be separated from your father and mother for 7 years is...I don't know. I think all the Kibei feel the same way. I think I had better explain to you the Kibei's mental status" (Embrey et al., 1986, p. 2). Listening to Ueno converse with Embrey and myself for the next 2½ hours (and correlating his discourse with what I had read about Kibei deportment in the wartime camps)[12] made me realize that, had Lyman's early socialization with second-generation Japanese Americans been with Kibei-Nisei rather than Nisei bereft of a prolonged stay in Japan, his essay would have assumed a substantially different complexion. I now appreciated in a more profound sense than before Embrey's observation during our interview that many Kibei, upon their return to the United States, never made the adjustment to Nisei society (Hansen, 1991).

There was one notable point in Ueno's interview, however, when he sounded characteristically Nisei. Because of its centrality both to the Manzanar Riot and Ueno's interpersonal style of communication, it merits our careful attention.

AH: All of a sudden on the night of December 5, 1942, Fred Tayama was beaten by some masked people, and you were accused of being one of them. The attackers had something over their heads. Fred Tayama and his wife identified you. They said they could identify your eyes. Later, Joe

---

[12]The War Relocation Authority administration distrusted Kibei as a group and regularly castigated them as "troublemakers" and "disloyals." The wartime situation of the Kibei has been accorded fictionalized representation (Templeman, 1979).

Kurihara claimed that he was behind the beating, that he had master-
minded it, and did not indicate whether you were included or not. But you
were accused of the beating and, on the basis of that accusation, you were
picked up and taken out of Manzanar. Now I would like to ask you very
pointedly, were you involved in the beating of Fred Tayama?

HU: No, not me. And I don't think Kurihara was either.

AH: He didn't say that he was there.

HU: If he were involved, he probably would have told me—we were so close
right after the incident.

AH: Do you know who did beat Tayama up?

HU: No, no. I don't think so.

AH: You didn't hear anything from anybody at the jail, or later at Moab, or at
Leupp, any speculation as to who was involved? Was Ben Kishi there?

HU: I don't know.

AH: You didn't hear any speculation from anybody? It seems odd, because
rumors would go around the camp and people would talk about them.

HU: I know, but I think we felt that we didn't want to discuss it. You know
what I mean?

AH: Do you mean that you know who did it, but you're just not saying?

HU: Well, maybe I know and maybe I don't. I think there are a lot of things
that we don't want to discuss unless we have proof, you know. (Embrey
et al., 1986, pp. 48–49)

Here, it would seem, was a prime example of the indirection, circumlocution, and
confabulation in Nisei speech that Lyman had postulated and which projective tests
with those in that generation had confirmed. Still, it appears more plausible to infer
from this uncommon exchange that Ueno was exercising prudential restraint out
of concern for the reputation and security of others and not merely engaging in
prototypical rhetorical management. As with Embrey, Tanaka, and Yoneda, Ueno
represented an exception that made the rule problematic, at best.

We now need to exploit this case study of the Manzanar Riot involving one
racial-ethnic group, Japanese Americans, in the interest of generating useful
knowledge about all such groups and, more specifically, of postulating some
provisional guidelines for transacting oral-historical fieldwork within racial-ethnic
communities in the United States.

Two decades ago British historian Eric Hobsbawm (1971) shrewdly observed
that studies of social conflict, ranging from revolutions to riots, require more careful
assessment than other historical topics because they dramatize crucial aspects of
the sociocultural structure. In the case of the Manzanar Riot, our investigation has
revealed, minimally, that the racist assumption underpinning the Japanese American Evacuation—"A Jap is a Jap"—was not only pernicious but egregiously false.
Among primarily the Nisei generation at one concentration camp alone, we have
encountered differences in ideas, values, and behavior so acute as to result in
extreme acts like social ostracism and death threats. Moreover, we have seen that

even seemingly compact generational coteries at this camp were fractured during pivotal moments when latent disparities in socialization and attendant cultural style were forced to the surface or when the mise-en-scene shifted from the public to the private domain.

Although the sheer "discovery" of intracultural variation among Japanese Americans should hardly be surprising, the considerable degree of heterogeneity disclosed in this racial-ethnic group, especially when one considers their historical legacy and wartime situation, is significant both in itself and for what it suggests about the composition of all such American subcultures. Nonetheless, before pursuing this point I want, for heuristic purposes, to set aside the manifest diversity within the Nikkei population and argue that their plight, at least after World War II, embodied an extreme case scenario of the socialization process of other racial-ethnic groups in which normative behavior inordinately molded actual behavior.

As Fugita and O'Brien (1991) showed, structural constraints—stemming both from the cultural legacy that Japanese immigrants (Issei) brought with them to the mainland United States and from the conditions they and their offspring (Nisei) encountered in American society—produced a personality type that was remarkably uniform as against that found in white immigrant groups from Europe (an observation that I would extend to embrace "persons of color" coming from the rest of the world).

On the one hand, Japan was a very small island nation made up of mostly small agricultural villages inhabited by culturally homogeneous people. "As early as the seventh century, the Japanese saw themselves as a single people living in a unified nation" (Fugita & O'Brien, 1991, p. 4). Moreover, for two centuries prior to the 19th-century Meiji Revolution and decision to Westernize, the ruling Tokugawa Shogunate had permitted neither immigration into or emigration out of Japan. Thus, the Japanese immigrants who came to the United States chiefly in the four decades extending from 1885 to 1924 (when the Immigration Exclusion Act was passed) and largely from four southwestern prefectures (Hiroshima, Yamaguichi, Fukuoka, and Kumamoto)[13] were mostly experienced farmers (augmented by a substantial number of students and merchants) seeking to better their economic situation (Ichioka, 1983, 1988; Wakatsuke, 1979).

On the other hand, once they arrived in the mainland United States, the overwhelming percentage of the always numerically insignificant Japanese immigrant population lived in the western states of Washington, Oregon, and (most especially) California. There, owing to intense discrimination against them in housing and employment, they resided and worked in re-created traditional communities in rural areas and urban centers that insulated them from mainstream American society. Although the Japanese immigrants and their Nisei children "did not experience the kind of complete isolation enforced upon

---

[13]The families of Karl Yoneda and Harry Ueno came from Hiroshima Prefecture, whereas Togo Tanaka traced his family roots back to Yamaguichi.

blacks...they did nonetheless live apart from white society in many significant ways...and their most intimate relationships and institutional affiliations were found within the ethnic community" (Fugita & O'Brien, 1991, pp. 34–35). Additionally, anti-miscegenation laws and community pressure conspired to minimize outmarriage and to strengthen the sense of peoplehood of Japanese America, as did the special character of the ethnic economy revolving around small business enterprises and labor-intensive agriculture.[14] This "concentrated" community existence was exacerbated by the rise of legal and extralegal discrimination against people of Japanese ancestry and culminated in the World War II policy of exclusion and concentration camp detention.

In the late 1950s and early 1960s when many Americans indulged themselves in a wave of self-congratulatory democratic liberalism, a profusion of articles appeared in mass-circulation magazines announcing that the Japanese American Evacuation had been for the Nikkei a "blessing in disguise," for it had broken up their ethnic enclaves, relocated them geographically to other parts of the country, and precipitated not only their assimilation into the larger society but also set them on a course leading to their status as America's "model minority." At the time I did not appreciate the perversity of the logic informing this line of thought and, unwittingly, became a temporary captive of it.

The "blessing in disguise" for me came a decade later when I again took up the topic of the Japanese American Evacuation and, by chance, came to study it via the method of oral history and through the madness of the Manzanar Riot. Talking on tape to Japanese American participants in this event forced me to realize an important truth: Notwithstanding a historical legacy, socialization process, and public policy that worked to stylize Nikkei thought and behavior, there was still ample scope for subcultural diversity and individual differences (even during a time of extreme crisis when the expectation would be minimal normative deviation). The realization of this truth, in turn, made me appreciate that the same situation would obtain for transacting interviews in any other racial-ethnic community, that the racist myth of homogeneity would have to be supplanted by a strategic, humanistic quest for and appreciation of heterogeneity. Or, put another way, those of us studying such communities would have to attend to age, generational, class, gender, and ideological divisions within them if we wanted to gain a more complex sense of past reality and avoid the charge of racism. Furthermore, my early interviewing experiences with Nikkei survivors[15] of the Manzanar Riot like Togo Tanaka, Karl Yoneda, and Harry Ueno, impressed upon me the fact, too often ignored by scholars and lay people alike, that time is a critical

---

[14]The short stories by the late Nisei writer Toshio Mori nicely capture life in pre-World War II Japanese America (Mori, 1985).

[15]I employ this term here not in the histrionic, politically correct manner of some Evacuation scholars, but because it is descriptive of the historical reality experienced by Togo Tanaka, Karl Yoneda, and Harry Ueno.

dimension in the study of racial-ethnic communities, as with all others, and that oral historians working in these communities must exorcise the bogeyman of not only homogeneous racial-ethnic communities but that of unchanging ones as well.[16]

REFERENCES

Barnhart, E. N. (1958). *Japanese American evacuation and resettlement: Catalog of material in the General Library.* Berkeley, CA: University of California General Library.
Chuman, F. (1975, January 6, 13). Interview by A.A. Hansen, O. H. 1475a, 6.
Conroy, H., & Miyakawa, T. S. (Eds.). (1972). *East across the pacific: Historical and sociological studies of Japanese immigration and assimilation.* Santa Barbara, CA: ABC Clio Press.
Daniels, R. (1971). *Concentration camps U.S.A.: Japanese Americans and World War II.* Hillside, IL: Dryden Press.
Embrey, S. K. (1973a, August 24). Interview by A. A. Hansen & D. A. Hacker, O. H. 1366a, OHP-CSUF.
Embrey, S. K. (1973b, November 1). Interview by D. J. Bertagnoli & A. A. Hansen, O.H. 1366b, OHP-CSUF.
Embrey, S. K., Hansen, A. A., & Mitson, B. E. (1985). Dissident Harry Ueno remembers Manzanar. *California History, 64,* 16–22.
Embrey, S. K., Hansen, A. A., & Mitson, B. K. (1986). *Manzanar Martyr: An Interview with Harry Y. Ueno.* Fullerton, CA: Japanese American Project, Oral History Program, California State University, Fullerton.
Fugita, S. S., & O'Brien, D. J. (1991). *The Japanese American experience.* Bloomington: Indiana University Press.
Fukasawa, G. (1974, August 12). Interview by A. A. Hansen, O. H. 1336, OHP-CSUF.
Hacker, D. A., & Hansen, A. A. (1974). The Manzanar riot: An ethnic perspective. *Amerasia Journal 2,* 112–157.
Hansen, A. A. (Ed.). (1991). *Japanese American World War II evacuation project: Part I: Internees.* Westport, CT: Meckler.
Hansen, A. A., & Mitson, B. E. (Eds.). (1974). *Voices long silent: An oral inquiry into the Japanese American evacuation.* Fullerton, CA: Japanese American Project, Oral History Program, CSUF.
Hirabayashi, J. (1975). Nisei: The quiet American? A re-evaluation. *Amerasia Journal, 3,* 114–29.

[16]Recently, a U.C. Berkeley professor celebrated for his innovative approach to African-American cultural history capsulized the larger point of this chapter:

Contemporary scholars have demonstrated again and again that, in penetrating the culture of a neglected group, historians often find more than they bargained for. What looked like a group becomes an amalgam of groups; what looked like a culture becomes a series of cultures. Americans on the eve of World War II might have seen only a monolith when they looked at Japanese Americans, but historians must see something vastly more complicated: The *Issei* born in Japan and legally barred from becoming U. S. citizens, the *Nisei,* born and raised here and thus citizens by birth, the *Kibei,* born here but raised in Japan and thus legally Americans and culturally Japanese, as well as those who lived in cities and those who lived on farms, those who struggled to maintain the old ways and those who hungered for acculturation. The complexity I speak of is not the complexity of specialized languages or esoteric methodologies but the complexity of people and the cultures they create. (Levine, 1993, pp. 11–12)

Hobsbawm, E. J. (1971). From social history to the history of society. In F. Gilbert & S. R. Grubard (Eds.). *Historical studies today*. New York: Norton.

Hosokawa, B. (1969). *Nisei: The quiet Americans*. New York: William Morrow.

Ichioka, Y. (Ed.). (1989). *Views from within: The Japanese American evacuation and resettlement study*. Los Angeles: Asian American Studies Center, University of California at Los Angeles.

Ichioka, Y. (1983, November). Recent Japanese scholarship on the origins and causes of Japanese immigration. *Immigration History Newsletter 15*, 2–7.

Ichioka, Y. (1988). *Issei: The world of the first generation immigrants, 1885-1924*. New York: Morrow.

Ishida, S. (1974). Interview by A. A. Hansen, O. H. 1338, OHP-CSUF.

Kikuchi, Y. (1974, July 29). Interview by A. A. Hansen, O. H. 1340, OHP- CSUF.

Kitano, H. H. L. (1969). *Japanese Americans: The evolution of a subculture*. Englewood Cliffs, NJ: Prentice-Hall.

Larson, R. L. (1975). *Doho: The Japanese-American "Communist" Press, 1937-1942*. Unpublished Manuscript, Japanese American Project of the Oral History Program, California State University, Fullerton.

Levine, L. W. (1993). The unpredictable past: Reflections on recent American historiography. In L. W. Levine (Ed.), *The unpredictable past: Explorations in American cultural history*. New York: Oxford University Press.

Lyman, S. M. (1972). Generation and character: The case of Japanese-Americans. In H. Conroy & T. S. Miyakawa (Eds.), *East across the pacific: Historical and sociological studies of Japanese immigration and assimilation*. Santa Barbara, CA: ABC Clio Press.

Lyman, S. M. (1988a). On Nisei interpersonal style: A reply to S. Frank Miyamoto. *Amerasia Journal, 14*, 105–108.

Lyman, S. M. (1988b). "American" interpersonal style and Nikkei realities: A rejoinder to S. Frank Miyamoto. *Amerasia Journal, 14* , 115–123.

Lyman, S. M. (1988c). Growing up among ghetto dwellers. In P. C. Higgins & J. M. Johnson (Eds.), *Personal Sociology*. New York: Praeger.

Merritt, R. P. (1987). *Death Valley—Its impounded Americans: The contributions by Americans of Japanese ancestry during World War II*. Death Valley, CA: The Death Valley '49ers, Inc.

Mitchell, W. E. (1988). A goy in the ghetto: Gentile-Jewish communication in fieldwork research. In J. Kuglemaas (Ed.), *Between Two Worlds: Ethnographic essays on American Jewry*. Ithaca, NY: Cornell University Press.

Miyamoto, F. (1972). An immigrant community in America. In H. Conoy & T. S. Miyakawa (Eds.), *East across the pacific: Historical and sociological studies of Japanese immigration and assimilation*. Santa Barbara, CA: ABC Clio Press.

Miyamoto, F. (1984). *Social solidarity among the Japanese in Seattle*. Seattle: University of Washington Press.

Miyamoto, S. F. (1986/1987). Problems of interpersonal style among the Nisei. *Amerasia Journal, 13*, 29–45.

Miyamoto, S. F. (1988). Miyamoto reply to Stanford Lyman. *Amerasia Journal, 14*, 109–113.

Mori, T. (1985). *Yokohama, California*. Seattle: University of Washington Press.

Oda, J. (1980). *Heroic struggles of Japanese Americans: Purtisan fighters from America's concentration camps*. Los Angeles: Privately Printed.

Ogawa, D. (1971). *From Jap to Japanese: The evolution of Japanese American stereotypes*. Berkeley, CA: McCutchan.

Peterson, W. (1970). Success story, Japanese American style. In M. Kurokawa (Ed.), *Minority responses*. New York: Random House.

Peterson, W. (1971). *Japanese Americans*. New York: Random House.

Raineri, V. M. (1991). *The red angel: The life and times of Elaine Black Yoneda, 1906-1988*. New York: International Publishers.

Rosaldo, R. (1989). *Culture and truth: The remaking of social analysis*. Boston: Atheneum.

Stephenson, S. E. (Ed.). (1985). *Oral history collection: California State University, Fullerton.* Fullerton: Oral History Program, California State University, Fullerton.

Tachibana, J. (1980, December 20). Indefinite isolation: The World War II ordeal of Harry Yoshio Ueno. *Rafu Shimpo.*

Takahashi, J. (1982). Japanese American responses to race relations: The formation of Nisei perspectives. *Amerasia Journal, 9,* 42–51.

Tanaka, T. (1942). *A report on the Manzanar riot of Sunday, December 6, 1942.* Unpublished manuscript. University of California, Berkeley.

Tanaka, T. (1943). *An analysis of the Manzanar incident and its aftermath.* Unpublished manuscript, University of California, Berkeley.

Tanaka, T. (1973a, May 19). Interview by D. A. Hacker & B. E. Mitson, O. H. 1271a, OHP-CSUF.

Tanaka, T. (1973b, August 30). Interview by A. A. Hansen, O. H. 1271b, OHP-CSUF.

Tanaka, T. (1974). How to survive racism in America's free society. In A. A. Hansen & B. E. Mitson (Eds.), *Voices long silent: An oral inquiry into the Japanese American evacuation.* Fullerton, CA: Japanese American Project, Oral History Program, CSUF.

Tateishi, J. (1984). *And justice for all: An oral history of the Japanese detention camps.* New York: Random House.

Templeman, M. (1979). *Kibei.* Honolulu: Daimax.

Ueno, H. Y. (1976, October 30). Interview by S. K. Embrey & A. A. Hansen, O. H., 1518a, OHP-CSUF.

Uyeno, T. (1973, August 22-October 20). Point of no return. *Rafu Shimpo.*

Wakatsuke, Y. (1979). Japanese emigration to the United States, 1866-1924: A monograph. *Perspectives in American History, 12,* 387–514.

Wilson, R. A., & Hosokawa, B. (1982). *East to America: A history of the Japanese in the United States.* New York: Morrow.

Wise, G. (1973). *American historical explanations: A strategy for grounded inquiry.* Homewood, IL: Dorsey.

Yoneda, E. B. (1974, March 2). Interviewed by A. A. Hansen, O. H. 1377b, OHP-CSUF.

Yoneda, K. G. (1974, March 3). Interview by R. L. Larson & A. A. Hansen, O. H., 1376b, OHP-CSUF.

Yoneda, K. G. (1983). *Ganbatte: Sixty-year struggle of a Kibei worker.* Los Angeles: Asian American Studies Center, University of California at Los Angeles.

Yoneda, K. G., & Yoneda, E. B. (1973, December 19). Manazanar: Another view. *Rafu Shimpo.*

8

Envisioning Homestead: Using Photographs in Interviewing (Homestead, Pennsylvania)

Judith Modell
Charlee Brodsky
Carnegie Mellon University

All photographs in this chapter were taken by Charlee Brodsky.

142   Modell and Brodsky

This is a chapter about memory, and about eliciting memories through the use of photographs during an interview. It is also about the visual construction of a community over time, a community that has been pictured in a variety of ways.

The community is Homestead, Pennsylvania, one of the most well-known "steeltowns" in the United States. The Homestead strike of 1892 provided a dramatic rendering of labor–management relationships that has framed conventional views of a one-industry town for nearly a century. Homestead is located 8 miles from downtown Pittsburgh, along the Monongahela River; its population contains the ethnic mixture typical of steel valley towns in Western Pennsylvania: Irish, English, Eastern European, and an African-American population that has been increasing in number and in proportion since the closing of the USX (formerly United States Steel) mill in 1986.

The mill dominates the landscape and it was partly that visual dominance that suggested the project to us in the first place. Four miles long and one and a half miles wide, the mill occupies the flat lands along the Monongahela River and is an unavoidable presence in the Homestead scene. Like other towns in this area, the rest of the town moves up the hills: Worker housing clustered near the mill, middle-class and manager housing farther up the hill. Byington (1910/1974), in the opening paragraphs of *Homestead: The Households of a Mill Town*, wrote:

> On the slope which rises steeply behind the mill are the Carnegie Library and the "mansion" of the mill superintendent, with the larger and more attractive dwellings of the town grouped about two small parks. Here and there the towers of a church rise in relief. The green of the parks modifies the first impression of dreariness by one of prosperity such as is not infrequent in American industrial towns. Turn up a side street, however, and you pass uniform frame houses, closely built and dulled by the smoke; and below, on the flats behind the mill, are cluttered alleys, unsightly and unsanitary, the dwelling place of the Slavic laborers. (p. 3)

Byington's account is accompanied by photographs taken in major part by Lewis Hine, also part of the Pittsburgh Survey and as reflective of progressive social commentary as is Byington's prose. Nearly 80 years later the social, economic, and cultural shape of the town can still be evoked through a combination of verbal and visual portraiture—and the history of the town is, we discovered, told that way by the people of Homestead.

METHOD

Interactive interviewing refers to an interaction between interviewer and interviewee—a conversational, open, or loosely structured mode, in which give and take is emphasized during the encounter and made an important aspect of subsequent analysis. That only partially describes our strategy. We introduced a third element into the encounter, photographs. But we used these in a particular way. We did not present the photographs during the interview and ask people to tell their story around the photos; we did not want to use pictures simply as reminders, or illustrations of a story, or as "indicators" of significant places, events, and persons.

Nor did we understand photography to serve the conventional anthropological purpose of extracting more data from an individual. "There really are no other ways to use photographic records scientifically except to use photographs as stimuli in interviewing. Certainly the projective use of photographs offers a rich recovery of data" (Collier, 1967/1986, p. 213). And we did not stop with the historian's goal: "This technique of interviewing with photographs elicits much more complete and precise information from respondents" (Borchert, 1982, p. 274). Beyond the recovery of more and, perhaps, more precise data, we assumed photographs could inform us about how individuals themselves understand and communicate "data."

We encouraged people to tell the story of Homestead as freely as possible and then after giving a verbal account to respond to the photographs we presented to them or they showed to us. We did, however, introduce the project by explaining our use of photography—the visual component of our inquiry and analysis—and by suggesting the importance of their perceptions of the community as documented in "images" taken, saved, and displayed. We described the photographs we had: Brodsky's documentary portraits of the town and its people (a documentation that began in 1986 with the mill closing); archival photographs from the University of Pittsburgh Hillman Library Collection (from approximately 1900 through the early 1940s). We also told people that we wanted to see and talk about their photographs; these included studio and other formal portraits, snapshots, family albums, pictures displayed in the house—the "private" visual documentation. Some people had their family photo collections out and ready when we arrived; others claimed it was "hard" to find the photographs. Almost everyone we interviewed at home had some photographs displayed on walls or mantelpieces (cf. Csikszentmihalyi & Rochberg-Halton, 1981).

We let each interviewee hold the photographs and look at them at her or his own pace. The archival photographs were uniform in size (8 x 10), as were Brodsky's documentary photographs (11 x 14). In essence, the interviewee was presented with a stack of photographs, all black and white (a contrast with their own) and all mainly focused on a scene: a street or corner, building or panorama. Individuals were visible in some of the old photographs; occasionally we showed Brodsky's portraits of people, particularly if she had photographed a member of the interviewee's family. (We also made prints of both the archival and Brodsky's photographs to give to people.) The family photographs people showed us were kept in various ways, from albums to shoeboxes (cf. Chalfen, 1987). People generally took snapshots out of the boxes for us to see and often turned the pages of the albums, guiding us through the collection. We also walked around with people and discussed the pictures they had displayed in their houses.

Our intention was to let people tell the story of the town in their own words—construct a response to changes in Homestead as they interpreted these changes before exposing them to "memory jogger" provided by photographs (Chalfen, 1987). We wanted to go beyond the assumptions made about photographs, that they "revive" peoples' memories, that they organize the past, and that they inspire interpretations of "life" (Lesy, 1980). We assumed that by analyzing the relationship between verbal accounts and a visual story we would not only expand a method—using photographs during interviews—and refine a theory—visual representations carry "different" information from verbal representations—but also provide insight into peoples' construction of the links among economic, social, and personal changes in a one-industry town.

People in Homestead felt they had been studied but not heard and our presentation of the project as one that intended to capture their views of the town pleased them. Our research strategy tapped a popular sense that the mill closing had brought "professionals" to Homestead who ignored the voices of inside experts; this, combined with the reassurance provided by the tangibleness of photographs, laid the foundation for trust and for rapport. I explained my discipline of anthropology as one that attended to people's perceptions of their lives and Brodsky emphasized the importance of their snapshots to her vision of the town. (We did interviews in several ways: occasionally together; sometimes Brodsky was present only when the photographs were being discussed, and often I did the full interview by myself.) Our presentation of our professional undertakings further confirmed the contrast with other researchers people in Homestead encountered.[1] In focusing on photographs, too, we duplicated a way of telling history that was familiar to our informants, and our interviews (mostly at people's houses) resembled the kind of "do-you-remember" exercise that ordinarily accompanies a display of photographs. Questions and answers over a "bunch of pictures" did not seem

---

[1] We also came from a prestigious university and that validated our apparently unusual and informal approach to interviewing.

intrusive or hierarchical. The interview partook of the composite creation of history people from time to time engage in; we became part of a conversation about the past. In the course of interviewing, we discovered how powerful a conceptual device photographs can be. After our introductory statements virtually everyone told their "free" stories with pictures in mind. The presence of the idea of "photograph," even without the actual artifact, resulted in a story differently shaped and differently told from the conventional oral history narrative: Episode and scene modified the chronological or autobiographical structure; characters, it seemed, were remembered as portraits; changes in Homestead were portrayed through "imagistic" contrasts—a before-and-after view of the town. The interaction in our interviews was produced by the concept of photography—thinking about pictorial representations—and not, immediately, by the presence of photographs.

This does not seem to be a common use of photographs. A search of the literature did not provide many guidelines, although it did provide beautifully illustrated oral histories of a city, an industry, a one-industry town like Homestead and, as well, artistic photography books illuminated (and enlivened) by quotations from the subjects. Hareven and Lagenbach's (1978) social history, *Amoskeag: Life and Work in an American Factory City*, may come the closest to wedding interview to photography in processual not just "post facto" terms. Hareven and Langenbach used photographs not only to add information but also to explore people's notions of themselves as informants.

> Interviewing gained new meaning with the opening of Randolph Langenbach's exhibit, "Amoskeag: A Sense of Place, A Way of Life...."... The exhibit evoked an overwhelming response from former Amoskeag and Chicopee workers, some of whom visited the show over and over.... The former workers of the Chicopee whose portraits were displayed in the exhibit had become historical symbols. As soon as they realized this, it was no longer necessary to explain why their lives were important, why we wanted to interview them, and why we were writing this book. (Hareven & Langenbach, 1978, p. 31)

We took a further step by using the photographs to explore the nature of narrative, of memory, and of "re-viewing" verbal history with visual images. Furthermore, by merging several kinds of photographs during the interview we probed into strategies of interpretation and of linking private and public history, as well as into the process by which people establish themselves as informants.

INTERVIEWS

Joe R. was our first informant. We met him by chance in the Carnegie Library in Homestead.[2] We had asked the librarian for material on Homestead and she gave us a collection of newspaper articles. (Hers was not a friendly response and she told us later, "Homestead has been studied so much by outsiders who never show

---

[2]The library is actually located in Munhall, and our study in fact includes three boroughs: Homestead, West Homestead, and Munhall. There are significant political and socioeconomic differences among the three communities, which are important but not pertinent to this chapter. For our purposes, "Homestead" refers to the three communities inasmuch as their fortunes were tied to the fate of the U.S. Steel Homestead Works.

us what they do; they just disappear"—a warning we have taken to heart, giving the library reports and arranging to display photographs in the community.) Joe looked across the table and spotted the photographs that illustrated most of these articles. Without hesitation he began identifying, elaborating, and weaving a story around each of the photographs. We listened, then explained our project. Considering himself a historian of Homestead, he was happy to help—and offered his family as our first set of informants.[3] The family has been in Homestead for three, going on four generations. Joe's father owned a store that was originally located "below the tracks," in the mill neighborhood. With mill expansion in 1941, the store was forced out and moved up the hill into a residential neighborhood. Joe now owns the store and lives right next door. His brother worked in the mill all his life (combining that with a job on the police force), and his sister married a steelworker who worked for an Ohio mill. Their children experienced the collapse of the mill as an economic resource and they have chosen other jobs and careers.

We have, at this writing, interviewed Joe, his wife, and three of their five children. We have interviewed Joe's brother Dave, his wife, and two of their eight children. And we have interviewed people suggested by these early contacts. An initial plan was to focus on families who had been in Homestead for more than three generations and that remains one of our strategies for conducting interviews. We also discovered that Brodsky and her camera are an attraction and that people stop to tell her their stories of Homestead; I have begun following the networks created by these contacts. I arrange to interview the people encountered that way at a later time and in a place where I can use the tape recorder and talk for a relatively long period of time.[4] At the moment, then, we have a two-pronged approach to interviewing that combines family-based interviews with chance encounters. Three-generation interviews will be the core of a community portrait of Homestead in which the presence, dominance, and disappearance of the mill is the organizing theme.

Mrs. Joe R.—neither she nor her husband used her first name—was one of our first interviews. Her narrative and subsequent response to photos established several of the themes I discuss in this chapter: First the mill, portrayed scenically and as a place of work, and second the town—also a scene and a place of public activity, with Eighth Avenue, Homestead's main shopping street, the focus of discussion. Too, the way in which pictures "worked" became clear in this interview. Uncertain of what I wanted, Mrs. R. was led into memories of her family by my interest in her "old" photographs. She used her life story as an introduction to (and context for) the collection of photographs—in this case in a box—she would display at the end of the interview. The box sat in front of us, incidentally obscuring the tape recorder (and the taping) as well as holding its apparently usual place for times of family reminiscence. And it became apparent that as keeper of the box, Mrs. R. was keeper of the private history that complemented her husband's more public history of the town.

---

[3]Strauss (1961) commented on the emergence of self-styled amateur historians in ethnically diverse urban settings.

[4]All interviews were tape recorded and the tapes subsequently transcribed. In this chapter, all names have been changed to protect confidentiality.

THE MILL

Mrs. R. was born in Braddock, a neighboring steel town, and she started her story there. She described a setting not unlike Homestead: The mill along the river, houses running up the hill in geographic correspondence to socioeconomic difference. Her family resembled the Irish described by Byington; her father was an open hearth worker in the mill and her mother the canny, clever manager of household resources. In the middle of the interview Mrs. R. brought out a novel written by a relative, deferring to his portrait of Braddock (O'Malley, 1962). In the novel one Irishman complains to another:

> Oh, they write up in the company magazine about the interest they take in improvin' things, an' "Make Pittsburgh Beautiful" an' so on, an' then all day long the bastards have those smokestacks throwin' out all that soot in big dirty clouds an' those sewers pourin' that shit into the river. Not that I mind the mills goin', mind ye—I'm all fer work. (p. 90)

Smoke, dirt, and yellow dust represented the mills at work and a prosperous town. As suggested here, smoke was also a multivocal symbol, representing the conditions of work, worker–owner relationships, and an intrusion into the landscape. For Mrs. R. smoke meant dirt and the lines of laundry through which she remembered her childhood. "Most of the housewives did their, every Monday was, you know, washday. Everybody hung out their wash on Monday, and you were almost considered an outcast if you didn't have your wash out there early on Monday. Tuesday was ironing day." In his interview, Joe said: "I'll tell you how living next to the mill affected me.... I remember walking out from Fourth Avenue to Tenth Avenue and by the time I'd get to school and I wiped my face, it was all full of soot." Thinking back to when the mills were in operation, people pictured themselves covered with the residue of the mills; "now the rivers are all cleaned up; I remember when we used to swim in there and we'd come out all covered with filth." Dirt remembered represented a kind of unity within the steel valley towns. "The whole Allegheny County was like that. If you're going to hang clothes, you hang your clothes out and get coal dust all over them."

Women's activities took place outside the mill and involved keeping the households clean against the onslaught of the mill's dirt. When we interviewed the oldest R. daughter, Kathleen, she recalled her Serbian grandmother sweeping the porch three times a day.

> That I do remember growing up, I definitely remember that, how filthy it was around here. My grandmother used to sweep the front porch off three times a day. I mean the soot on the front porch was just incredible. I mean we were always dirty. We always had that, you know, the shiny stuff, the soot, all over your hands and everything like that.

Throughout the interviews, people used an image of dirt and the struggle against dirt to evoke a period of time, a set of characters, and a community spirit. Men were pictured— and pictured themselves—as continually and inevitably covered with dirt, whether they were actually millworkers or not. The women portrayed themselves as creating a clean space, an undusty domain for those who had been exposed to the soot and filth.

The complex significance of smoke and dust became even more apparent when we showed people the archival photographs.[5] One after another, people remarked on the smoke in the sky, sometimes noticing a puff of dark cloud neither Brodsky nor I had seen in the picture. Our surprised response to the previously unnoticed detail prompted a prolonged conversation about its significance. And into this came appreciation of the meaning of the smoke: For our informants, smoke symbolized "good times," neighborhood cooperativeness, and ethnic integration—sometimes in the face of heartless mill policies. Responses to the smoke evident in old photos, as it was not in new ones, resembled the reaction a person had to pictures of childhood, when they were happy, innocent, and gullible (Harris, 1987). "When I was a wee little kid I used to look at the smoke, and I thought the smoke made the clouds," said Mrs. B. when she looked at the archival photos.

"Contemporary photographs and panoramic views of the city in this period [early 1900s] invariably showed belching furnaces and haze obscuring the workers' housing nearby" (Kleinberg, 1989, p. 66; cf. p. 339, note 4). Our interviews revealed that the people of Homestead "saw" a different picture in the smoke and dirt; for them smoke did not obscure but highlighted the details of lives and places. Looking at the photographs, people told the town's and their own histories with smoke and haze as key interpretive devices.

---

[5] Taken by the Pittsburgh and Lake Erie Railroad Company, they show the "crossings" in the mill neighborhood and incidentally provide a fairly substantial portrait of that part of Homestead; Hillman Library Collection, University of Pittsburgh.

The other aspect of the story of the mill were the human lives involved in mill activity—the men who worked in the mill, the people who supported the working of the mill, the women who kept households going. The mention of photography at the beginning of our interviews led people to translate memories into snapshots. Mrs. R. once again borrowed from her cousin's book in working out a picture of her own father, the open hearth worker.

In *Miners Hill*, the millworker is described through the eyes of his son.

[H]ere's a back to pit against the earth, to pit against huge quivering walls of clay, thick seams of coal; a back to stand on the lip of the roaring furnace and shovel nourishment into its white-hot throat—yes, here's a back for steel, equal to steel, deserving of steel, for the tall hungry glory of the blast furnace belching red-gold light high into the smoky midnight sky; for the furnace's glowing scarlet maw, to keep it spewing steel...(p. 89)

Mrs. R. described her father:

He was called a first helper. He, at the open hearth, so it was a fairly responsible position. He had to, I guess, know when the steel was ready and, you know, take tests and things—. But it was also very hard because he worked and it was very warm there. I mean, it was extreme heat and there were times when he got, I know there were a few times when he got, a few times he'd come home with big burns on him.... My father was, too, he was very proud that the heat never bothered him, you know, got to, well it got to him in that he felt hot and everything. But he never passed out.... Also his hands were very, his skin was very tough on his hands. And he could touch hot things that you or I would get burnt right away if we touched them.

At the end of the interview she showed us a photograph of her father. It was a retirement picture and he stood formally, stiffly, clothed conventionally in a suit and tie. "Well, it must of been on display for a while because it is in a frame and that, so yeah, they [her parents] must have had it there. I guess for awhile after he retired, they must have had it on display." In some sense, the photograph was untrue: it matched neither her memories nor her recently presented verbal portrait of her father. And rather than revise the verbal portrait, prompted by the contrasting image Mrs. R. reiterated the earlier characterization.

He did work that not all, a lot of men couldn't do. He was very, very hard, I mean his body, he was very strong. Not that he was a huge man or anything, you know, but he was very strong. The type of work that he did he had to work up against a tremendous heat and a lot of men couldn't take it. They would just pass out.

She had a box full of photographs, not an organized family album, and she expressed surprise as she pulled out one picture after another. The images served less to spark her memory than to confirm what she had described in her narrative even when, as was the case with her father, the photograph did not match what she had said. Then she used the very contrast (or "untruth") of the picture to substantiate her "truthful" verbal description. This was a consequence of our approach, inasmuch as we responded to the photos with the information we had already received from a verbal account. And whether or not we actually said anything—and we usually did ask for an explanation of content and of fit into the narrated history—we clearly shared knowledge of the picture's references based on the story we had just heard. A now common experience with the interviewer structured Mrs. R's interpretation of the snapshots and studio portraits she displayed. My presence as interlocutor in the earlier exchange turned me into an informed viewer of family pictures; it also made Mrs. R. a particular kind of historian for whom pictures became not the whole story but a piece captured briefly and from the point of view of the taker. Mrs. R. had become a critic of photographic evidence.

When she found pictures of her mother, Mrs. R. again pointed out the details that filled in or "colored" her verbal description. The unsentimental and documentary strategy for looking at the photos in turn increased her confidence as a reporter of the past. The box contained several snapshots of her mother, including one in which her mother stood with, as she put it, "the girls who came from Ireland." "This is one of the girls that we took off from Ireland [her mother ran a kind of boarding house], remember I told you we took different ones, that was one of them."

Then, pulling out another snapshot: "This is a picture of mother with the three of us [Mrs. R. and her siblings]...." The pictures of her mother were closer to what she had said than were those she found of her father, but Mrs. R. considerably changed her tone in talking about her mother when the photos were lying on the table in front of us. Her admiration, clear when she spoke of the open hearth worker, now came out when she talked about the household manager, renter, and parent.

> I don't know if you are interested in this part or not but at the time when we were growing up, ok, dresses, my mother would have, there was a lady and she would have her make our clothes and this particular dress [in the photograph], I can remember the material my sister had, hers was the whole thing, mine has white on top because they ran out of the blue and white so they just put white on the top. But at the time it was cheaper for her to buy the material and have this lady make them, because she would only charge a dollar a dress.

We did not change our approach to interviewing in the presence of the photographs, either theirs or the ones we brought. As in the earlier half of the interview, we encouraged each "storyteller" to construct his or her own account around the images, our part being less the interviewer than the listener as interaction focused on the visual material. In addition, people always had control over the photographic display: They turned the pages of the albums, took the snapshots out of boxes, or flipped from one to the other of the photographs we brought. Through managing the visual component, interviewees controlled the interaction and compelled us to follow their rhythms and sequencing of subjects. This also fit with the way the project had initially been presented and justified the trust they had shown in us as interviewers. People gave attention to the range of photographic materials at their own pace, just as they had told the narrative, but their interpretation of visual imagery was clearly dependent on the form and content of the narratives. Like Mrs. R., people chose those aspects of a scene, a portrait, or a pictured event that affirmed an articulated memory. They ended up combining "visual and verbal language" so that one "inspired" and "empowered" the other (Harris, 1987). The words changed the images, just as the idea of image had so strikingly changed the verbal narrative.

We were not completely silent and when Mrs. R. brought out an elegant wedding photo; we commented:"oh, that's beautiful." The subjects were her parents, formally dressed and carefully posed. Mrs. R. responded to the portrait by referring to the themes she had already established in her narrative.

Yeah, I think that they did pretty good in those days, having no parents here with them or anything, that they managed to have a fairly nice wedding and things like that, you know.... That they went through and did all of these things, you know, at the time, which was the right way, I guess, had pictures and a wedding. Mother had her wedding gown for many years. The whole front of it was, they're not exactly jewels, not rhinestones, all beaded, all different types of beads, the whole front of it. I don't think you can tell there [in the photograph] but it was a whole separate piece that connected.

The clothing, like her father's "hardness," visually represented a person's character and also evoked the times in which people exercised strength—old times, from her point of view. In the course of the conversation, Mrs. R. decided she might have the wedding picture redone so she could add it to the mantlepiece that was crowded with pictures of the R. children.

She had not lost sight of the mill. Throughout her interview she portrayed it not as a physical symbol but as the environment in which her parents' lives evolved and a community prospered. The mill cast its shadow over the personal details of her life history, and as an interpreter of photographs she read into family snapshots and studio portraits signs of the stamina and energy associated with a steel mill town.

THE TOWN

"Well, gee, when I first moved over here, thirty years ago, there were so many nice dress shops." I had asked Mrs. R. to talk about Eighth Avenue, Homestead's main shopping street. "There was like this Half Brothers, it sold furniture, it was like a five- or six-story building. Everything was thriving. And, of course, through the years then you would just slowly see, you know, this one closing down and the following year another one closed down." In virtually everyone's interview, discussion of Eighth Avenue was the most "scenic" and contrastive part of the story—from busy town to ghost town.

In their accounts, people imaginatively walked up and down Eighth Avenue, envisioning the street, naming the stores, and pinpointing the changes that had occurred over the past decade. We interviewed two R. sisters at the same time, the daughters of Dave. In their 30's, they had lived in Homestead all their lives and were close friends. Together they visualized downtown Homestead, competing in their ability to remember and identify each existing store and what had been there before.

A: Yeah, it's there, the sign is there, but the store has been empty for about, what, twelve, fifteen years now.
B: No, no. Morris Greenberg's is still there. It's all kids clothes still. Yes, it is! It's right next to that office shop. I go there every day.
A: No, that's Freelander's, hon, that's Freelander's.

People amazed us with their seemingly total recall of businesses (something we both knew we could not do for the towns we grew up in). Prompted by a pile of photographs on the restaurant table—which she did not, however, look at—a waitress went up and down the nearly 10 blocks of "down street," naming the stores that had survived, the new ones, the ones that had disappeared with the closing of the mill. She refused the mnemonic to her memory, knowing she could visualize Eighth Avenue accurately without the pictures.

In her interview, Dave's wife remarked:

But it's, it's just so sad when you go down into Homestead now. It's just, it's as though, you know, you see the town as a whole but the body, it's empty, there's something so sad, so depressing about it. And it's hard, you know it's hard to believe.... It's just incredible to believe that there would never be any more steel produced.

And she expanded:

And it was a, I mean that was a big treat going into Homestead, you know. It was, it was important, it was exciting to be able to shop in all those shops thriving. Now, you know, it's as if you—the farther down you go into Homestead just, I don't know, there's just something that's—it's not there any more. The theater, they had the theater down there. They had a big article about that, I think a few years ago when that was all taken away. To me, it just seems like when you see those, whatever they call them, Uni-Marts that are now on the corner, it takes away from it, from architectural, the whole theme of the town and that. It just doesn't fit. It just doesn't seem right to me anyway or to David.

Like smoke in the sky, the replacement of a movie theater by a convenience store became symbolic for people in their reconstruction of down street. The Leona Theater had been a significant part of Homestead's history. It was the theater people remembered seeing their first movies in and the place people considered Homestead's link to a Hollywood-created world of glamour and excitement; the "stars" who came and the crowds who watched completed the description of a monumental and stately structure. "Movies for 11¢. It was hard to get 11¢. That was one of the—old time movies, too, were really entertaining. The Leona Theater cost $1 or $2 million to build. That old place should have been an historical landmark." In one of the archival photographs there is a small representation of a movie poster. People pointed it out to us, and used it to elaborate on the importance of the Leona in Homestead, sign of a town's prosperity and worldliness. The image also reminded people that there had been "five movie theaters in Homestead" and, another demonstration of memory, they named the theaters in geographical order. Places, buildings, shops were described, an evocation of the "look" of the town, as much as any activity they would have participated in there. To remember the sight of Eighth Avenue, in full detail, was to picture Homestead's good years.

But Eighth Avenue had changed: The Leona was a casualty of the recent mill closing. As people outlined the changes and described the businesses that had died, they were thrown back in memory or in an analogy to the flattening of the area around the mill during World War II. Then the mill had expanded, taking over the neighborhood of "below the tracks" in which many of our first generation of interviewees had spent their childhood.[6] The narratives, organized by scene and image, brought the two events together: The intrusion of the mill into the landscape substantially and inevitably modified its contours.

> They tore the whole thing down, flat.... They flattened everything out. They tore down everything. There's one building left, it's, I think it's something like the Russian Club that's still standing. My dad used to open up the store at five o'clock in the morning. Guys going in the mill, they get their lunch cake, or this and that.

Archival photographs of "below the tracks" before and after mill expansion reminded people not only of a past but also of the present decline, with closed stores and empty blocks. Even for those who had not lived through mill expansion, the pictured gap in the landscape evoked the current crisis.

The old and new photographs we brought constituted a dramatic rendering of the mill's impact on the town, either illustrating memories or creating a scene for those who had not witnessed that change. The pictures made a powerful impression; people explained and interpreted them for us and, as well, used them as a way of reseeing their own photographs of the town. Interacting with the archival photographs, informants became the historians we could not be. In noticing details we had not noticed and in being able to explain the picture for our evident enlightenment, people of Homestead did not become simply more accurate historians; rather, they constructed a more complex view of the history they knew. In addition, our responses to descriptions of the content of an archival photograph led people to take the same tone when

---

[6] The phrase "below the tracks" was used fondly, a recall of a neighborhood in which different ethnic groups lived side by side, cooperative and neighborly in their activities.

describing their family snapshots. Our role as listeners blurred the distinction people made between official photographs and family pictures as material for a history of Homestead. Not only tone but viewpoint was transferred from one to the other, and people looked through their family albums (or boxes) from the perspective of abrupt and sweeping change, emphasizing the pictures they had of below the tracks: a church, the backyard of a house, the old elementary school. "Here she [mother] is, this is the playground over on Second Avenue. She was a teacher over there.... Playground, right by the river." Then, making sure I had noticed: "Did you see what I passed to you, 1939?"

Prompted by our photographs, one woman brought out snapshots she had taken of the mill area from the Homestead High Level Bridge, including some pictures of the damage done by the 1936 flood. Looking at those pictures recalled the devastation brought by the mill expansion into residential neighborhoods four years later. The second leveling of buildings, occurring in the late 1980s and early 1990s, seemed to our informants like an eerie echo of the first, and people we interviewed had begun to document the destruction of the mill in photographs and on videotape. A next phase of our interviewing will involve talking with people about these recent, purposeful records of collapse. "I was telling her [me] how when you go down into Homestead now, it just seems like a town like with an empty shell inside," Mrs. Dave R. said to Dave when he came into the room. Looking down from the High Level Bridge, the piece by piece destruction of the mill presented a sharpened and physical version of the desolation of Eighth Avenue: "Homestead used to be packed but now it's a ghost town."

PRIVATE HISTORY/PUBLIC HISTORY

"They're just parties and stuff, just my friends." Using different kinds of photographs in the interviews revealed an interesting relationship between private and public history. People tended to assume that family photographs were private: snapshots about a person or an event that was special to one individual or one family but not part of public record. Yet we were asking about Homestead the town and drawing on their snapshots as information. Participating in our project changed the way they ordinarily looked at a photograph collection, as an amusement to be shared with kin or with friends. At the same time, in their experiences, personal photo collections told a life story and, under the thrust of our conversation with them, people began to intersect this presumably private history with the public one they presumed we wanted to know for our book.[7] People adopted different strategies in order to place their own photographs in a public context—a context that was especially vivid to them inasmuch as they had just finished telling the town's history through their perceptions of changes in it.

Some people "publicized" their photos. They went through their personal collections looking for photographs of a public event—a parade or graduation or ethnic festival. In other cases, they found published materials that contained a picture of someone in their family. "Excuse me one second," said Dave R. in the middle of my interview with his wife. "Uh, my brother has a book from when the people start coming over and they meet down in the ward and they ask for their pictures in there. So I'm going to get it for you." "That would be great," I said. "The daughter said it was all right for you to take it with you but make sure she gets it back." I assured him I would.

Joe's friend Steve, another amateur historian, showed me a newspaper picture of his son in the Honor Guard for Truman's funeral and was not eager to show me family photographs. (He was one of the few Homestead people we talked with who did not want to be interviewed at home, each time arranging to meet in a local restaurant. I suspect he did not want his wife to interact with us during the interview. Later, when I interviewed her, I discovered she was an outspoken and articulate narrator of both public and private history.) He also brought us his high school yearbook, and pointed out the ethnic diversity of his classmates along with the football stars. "This is what we had when we had our banquet, football banquet." Modell: "You were on the team?" "Yeah, I played quarterback. You'll see a lot of familiar names in there [the photograph caption] that, from the Steelers and that." In our second interview with him, Steve had his pictures all ready for us both to see (I had been alone during the first interview). And once again, he publicized the personal pictures by quickly looking for shots of events that were "officially" significant. He pulled out a snapshot of a house in the mill neighborhood. We asked, "Is this where you lived?" "No, that's, yeah, that's where they used to have, you know, like the people we lived with that time, they used to grow a lot of grapes.

---

[7] People asked what we were going to do with all the "stuff" and we told them we expected to publish a book that we hoped would represent their points of view.

And this is when I played football, this is our banquet at Jack Dunn Hotel. This is around, oh latter part of '42."

Everyone had wedding pictures, in albums or framed, formal portraits and informal "candids." When people could, they showed us the wedding picture that had been printed in the local newspaper, the *Homestead Messenger*. Kathleen R. showed us hers: "They do this for people in the area, they put the thing [photograph] in the paper and they mount it for you and it's a little remembrance." She also found the picture that had been printed in the *Pittsburgh Press*, and compared the two images; "the big one is probably Homestead, yeah." By contrast, she dismissed her own snapshots as "the party years, volume 1, 2, and 3."

It was as if personal photo albums and collections were too idiosyncratic, not worthy documentation of a town's history unless the content was somehow "significant." That was true no matter how much we tried to persuade people that we wanted to see all the family snapshots. They willingly showed us pictures of family members in public places or at public events: the local amusement park or a parade through town. "That's Fourth of July, that's Uncle Sam." Pictures that portrayed what was already defined as public and important were shown, no matter how private or intimate the content. "That's my christening," Kathleen informed us about a classic baby picture. Weddings fit this category perfectly, merging a private dimension with a publicly recognized event—a celebration of one's own life-course but also of ethnicity and "good times," themes that had been raised in the narratives. And as people looked at these semi-official photographs, interpreting them for us, they discovered new information. "Dottie, go in my bedroom and there's that picture of me and you and Grandma at my shower." Then looking at several pictures together: "Look at that, they're both on one street." Brodsky: "This is the store that's still here." "Yeah, that's the store there."

Similarly, "old" pictures of a grandmother, a mother's brother, or, even, of oneself as an infant were also considered worth showing. These snapshots would be construed as historical. "Here's me and Daddy. I was the first one [laughing]. That was in a garden, Grandma's garden." Steve, who had been reluctant to show us anything personal unless when he did he could give it a larger significance, found a baby picture in one of the manila envelopes he had brought to the interview. "Here I am when I was a baby. I must have been about two years old. That was 1925 or 26." Slowly he warmed to the story the photographs told of his family's past. "And this is my uncle and my brother and that's his boy. He was a county policeman. In fact, this one down here was a policeman in Homestead." As we talked, people came to see more recent snapshots as a kind of history: "I was a candy-striper at the Homestead Hospital. It's not the best—it's not the greatest picture." Brodsky: "Oh, I love the skirt." "Do you like that? That's when things were like, when things like that were in style." She had been a candy-striper no more than 10 years earlier.

What happened as we talked was that the public inserted itself into further reaches of the private. Interpreted, as Steve did, a baby picture could be a historical document, reflecting changes in Homestead. Simultaneously people linked the stories of their lives to developments in the town, imbuing the private with the capacity for demonstrating and, even, "proving" those developments. The presentation of photographs and the replication of conventional ways of using photos to recall the past meant our interviews resembled conversations they had had in which one person, "holding" the evidence, related pictures to past events and designated changes in individual lives that represented differences from decade to decade. Mrs. R. did not just explain who was in the elegant wedding portrait she showed us but used that to compare the past, when people "did that sort of thing," with the present when, presumably, they did not. Our approach of paying equal attention to snapshots, formal portraits, and newspaper clippings—all, without distinction, included in family albums—also encouraged people to consider their collections significant to the history of Homestead. Through the talk over pictures an informant appropriated the interlinking of private life story with public history that I had presented as my goal at the beginning of an interview. Discussing the photographs, people assumed that the "truth" in a personal snapshot documented the past as public event.

People translated the snapshot into a public document, too, when they did not distinguish their photos from either the archival photographs or Brodsky's artistically and ethnographically conceived portraits of the town. This was not a failure to see difference in content and style so much as an interpretation of the links between pictured images and a town's history. With that in mind—and we had put that into people's minds—the precise provenance of the photo did not so much matter: all could be read as evidence for the rightness of their story of Homestead. Practically no one commented on the beauty of either the archival photos or Brodsky's, despite the fact that some of the people we talked with had seen her photographs exhibited in a gallery. Praise came in very general terms: "those are great" or "they are really terrific pictures." Mainly they read the photos we brought for content not for form. They found details in the archival photographs to substantiate the memories they had recounted and they remarked on the subjects of the recent (i.e., Brodsky's) photographs in order to re-draw a town they had recently pictured in words. Moreover, seeing the old and new photographs together completed the story: People used scenes to convey the changes and the continuities that characterized a one-industry town.

We did not ask questions that would alter this "blurred genres" approach to the photographs, never suggesting our own sharp sense of difference between the three types of photographs or in any way requesting judgment of quality. A few people tested our ability to read photographs by asking us to find them in crowded scenes of a confirmation or school graduation, thus redressing a balance in the interview. "Here's when I was in Sixth grade. See if you can find me." And again compelling us to interact with the photographs: "We made our First Holy Communion. See if you can find me on there."

Shown after a narrative, the photographs provided insight into the way people reaffirm their memories in the process of discovering concrete representations of those memories, whatever the source. Steve was an exception that, in fact, strengthened our assumption about the links between verbal and visual narratives. He insisted upon looking at his snapshots during the interview and clung closely to the visual material, moving rapidly between one sort of photograph and another, adding newspaper articles and baptismal certificates, prize ribbons and postcards. At moments in the interview with him visual material became equivalent to an extensive souvenir collection. There was little free-flowing narrative as he continually offered us another "thing you will like." Self-deprecating about his narrative, he became confident as soon as something visible (tangible) sat between us on the table.

Without bringing aesthetic or critical commentary to bear on the distinction, people did recognize that the content and context of their photographs differed from the ones we brought. And they showed us personal photos with a sense of the special truth of these images compared with ones done by a railroad company, a newspaper, or a documentary photographer (cf. Chalfen, 1987). As they talked about all the photographs, our interviewees revealed a conviction that unplanned and spontaneous picture taking provides a better mirror of reality than a railroad company's official records of "below the tracks" or a professional photographer's (Brodsky) artistic portraits of Homestead in the 1980s and 1990s. The haphazardness of a family album as well as the continued interaction people carried on with their own snapshot collections underlined the reality these visual images had for people. Modell: "She [Mrs. R.] wants all the pictures taken out?" Kathleen: "Well, I don't think she'd mind pictures like that if she looks okay in them." The interviews demonstrated to people in Homestead the significance of their own photographic portraits in the context of a town's history. The project gave them a new outlook on their collections of pictures and on the relationship between their "views" of the town and the town's history. The empowerment of word by image and of image by word demonstrated to them as well as to us the way in which an elicited envisioning links personal experiences with the story of a steel town.

CONCLUSION

Our method of interviewing elicited first a story in words and then a verbal response to a set of visual images. The two histories were, not surprisingly, neither the same nor exactly parallel. The interweavings were more complex than we had anticipated. The extent to which "picture" framed the narrative a person constructed or an idea about photography organized a life story varied from one person to another. The content of our interviews, however, suggested that thinking about pictures invariably (if diversely) shaped the telling and confirmed for the teller her or his reliability, accuracy, and insightfulness. During the second phase of the interview, when we concentrated on photographs, individuals brought out the linkages they had made: finding in pictures affirmation of a point made in the verbal narrative or returning to an earlier point with an expanded perspective on what they had just finished saying. Reluctant as some people initially were to show us their snapshots—"But I just have tons and tons. I take pictures everywhere I go"—when they did, they used these as indicators of the truth of their perceptions of Homestead.

The people we interviewed were not using photographs to illustrate points they had made—they did not simply show what they had said—rather, they used the photographs to make these points "history." With an array of photographs in front of them, they placed their lives in a wider context and accorded significance to the information they had provided. In the process of interpreting photographs, they took on the status of informant rather than interviewee or storyteller; some were evidently more comfortable in the role of offering information rather than just "talking about" Homestead. Most people expressed confidence in their ability to identify pictures, regardless of the source, and this retrospectively validated their portrait of the town and, our focus, of the changes in the town. Homestead was a place they knew inside and out, up the hills and "down street." Just as almost anyone could walk along Eighth Avenue in her or his imagination, so virtually everyone we talked with confidently interpreted the images created by others—and by themselves, in the past.

Interactive interviewing, as we have described the technique, includes the complex interaction not only of interviewer and interviewee but also of interviewee with a third element, visual images. People interacted with the photographs, using visual imagery to reexamine their previously told narrative and to underline its truth and vision. The photographs (whatever their source) became another voice in the encounter, to which individuals responded actively, creatively, and confidently. The presence of photographs illustrated, too, the way in which memories work to construct a history. Going through albums and boxes with little interference from us, people wove strands of private and public together, composing a history of several dimensions and coming to a new awareness of themselves as amateur historians. The history of Homestead we heard was not simply parallel with but constructed out of private histories, just as the private became public under the impetus of our expressed interest in the town. This approach to history became apparent as people responded to the several stimuli in the interview encounter. And they regarded my role less as interviewer than as part of a conversation—but a conversation that I as researcher would communicate to others. For the people who participated, the goal of the project was to have our presentation of their viewpoints influence political and economic plans for Homestead's future.

A strategy of talking around photographs may be especially significant in a town like Homestead whose shape and space were so completely dominated by the mill and its intrusive residue. With their own photographs, people established an alternative view not only of time passing but also of space changing. Through photographs, albums, collections, framed "remembrances," people of Homestead established an image of the town that put the presence of the mill into a domestic framework. Through photographs, too, they saw their own life stories as data in Homestead's history. Interviewing changed, from "us" asking for or eliciting information from "them" to an interaction over a third element—pictures—and a consequent self-consciousness about the workings of memories, the "images" that jog memory, and the accuracy of personal recall. In the end, our expectation is that this self-consciousness will lead forward: Everyone who brings a camera or videotape to the Homestead High Level Bridge to record the destruction of the mill may help keep the current "flattening" from bringing a total disappearance of landscape and scene. What we discovered in this project, through the particular approach to interviewing that we adopted, indicates that Homestead has a history which the townspeople, not only the photographer and anthropologist, record "visually."

REFERENCES

Borchert, J. (1982). *Alley life in Washington: Family, community, religion and folklife in the city, 1850-1970.* Urbana: University of Illinois Press.

Byington, M. (1974). *Homestead: The households of a mill town.* Pittsburgh, University Center for International Studies. (Original work published 1910)

Chalfen, R. (1987). *Snapshot versions of life.* Bowling Green, OH: Bowling Green State University Popular Press.

Collier, J. (1986). *Visual anthropology: Photography as a research method.* New York: Holt, Rinehart & Winston. (Original work published 1967)

Csikszentmihalyi, M., & Rochberg-Halton, E. (1981). *The meaning of things*. New York: Cambridge University Press.

Hareven, T., & Langenbach, R. (1978). *Amoskeag: Life and work in an American factory city*. New York: Pantheon Press.

Harris, A. (Ed.). (1987). *A world unsuspected*. Chapel Hill: University of North Carolina Press.

Kleinberg, S. J. (1989). *The shadow of the mills*. Pittsburgh: University of Pittsburgh Press.

Lesy, M. (1980). *Time frames—the meaning of family pictures*. New York: Pantheon Press.

O'Malley, M. (1962). *Miners hill*. New York: Harper.

Strauss, A. (1961). *Images of the American city*. New York: Doubleday Anchor.

Afterword to Chapter 1

Ronald J. Grele

Columbia University

This chapter was originally prepared in the early winter of 1990. Rereading it now in 1994 is disturbing because, like most people, I have worked and reworked these ideas over the intervening period. There is little to do about what I now see as major problems in the presentation, but I would like to point out two areas of the chapter that now seem problematic.

First, the transition from the extended discussion of the problems of fieldwork to the very brief outline of recent work in oral history and its meaning for that debate now seems to be too brief and facile. The connective thread I would now use would be derived from the work of Bernstein (1988) and Carr (1986), especially Bernstein's discussion of a shared "universe of discourse and concern" (p. 176) and Carr's argument for the origins of narrativity in experience itself. That discussion is outlined in greater detail in a forthcoming article.

Second, the works in oral history cited do not close the argument. They simply point to a direction in our discourse about ourselves as historians. Most bothersome to me now is the assumed nature of the value of rational dialogue. Although this may be a pragmatic scientific principle, it is often not a cultural one. I can conceive of many instances where such a stance would act against the deepest held values of both historians and citizens.

Two examples will suffice. In gathering the stories of political prisoners and their captors do we serve history, the past, or the future best by granting a democratic difference and equality to both sides? Isn't it an easy liberalism that condemns the filmmakers of *Shaoh* for tricking former Nazi jailers into testifying?

Or, what are we to do in situations such as now prevail in Bosnia? It may be that in many cases, not all of them so extreme, that the assumptions of fieldwork relations outlined in this chapter simply do not prevail.

Both of these issues are beyond the scope of this brief comment. They do, however, point to problematic areas that are still open for argument and counterargument.

REFERENCES

Bernstein, R. (1988). *Beyond objectivism and relativism: Science, hermeneutics and praxis.* Philadelphia: University of Pennsylvania Press.

Carr, D. (1986). *Time, narrative, and history.* Bloomington: Indiana University Press.

Author Index

Numbers in *italics* denote complete bibliographic references.

A

Abelson, R. P., 51, 55, 57, *61*
Aberbach, D., 31, *45*
Allport, G., 54, *59*
Althusser, L., 63n, *80*
Anderson, K., 6, *17*
Anguera, K., 4n, *17*
Appleby, J. O., 14n, *17*
Applegate, J. L., 51, *61*
Archer, D., 51, *61*
Argyle, M., 50, *59*
Armitage, S., 6, *17*

B

Baddeley, A. D., 54, *61*
Barnhart, E. N., 121n, *137*
Bartlett, F. A., 53, 54, *59*
Bates, E., 56, *60*
Beavin, J. H., 49, *61*
Becker, C., 53, *59*
Bell, C. S., 65, *80*
Bernstein, S., 56, *60*
Bertaux-Wiame, I., 84, *105*
Black, J. B., 55, 57, *61*
Borchert, J., 143, *160*
Brady, R. M., 51, *61*
Branch, T., 33, *45*
Bransford, J. D., 50, *59*
Brehm, S. S., 57, *60*
Briggs, C. L., 64–65, 67, 73, 75, 79, *80*
Brown, P., 91, *105*
Brown, R., 56, *59*

Bruner, J., 39, *45*
Burgos, M., 10–11, *17*
Burke, K., 20, 30, *30*
Burleson, B. R., 52, *59*, 87, *105*
Buss, A. H., 50, *59*
Byington, M., 142, *160*

C

Cagin, S., 43n, *45*
Caplan, P., 2, 15, *17*
Carlston, D. E., 55, *59*
Carson, C., 31, 35, *45*
Cass, J., 33, *45*
Castle-Scott, D. J., 38, 39, 42, *45*
Chalfen, R., 144, 158, *160*
Chase, S. E., 65, *80*
Chestnutt, J. L., Jr., 33, *45*
Christie, L. S., 52, *60*
Chuman, F., 132, *137*
Cicourel, A. V., 85, *105*
Clark, E. C., 20, *30*
Clifford, J., 2, *17*
Collier, J., 143, *160*
Collins, R., 37, 42, *45*
Cone, J. H., 43, *45*
Conkin, P., 11, *17*
Conroy, H., 110, *137*
Corsino, L., 67n. 2, *80*
Corty, E., 51, *61*
Crane, M., 56, *60*
Crenshaw, K. W., 15, *17*
Csikszentmihalyi, M., 144, *161*

165

Kline, S., 87, *105*
Koffka, K., 54, *60*
Korstad, R., 1, *18*
Kraut, R., 51, 52, *60*
Kuiper, N. A., 57, *60*
Kulik, J., 56, *59*

L

Labov, W., *18*
Langellier, K. M., 2, 4, 14, *18*
Langenbach, R., 84, *105, 145, 161*
Lanzetta, J. T., 51, *60*
Larson, R. D., 122n, *138*
Leloudis, J., 1, *18*
Lesy, M., 144, *161*
Levine, L. W., *138*
Levinson, S., 91, *105*
Lewicki, P., 57, *60*
Lewis, D. J., 56, *60*
Lewis, S. H., 51, 52, *60*
Leydesdorff, S., 31, *45*
Lifton, R. J., 31, *45*
Lindsay, P. H., 53, *60*
Linge, D. E., 4, *18*
Loftus, E. F., 54, 56, *60*
Loftus, G. R., 54, *60*
Lomax, J. W., 19, *30*
Lombard, R., 36, 38, 39, 40–41, 43n, *45*
Lorber, J., 66, *81*
Luce, R. D., 52, *60*
Lyman, S. M., 111–114, 116, *138*

M

MacWhinney, B., 56, *60*
Macy, J., Jr., 52, *60*
Marcus, G. E., 2, *17, 85, 105*
Markus, H., 52, 56, 57, *60*
Mayhew, D., 56, *60*
Mbilinyi, M., 67n 2., *81*
McAdam, D., 33, *45*
McCann, D., 56, *59*
McCann, L. I., 43, *45*
McCormack, S. A., 91, *105*
McDonald, M. R., 57, *60*
McMahan, E. M., vii, *ix*, 3, *18, 85, 105*
Mead, G. H., 53, *60*
Mehrabian, A., 50, 51, *60*
Merritt, R. P., 129, *138*
Mies, M., 64, *81*
Mintz, S. W., 9, 10–11, *18*
Mishler, E. G., 5, 6, *18*, 59, *61*, 79, *81*
Mitchell, W. E., 131n, *138*
Mitson, B. E. [B. K.], 108, 108n. 2, 126, 132, 133, 134, *137*

Miyakawa, T. S., 110, *137*
Miyamoto, F., 110–111, *138*
Miyamoto, S. F., 111n. 3, *138*
Mollica, R. L., 31, *45*
Montenegro, X. P., 65, *81*
Mori, T., 136n. 14, *138*
Morrissey, C. T., 19, *30*
Mullener, E., 43n, 44, *45*
Murphy, M., 1, *18*

N

National Center for Education Statistics, 65, *81*
Neisser, U., 53–54, 55, 56, *61*
Neuliep, J. W., 52, *61*
Norman, D. A., 53, *60*
Novick, P., 2, *18*
Nowell-Smith, P. H., 53, *61*

O

O'Brien, D. J., 135, 136, *137*
Ochberg, F. M., 31, *46*
Oda, J., 122n, *138*
Ogawa, D., 109, *138*
O'Keefe, B. J., 86, 87–89, 90, 91, *105*
O'Keefe, D. J., 52, *61*
O'Malley, M., 147, *161*

P

Passerini, L., 1, *18*
Pearlman, L. A., 43, *45*
Peck, J., 33, *46*
Perkowitz, W. T., 50, *59*
Peterson, W., 109, *138*
Piliawsky, M., 42, *46*
Planalp, S., 50, *61*
Polkinghorne, D., 32, *46*
Portelli, A., vii, *ix*, 1, 14, 16, *18*, 20, *30*
Postman, L., 54, *59*

R

Rabinow, P., vii, *ix*, 9, 15, *18*
Raineri, V. M., 108, 130, *138*
Raines, H., 33, *46*
Reed, H., 50, 51, *60*
Reisser, B. J., 55, 57, *61*
Ricoeur, P., 15, *18*
Riessman, C. K., 67n. 2, 79, *81*
Robinson, J. A., 57, *61*
Rochberg-Halton, E., 144, *161*
Rogers, K. L., 31, 32, 33, 41, 43, 44, *46*
Rogers, P. L., 51, *61*
Roos, J. P., 15, *18*

Subject Index

169